The Orrible Synne

by the same author
QUEEN OF THE BAUDS

The Orrible Synne

A Look at London Lechery from Roman to Cromwellian Times

E. J. Burford

Calder & Boyars
London

First published in Great Britain in 1973
by Calder & Boyars Limited
18 Brewer Street
London W 1

ISBN 0 7145 0978 7 Casebound Edition

Typeset in Great Britain by
Specialised Offset Services Ltd., Liverpool
and printed by Whitstable Litho

Contents

A Twelfth Century Introduction to Lechery

The Branches of Lechery

The Synne of lecherie is departed in many braunches as after the staates of persones that doth it, and euere it clymbeth vpper and vpper and alwey wors and wors.

The First is of man and womman that beth not bounde bi a vow, ne by mariage, ne bi ordre, ne bi religioun, ne bi othere weies. Yit is this the first dedly synne of lecherie, who-so doth it.

The Secounde is with a comune womman. That synne is wel more, for it is fouler. And for suche ben ofte of religioun and forsaketh no man, that is to seye brother ne cosyn ne fadre.

The Thridde is a man vnbounde with a womman bounde bi a vow.

The Ferthe is with a mayde.

The Fifthe is with a womman maried, that is cleped in holy writ auoutrie; that is a wel greuous synne, for ther is brekyng of oure bileue and trewthe that that on schal bere to that other, also ther is the synne of sacrilege, whan a man breketh the sacrament of holi chirche, that is of mariage. And ther-of cometh ofte disheritynges and fals heires and wrongful mariages. And this synne doubleth otherwhile, as a man maried with a-nother mannes wif, and also a womman maried with a-nother man y-maried that is nouyt hire owne husbonde.

The Sixte is whan a man with his owne wif doth thing forboden and defended, ayens kynde and ayens the ordre of wedloke; for a man may slen hymself with his owne swerd, and also a man may do dedly synne with his owne wif, and therfore smot God Ozam, Iacobes cosyn. And the deuel that heiyt Asmodeus strangelede seuene husbondes of the holy womman Sare that afterward was yong Tobies wif. For alle the sacramentes of holy chirche scholde men fare clenly with and holde hem in gret reuerence and worschipe.

The Sevene is a man with his modre or with his douyter, or with the children of his godfadre or of his godmodre, for suche folke mowe not come to-gidre with-out dedly synne, not in mariage.

The Eiytthe a man with his kynnes womman, and this synne is grettere and smallere after that the kyn is nyy or feer.

The Nynthe is a man with his wyues kyn or the womman with hire housbondes kyn. This synne is wel perilous, for whan a man taketh a womman he may not after that wedde noon of hire coseynes; and yif he take any of hem, the mariage is as noon; and yif he take a womman and after taketh a-nother of hire kynne leseth the riyt that he had to his wif, in as moche that he may not dele with hire but yif sche bidde hym bifore-hond.

The Tenthe a woman with a clerke with-ynne holi ordre. That synne is grettere or smallere as the ordres beth gretter or smaller.

The Eleventhe is with a womman of religioun or a womman of the world with a man of religioun.

The Twelfthe is a man of religioun with a womman of religioun, and this synne is more or lasse after that the staat is of hem that doth it.

Preface

The Stynkynge Orrible Synne is of course Lechery, as a sin a comparative latecomer to the canon of human sins. It is a creation of the later Christian era, since the word 'lechery' does not appear in either testament of the Bible. Some of its manifestations, such as adultery, fornication and lust, indeed liberally bestrew the pages of these august Works, but the sin of lechery is not to be found there.

Lechery may be said without any argument to be the very oldest of the human passions after eating – indeed, there are not wanting earnest savants to assert that men will copulate rather than eat if that is an ultimate choice. There is not a human being alive in any generation, nor at any time in human history, who has not at some time in his life experienced the urge to lechery. The vast majority will have succumbed to it, even if only briefly or occasionally, but it will be very frequently in their thoughts and dreams.

Lechery, as a sin, is unknown among the early peoples. It is unknown amongst the Hebrews and the Semitic people, perhaps because of the wise precaution in their epochs of allowing polygamy by the payment on easy terms by instalments, for wives (with a power of return if the goods were unsatisfactory) and concubines, not to forget the always available female slaves. Lechery as a sin is not known in the Islamic canon, nor in the Hindu religion; it is peculiar in both senses of the word to the Christian canon, for these fleshly lustings were not regarded as a sin by the ancient Egyptians, nor the Greeks nor the Romans, all of whom sensibly arranged to channel the more obvious manifestations of lechery into suitable places, with suitable people; indeed, cleverly combining gluttony and slothful indulgence with carnal enjoyment and with sodomy thrown in to complete the tally. So long as it was not offending the susceptibilities of their contemporary Madame Maison Blanc and Frau Weisshaus, none would cavil; it might be sometimes a noisy nuisance but it was not a sin.

The earliest, if not the best and most useful, guide as to what is actually implied by the term 'Lechery', is set out as a Twelfth Century Introduction to this book, which was written by the old monk, Lorens or Laurence, in his 'Book of Vices and Virtues'.

The Christian conception of strict monogamy, coupled with the salvation of the soul, however, led to all sorts of theological gyrations, in order to put a curb and, hence, a punitive seal, on these natural human desires and their fulfilments. In consequence, they invoked spates of savage repression or proscription, and ghastly punishments, alternating with reluctant permissiveness, in turn creating vast psychological stresses and problems without in any way abolishing the sin itself, nor altering humanity's basically lecherous disposition.

It is only now, in this third quarter of the twentieth century after Christ, that the fig-leaf of Christian morality is slipping fast from the original genitalia which have always been under it; and this is manifested by the massive desertion from the established Churches by the post-war generations. They gaily and consistently ignore all the laborious theological moral canons, and proceed to indulge more publicly, and with somewhat greater honesty, in the various manifestations of sexual congress.

Wherever a man and a woman find themselves together, lechery will raise its head, whether it be satisfied or not. The difference today is that it is regarded as of less moral importance than it has been claimed to be for nineteen centuries. To be sure, cracks have appeared in this facade before. Sir John Harington, one of Queen Elizabeth I's young favourites, called it: '. . . the sweete synne of letcherie . . . whiche makes them so ofte break the sixt commaundement . . . ' because no one believed in it.

This book is intended as a history of lechery in the City of London and the ways in which the Lord Mayor and

Corporation and the royal authorities coped with it over a chosen period in our nation's history and that of our great capital city and its long-suffering satellite Southwark, as the cradle of the 'Stynkynge Orrible Synne yat Men cal Letcherie'. It does not set out to endorse or condemn the synne; merely to set out the facts for the serious enquirer for instruction and entertainment.

Chapter One

'Quo Loco Recta Via Ad Lupanar, Amicus?'

In the momentous year 54 A.D., an otherwise inconspicuous Roman general, Aulus Plautius, was entrusted by the Divine Emperor Claudius to cross the dark treacherous northern seas and teach the savages living there on an island, known as Britannia, a lesson they would not forget. His instructions included also the injunction to acquire the island and its inhabitants for the further glory of the Roman Empire in general and Claudius in particular, and the exploitation of the people and the land for the greater profit of the Emperor. Above all he was to bring the savages the great benefits of the Roman civilization, including law and order, without which no person in those days could be regarded even as human.

When the initial rather messy campaigning was over, the Divine Claudius would deign to come over and himself take command for the final vanquishing of the 'war mad savages', as the British were then described by the historian Strabo, and so earn for himself, his Praetorian Guards and his elephants a much needed, but genuine, Roman Triumph.[1] Claudius could only spare 16 days for the conquest of Albion.

Aulus Plautius and his legions accordingly footslogged their way from the coast until they came to a river whose banks were well defended by the savages, and, according to Dio Cassius writing, however, 150 years after the event, the British crossed because they knew the fords; his German auxiliaries swam across, while his Roman troops had to cross by a bridge which they found a little way up the river.

The bridge which General Aulus Plautius then threw across the river Thames was the umbilical cord for the newly

[1] Dio Cassius. *History*, LX.23.

created toehold which he presumably dubbed Londinium. From this small beginning sprang up eventually a new nation with all the benefits, and not a few of the disadvantages, of the Roman civilization, including one of that civilization's most interesting and always ultra-popular aberrations, the whorehouses and bagnios. Sexual aberrations were assuredly not novelties to the Celts, but till that time they had not thought up the idea of enjoying it in an organized fashion. It was the one unique aspect of Roman civilization which did not wither over the centuries, albeit trimmed suitably to the changing conditions of the subsequent two thousand years.

The area of the crossing was already from ancient times the focus of a network of tracks and ways which radiated throughout the island, though there is no known settlement. Thus this southern approach to the crossing became the assembly place for the legions, as well as people and goods wishing to cross the wooden bridge. For safety's sake the Romans would have established a small military settlement, perhaps even a small fort or earthwork to guard the entrance to the bridge, which certainly would have been protected by a fortified gate of brick and wood. The Roman guardians would certainly test the *bona fides* of would-be crossers and exact a toll. The traffic was undoubtedly heavy with soldiers, administrators and carpet-baggers rushing to seize the opportunities offered for plunder and exploitation.

Since every Roman legion of that time was accompanied by its cohort of camp-followers, the establishment of *Lupanaria* for the soldiers' lot and the satisfaction of their sexual needs would have had high and immediate priority in this settlement. Thus the southern *'sub urbs'* became established even before its greater and more famous partner over the water, even though for many centuries it had no known name. Its physical character hardly changed. The dank marshland, thickly studded with trees, was ideal for malefactors and people on the run who could find a hiding place where nobody was concerned to seek them out to bring them to justice. Southwark's lawless character was formed in these times and lasted for more than 1500 years.

These army and working-class brothels would have lined the small spit of solid land on the river strand hard by the bridge approach, and this site maintained its character for many centuries thereafter. The houses would have followed the Roman pattern, with construction allowing for the much damper northern climate. They were purely functional with rapid service, dispensing with all trimmings. In them would be found the *putae*, the common whores (the word is derived from the Latin 'puteus': a well or tank: *vide* Plautus '. . . a love tank . . .') and they are still known to this day in France as 'putains' and in Spain as 'putas'. Even in those early days there was competition from taverns, whose waitresses and maidservants would supply sexual services. Both were known as *assellae* because they usually accepted the smallest coin, the *as*, as befitted their lowly station.

On the northern side of the river, however, a very different Roman civilization developed very rapidly. Governors and their trains; administrators and their clerks; officers with their families and servants; merchants from all corners of the Roman world; commercial travellers; citizens and their families and dependents and slaves; all thronged to create the great commercial empire called Londinium. The very first reference to Londinium as a thriving city is recorded by Tacitus when describing Boadicea's avenging onslaught and her devastation of Londinium and the massacre of 70,000 people gathered inside it. It was, he said:

> *'a place not signified by the name of colonia but crowded with merchants and provisions . . .'*

and this describes the place a scant seven years after its foundation which shows how rapidly London had grown to eminence and riches.

300 years later, this city was to be given the accolade of *Augusta* (The Worshipful), when its immense wealth and importance could no longer be ignored by the imperial authorities in far-off Rome. Its shops and offices, its palaces and temples, its baths and theatres, and its substantial homes and villas became known within the Empire. Equally certainly this opulence must have been matched by the number and quality of its *Lupanaria* (public pleasure houses), its *Fornixes* (brothels), and its *Thermiae* (hot baths frequented by both sexes), in addition to the numerous

'To the Four Sisters', a frieze on a Roman Lupanar.

Meretrices[2] and *Prostibulae* – the independent whores. Amongst these were also the more primitive type of brothels, containing a wooden bed or bunk and a shabby blanket; for an extra penny or so a straw pallet was supplied. In these there were no facilities for refreshments; the client took his pleasure and left. If the Pompeiian examples be compared, there were even small shanties with a curtained entrance leading to small booths where the requisite performance could be quickly repeated at much cheaper rates.

That life was hard and unpleasant for the whores in these low class places is shown from an extract from Plautus' play *Pseudolus*, in which the jealous Hedylum tells his two concubines whom he accuses of unfaithfulness:

'I shall cause you to be carried away to the stews.

[2] from Latin *merere*, to earn.

There such a bed shall be given you as you shall find hard to sleep upon, even from exhaustion . . .'[3]

At the other end of the scale were the high-class *Lupanaria* patronized by the Roman-British nobility and gentry, which offered the greatest luxury, abundant willing attendants of both sexes for every kind of lubricity the human mind could conjure up; with copious refreshments and entertainments of all sorts.

The institution of *Lupanaria* is said to go right back to the actual foundation of Rome, to the she-wolf *Lupa*, who suckled the infants Romulus and Remus. Livy states that this animal was a symbol for the famous whore, Acca Laurentia, because the Romans called those women who gave their bodies to all comers, she-wolves – *Lupae*; hence the word *Lupanarium*, meaning a brothel as a House of She-wolves. There was annually an ancient Festival called the *Laurentia*, in honour of the wife of Faustulus who brought the two children to her, at which offerings of wine and milk were made to the participants.[4]

The respectable antiquity of the Roman brothel is evidenced in Horace's *First Satire*, when he advocates that young and noble rakes should slake their lusts rather in brothels than molest other men's wives and daughters – a sentiment and an excuse used long before his time by the Greeks, and by the worthy Aldermen of London centuries later to justify their own actions. Horace, however, was writing some fifty years before Christ and was only echoing the views of the Founding Fathers of the Roman Republic before them. These were men of quite different calibre, who demanded strict chastity of their wives and daughters as paragons of female and Roman virtue. Thus in their eyes the brothels and taverns for licensed whoredom fulfilled an acceptable and publicly endorsed useful function. Cato the Elder once remarked to a youthful acquaintance whom he

[3] Hayward. *The Courtezan*, p.232. Casanova Society, London 1926. (In Greece a whore was known as *Lupta*, the she-wolf, in the sense of her greed and covetousness.)

[4] H. Licht. *Sexual Life in Ancient Greece*, p.331. Routledge, London 1933.

saw coming out of a brothel 'Good! my boy', although when he saw the same youth a little while afterwards coming out of the same brothel he felt constrained to say 'When I said Good! to you I did not mean you should make the whorehouse your home!'

In Londinium, as elsewhere the woman who wished to become a prostitute had first to go before a Public Officer, the Aedile, and in making the application she had to give her name, date of birth, status, and the name under which she wished to trade.[5] Status was of importance because at one period ladies of very high rank were applying for such permission. The Aedile was meant to try and dissuade her but if she still persisted he had to grant her a licence, on which also was marked her proposed charges; which charges, if she frequented a brothel, were to be marked on the door of the cubicle. The registration gave her a legal right to get her fee, and if the client bilked her she could sue for her money. Thus it became a business like any other business.

In the *Fornixes* of the marble palaces and circuses and the public baths – under the colonnades – assignations were made and even sexual intercourse performed in public to the delectation of the passers-by. Hence the current description of this irregularity as 'fornication', which was changed to 'vokken' in Old Low German, where it was in common use as late as 1735 when S. Sewel's *Groot Nederdijtser-Engelsh Woordenboek* gives 'fokken' – to breed, with a cognate word 'vochelen' in the more vulgar sense, literally fucking underneath the arches. This word, so much debated today, has a very ancient and very respectable origin and history, and was commonly used in everyday speech for centuries. It came into the English language through the German 'ficken' – to copulate – as a distortion of the Latin 'fornicatio'.

Whoredom, too, has its respectable roots in deep antiquity, and brothels likewise. The Bible retails the Patriarch Judah's arrangement with a public harlot who sat by the wayside – although she turned out afterwards to be his daughter-in-law, Tamar, temporarily adopting the profession to teach him his duty.

[5] Tacitus. *Annales*, ii 85, *Loeb* ed.

As Londinium grew from strength to strength commercially, industrially and militarily, and as her garrisons came and went, her brothels flourished mightily, replenished frequently with female slaves captured from the native British population, and supplemented by a steady supply of women from various parts of the Empire, both amateur and professional. Roman law as well as Roman manners prevailed in all the Empire and the provincials aped the capital in fashions and morals. The Roman laws in imperial times reflected the outlooks, the whims and fancies of the respective periods. Caesar's Law was re-enacted in 90 A.D. by Domitian, without much effect, if Juvenal is to be believed. In his *Satires* he makes scathing and personal attacks on his contemporaries, parading their degrading and often revolting sexual habits in and out of brothels and bagnios, and claims these penetrated every walk of life. Indeed he went so far as to suggest that the ancient Republican Law *Lex Scantinia de nefanda Venere* (Scantinian Law against Abominable Sexual Practices) should be revived to counter the tremendous increase in the 'Eastern Vice', sodomy.

He describes the scandalous and lubricious goings-on in Baths and Bordellos, in some of which meals were served with bread rolls shaped like penises, called *colyphia*, *colyphium* being the gladiators' slang for penis. He mentions that women were customarily charged more to enter the public baths than men, possibly because they could always recover their money from avid clients. He mentions too, the '. . . whores who hang about the race course . . . ' and that the Circuses and Public Games were '. . . regular whores' beats . . . ' as indeed they are to this very day. In his *Ninth Satire* he says that the Temples, especially those devoted to goddesses like Cybele and Ceres, both of whom were enormously and fervently worshipped by women, were '. . . hot spots for easy women . . . '.[6]

In Southwark there is some evidence of a Temple to Isis, goddess paramount above all goddesses for women. This will assuredly have been a meeting place for local women of all descriptions, from the high-born Lady to the meanest

[6] All the above translations from Juvenal's *Satires* are by Peter Green, London 1947.

prostitute, all seeking sexual gratification of some kind, or help and advice about it from the priestesses, who themselves would have been practitioners of the art of prostitution when required. The women from the local *Lupanaria* would have gone to worship and participate in the fantastically lewd rites, as well as picking up clients.

The statuette of the Egypto-Roman god Harpocrates found under old London Bridge may be evidence of a phallic cult in Londinium. Several statuettes and small representations of this god have been found in Britain, in fact. Earlier statues of this god showed him with a penis three or four times his own height. Harpocrates was a bringer of good luck and a guarantor of immense sexual prowess as well as fertility. Figures with multiple penises were common in Rome and in the Empire. Lamps were made of figures whose penis held the oil or the wick; this luminous lamp-cum-phallus protected the paramours from evil demons lurking in the dark; they also helped them to redouble their amorous exercises. There were models of penises with wings: and penises would even be found engraved on the handles of workmen's tools.

Amongst the other necessary paraphernalia in early Roman-British Londinium would be the Herms which usually stood at principal street intersections. These were upright squared pillars of stone standing about 6 ft. high, with a bust of the god Hermes on the top, and a large and erect phallus complete with pendant testicles on one of the sides of the pillar. Hermes was a favourite god of women inherited from the Greek tradition, and the passing women would touch or fondle the stone genitalia or even kiss the phallus, soliciting the god's help in making them more sexually desirable to their males or to arouse passion in some specially desired paramour, or even to help them to become pregnant. This cult lasted for centuries and was a direct descendant of the very much earlier eastern temple phalli upon which virgins were encouraged to sit and secure divine deflowering.

The corollary of these were figurines with enormous *vulvae* or in attitudes of incredible turpitude: all designed to rouse the utmost concupiscence. In any major Festival a giant erect penis would be carried by bearers in the processions and

The God Hermes, facilitator of lechery.

would be followed by young girls carrying flowers and baskets of fruits, chanting a hymn to the Phallos himself, in earlier times the personified Penis of the Greeks later adopted in the name of Priapus, by the Romans, in their own similar festival.

All Juvenal's strictures would equally apply to Londinium. By this time it was a provincial city of considerable importance, comparable in size with Pompeii, which was destroyed in the year 70 A.D. by the eruption of Vesuvius. In Pompeii to this day visitors can see the *Lupanaria*, with the lewd pictures over the small wooden bunks intended to stimulate the clients' senses. Much the same would have been seen in Londinium. (It is a curious sidelight on modern Italian male morals that women visitors are not allowed even to peek into these ruined and empty Pompeiian brothels!)

Although few remains of Roman buildings in London have so far been discovered, it is certain that Londinium had its full quota of theatres, baths, pleasure houses and brothels, in addition to the Temples for the various Roman and indigenous cults. It is however strange that so far no trace of a Circus has been found: yet it is unthinkable that such a large and thriving Roman town should not have had such an essential social adjunct. It may yet be unearthed, possibly in Southwark, since most sites in the north and north-west have proved fruitless.

Remains of temples and shrines have been uncovered. The Romans never interfered with any religious cult unless it was suspected of being utilized for political subversion. But the brothels and bagnios, being of much lighter construction will probably never be excavated. There is plenty of evidence elsewhere of the magnificence of Roman public baths: and since the wealthy citizens of wealthy Londinium, as well as the *jeunesse dorée* and the *noblesse* would ape all Roman fashions and trends – much as Londoners today follow the trends of Paris and New York – the public baths would likewise perform the same functions of encouraging sexual promiscuity.

However it is doubtful if even the worst of them would have gone to the depths of depravity manifested by the Emperor Tiberius when in his old age he retired to Capri.

Suetonius describes the scene graphically in his *Histories of Twelve Caesars*, I. 43 and 44, transl. Philemon Holland, 1606.

> *' . . . but during the time of his private abode in Capri he devised a roome with seats and benches in it . . . for his secret wanton lusts. To furnish it there were gathered from all parts a number of young drabbes and stale catamites . . . such also as invented monstrous kind of libidinous filthinesse whom he terms* Spintriae *who being in three rewes linked together should abuse and pollute anothers bodie before his face, that by the verie sight he might stirre up his owne . . . fainting lust . . . '*

The Emperor's inventions were seemingly endless, for Suetonius next describes an almost unbelievable piece of lubricity:

> *' . . . hee shoulde traine up . . . fine boys the tenderest and daintiest . . . whom he called his little fishes to converse and play between his thighes as he was swimming and pretily with tongue and teethe to make unto his secret parts and there to nibble . . . howbeit as like unweaned babes he should set his privie member to sucke as unto the nipple of a breaste . . . '*

They were mainly places for social gatherings like present-day public houses, and bathing, although originally the main function, tended to be pushed into the background. The largest and most popular public baths would have had the modern equivalent of art galleries, boutiques, reading and reciting rooms and restaurants. (Roman moralists of the older generation often complained that the idea of daily bathing was a Greek corruption!) But even before they had become hotbeds of vice and prostitution the *thermiae* had often been used as overnight hotels, much as modern travellers put up at an all-night Turkish Bath instead of bothering to go to a Hotel.

Clustered around the baths were the *pervigiles popinae*, the all-night bars, which were frequently the scene of much rowdiness, raucous singing and often focal points for street fighting and brawls and even murders. Such must have been the scene nightly outside the Roman Bath House uncovered in Cheapside, which is complete enough to give a good idea of what it looked like, although the dressing rooms (*apodyteria*) and the exercise cum promenade yard (*palaestra*) have not been discovered.

A much larger and more pretentious public bath was uncovered in 1964 at Huggin Hill, on the Thames bank near Queenhithe. It appears to date from about the 2nd century A.D. Queenhithe, the very first of the Roman landing places, was known in mediaeval times for its large number of stews – both honest hot baths and bogus ones.

We may be sure that on the adjacent walls there were numerous lewd and humorous *graffiti* similar to those found plentifully in Pompeii, and as found in any public lavatory in London today. Plutarch mentions that the *palaestrae* of the baths were much frequented by homosexuals. The leather 'bikini' dredged up in the City of London some years ago may very well be the uniform of a local whore rather than the innocuous bathing garment of some local virgin, as the worthy City Fathers would have us believe.

Indigent people often were kept away from the baths sometimes because they could not afford the oil money for being rubbed down by the *sordidus unctor*, the oil attendant: and on one occasion an Emperor, Septimius Severus, issued an ordinance that oil money was to be distributed free in Rome, and doubtless the same bribe was offered to the British plebs during his sojourn in Britain.

As to the sexual proclivities of the pre-Roman Celtic population, there is no evidence of organized prostitution as such, although, of course, such common human foibles as fornication and adultery were practised no matter what the prevailing *mores* may have been. There is a clue in a short verbal passage-at-arms between the Empress Julia Domna, the Consort of the Emperor Septimius Severus (who spent some time in Britain and who died in York) and the wife of a Caledonian chieftain named Argentocoxus. The Roman thought that the sexual habits of the aborigines went a little too far. Julia, whose amorous proclivities were well known in Rome, teased the Scottish lady about the Caledonian habit of sharing women. The chieftainess snapped back:

' . . . we have intercourse openly with the best of our men; while you allow yourselves to be seduced in private by anyone including the worst of men . . . '

This was round about the year 155 A.D. and shows that at least in the untamed parts of the Celtic domains free-love was quite common and infers a very great amount of liberty for Celtic women.

The Roman historian, Strabo, had observed earlier that the British were war-mad, loving feats of arms:

' . . . their women fighting side by side with their menfolk and as bravely . . . '

The British menfolk did not treat their women as inferiors or playthings but as partners. Hence the Romans could not ever produce a Boadicea to lead their armies to death or glory, for no Roman Legionary would have fought under a woman's

Forestier's painting of London in the second century showing London Bridge in foreground and Bankside (on the left) upstream with the Roman fort, right of centre, around which the brothels clustered.

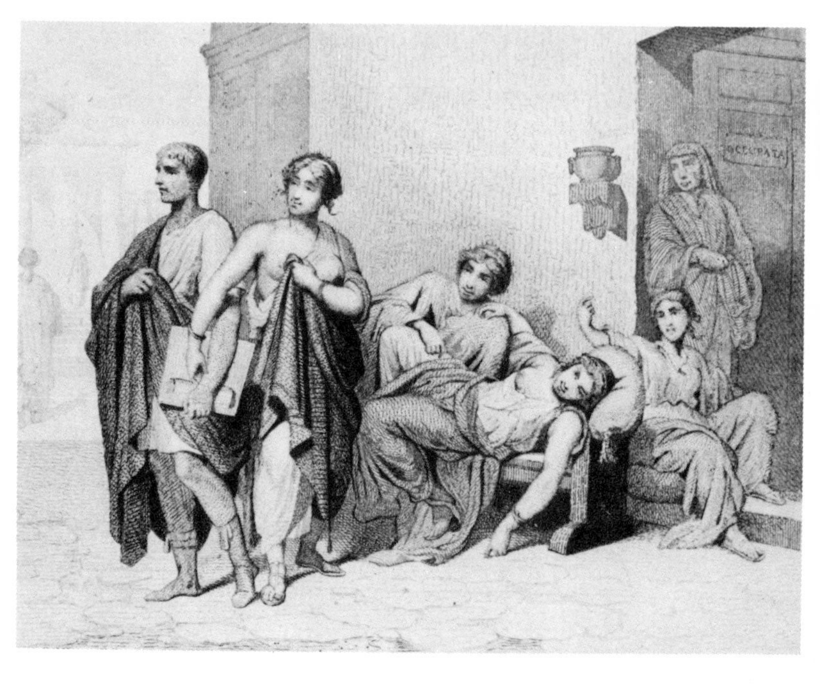

Soliciting outside a Lupanar *in Roman times.*

command. But the Romans eventually broke the back of the British resistance and at the end British women were reduced to slaves and prostitutes.

There was also a 'belt' of brothels in the North Western area of Roman Londinium, within its walls, and its origin is very typical. After Boadicea's savage revolt in 61 A.D., an increased Roman garrison was quartered in a fortified camp in the area of the present Aldersgate Street, Cripplegate and Moorfields, near the Guildhall. It was in a rectangular shape with one outer gate and at least two gates facing into the city. It goes without saying that wherever there was a Roman garrison there were whorehouses; and so, in the alleys later to

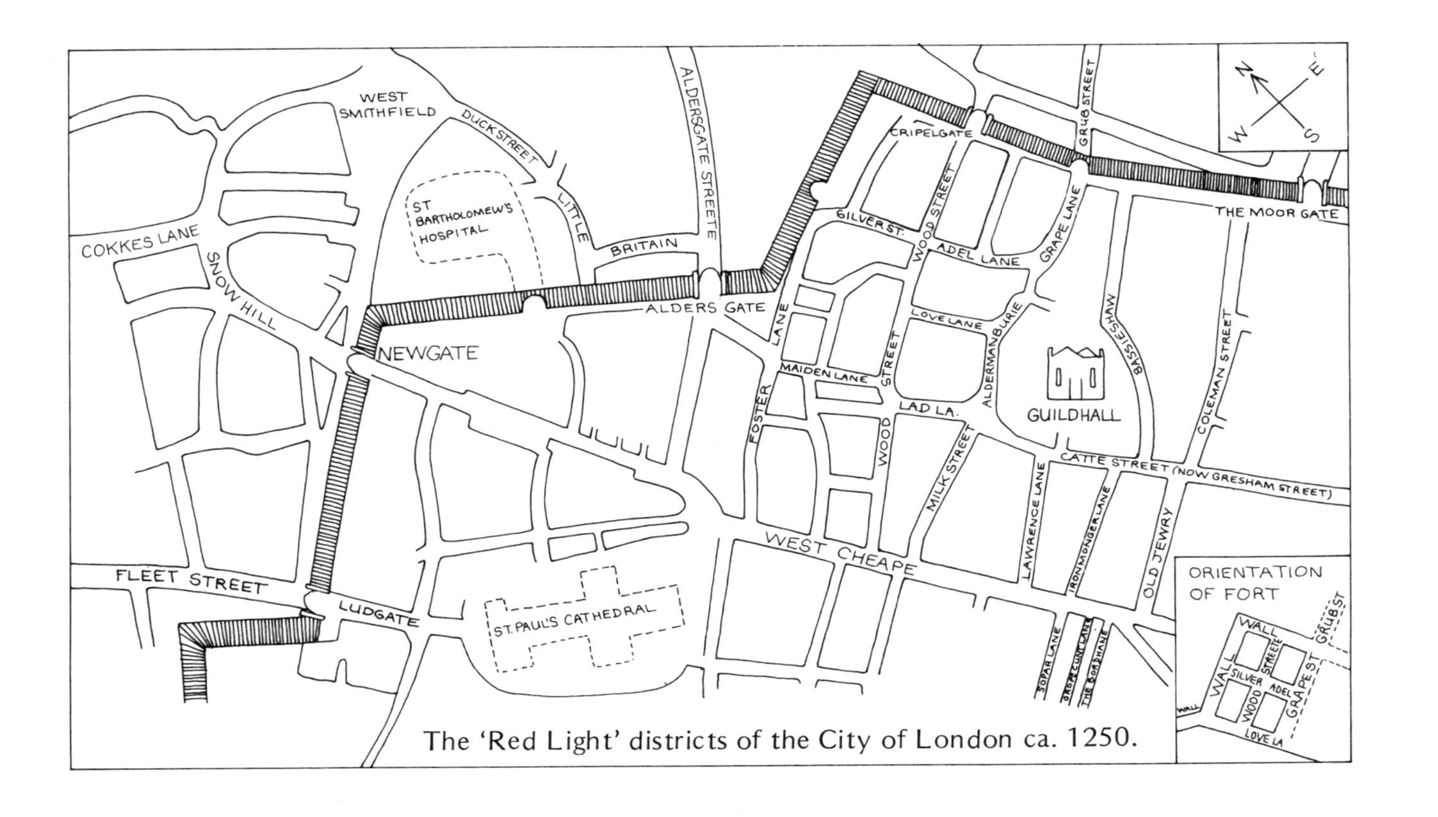

The 'Red Light' districts of the City of London ca. 1250.

be known as Maiden Lane, Love Lane, Golden Lane and Silver Street, and Grub Street, many houses of prostitution were established.

When the wall was extended about 200 A.D., the whole of the outer perimeter of the camp was incorporated, so that the brothels which clustered at the southern and eastern entrances were now willynilly included in the city's domain; thus finding themselves in company with all the other and higher-class *Lupanaria* nearer the city centre, for whom they were doubtless unwelcome competition, although their clientele was drawn from an entirely different social level. This 'belt' of streets and the 'stews' endured for centuries.

From the most ancient times, and in all parts of the world, prostitutes and brothels are found at or near the gates of cities or immediately outside their walls. The poor, the uprooted, the runaway slaves, the desperate peasant women, the deserting soldiers, the thieves and drunkards, the indigent honest as well as the indigent dishonest, all congregated at the City's gates, often because they would not be allowed in. For the girls and women, starving and destitute, or the simple country girls ignorant of the pitfalls of city life – (although it is not to be thought that adultery and fornication even in those days were the prerogative of the city-dwellers) – the descent into prostitution was usually immediate because there was no other outlet except slavery. Moreover, the ponces and pimps and whorehouse madams would be on the lookout for fresh unspoiled goods at the city gates, much as their modern counterparts frequent the railway termini to entice the girls coming up to town for the 'good life'! So, too, in Londinium business flourished mightily almost unchecked by any official actions; but about 200 A.D. a faint black shadow on the horizon was to be observed in the rise of the new religion of Christianity in the eastern part of the Empire, although as yet the Romans in the far west were not afflicted with Christian sexophobia. Moreover, by this time the first settlers, who had been of predominantly Italian or Romanized Gaulish or Mediterranean stock, had been diluted by repeated infusions of Celtic and Teutonic blood, often still speaking their native tongues and keeping their old pagan habits and *mores*; even though their speech would be bastardized with Greek and Roman phrases and words, they were still illiterate. Thus frequently there would be heard at the Bridge Gate the bastard-Latin equivalent of 'Which way to the *Lupanaria*, mate?'

The continuing growth of whoredom in Britain is evidenced by the attempts of the Emperor Hadrian to put down brothels and prostitution and to enforce old laws. According to Ammianus Marcellinus, Hadrian tried to ban the public baths in 370. During his sojourn in Britain the whores and their clients may have been a little more circumspect, only to come out into the open when the Emperor had finished his military pacification and left Albion's shores for ever.

According to current Roman law, the registered harlot still had to dye her hair blonde, apart from wearing a distinctive dress; although these rules must have been honoured more in the breach than the observance. These same basic rules derived from the time when Houses of Prostitution were first introduced by Solon many centuries before in Athens. Then they were a state monopoly and were known as *Pornai* (common brothels) for *Porneia* or *Dikteria* (common whores). It may derive either from an earlier tradition aimed at distinguishing the harlots from the universally brunette and olive-skinned Mediterranean women, or more likely from the importation of fair-haired and fair-skinned women much in demand by the cognoscenti like King Solomon and much later by the Caliphs. These would have been Celtic and Teutonic women captured in war or kidnapped on slaving expeditions. The *Porneia* are to be sharply distinguished from the later elegant, intelligent and cultured courtesans known as *Hetairae*, who were highly esteemed.

The *Hetairae* were also very carefully groomed, many of them serving as models for the famous Greek sculptors of ancient times; and since pubic hair is never seen on any of these statues, it must be inferred that they practiced depilation and carefully shaved their pubic parts for business reasons. This may have been a cosmetic device of high-born women also, since Lysistrata makes a jest about a young girl from the province of Boeotia who had come to support them

> *'. . . there never was much undergrowth in Boeotia; it is such a smooth place and this girl takes after it!'* Lysistrata also tells her women they must be prepared to meet their husbands after the 'strike' *'. . . with our Venus plaits plucked trim and neat . . .'*[7].

The Greek attitude may be best shown by an anecdote from Aristippus concerning the famous whore of Corinth, Lais, with whom Diogenes was in love. Aristippus asked Diogenes whether he thought it a disgrace to occupy a house in which others had lived. 'No!' replied the philosopher. 'Or a ship in which others have sailed?' 'No!' said Diogenes. 'Then neither is it disgraceful to be intimate with a woman whom others have used,' said Aristippus.

By the time the full force of Christianity struck the Eastern Empire, the Romans had withdrawn from Britain, so that its effect on the British good-time girls was as yet hardly felt. Originally, with the onset of Christianity elsewhere in the Empire, the prostitutes had no suspicion that they were about to fall victim to a worse persecution than ever they had experienced at pagan hands. Prostitutes generally had turned to the new religion readily because it offered some hope and compassion for the poor and downtrodden, on the basis of Christ's compassion to Mary Magdalene and others of her sisters in misfortune, and several prostitutes were later to be raised to sainthood for their martyrdom for the new faith.

They were not to know that Christianity was to turn what had hitherto been an accepted pleasant entertainment or diversion or hygienic necessity or whatever, into something 'wicked'. This may later on have added an extra spice, as well as a previously unknown element called 'sin'; which was the more peculiar because from time immemorial prostitution in temples and sacred places had been highly esteemed as an integral part of the religious way of life! The Church, intending then to destroy carnal pleasure, only succeeded in driving it underground and making it a somewhat furtive, although no less pleasurable, exercise.

Meanwhile Augusta Londinium went from strength to

[7] Jack Lindsay. *The Ancient World, Manners & Morals*. Weidenfeld & Nicholson, London 1968.

strength, receiving occasional visits from Emperors, and even on occasion electing or playing part in the choice of an Emperor. Visits of Emperors meant frequent ovations, necessitating much rejoicing and celebration. For ovations it was a good old Roman custom everywhere observed to utilize all the 'daughters of the city' in the processions, as well as for the later refreshment and delectation of the Legionaries and all celebrants from high to low. Augusta Londinium's whores could put on a show with the best of them. The long periods of peace under the Romans made every section of the Londoners richer and more avid for the most diverse forms of pleasure. All these functions therefore added to the revenues of the merchants and increased the incomes and profits from the brothels. There must have been a profusion of brothels, streetwalkers and baths, all stimulating the construction of even more and more splendidly furnished, luxurious and fully-equipped *Lupanaria*. Something else was flourishing side by side.

Venereal disease had reached Rome by about 150 B.C. supposedly from the soldiers returning from the eastern wars and campaigns. It is thought to have included syphilis: for although all infectious diseases were generically known as leprosy, a differentiation was early made for the *morbus indecens aie cunnientis*, the filthy disease of the cunt. This word was in standard use in ancient Rome and is derived from the Latin *cunnus*, the genital slit or *vulva*: and thence through Old Icelandic *kunta* into standard English. We shall deal with this matter more fully in a subsequent chapter.

It is very probable that some of the early Roman laws for the registration of harlots may have been an attempt to control the diseases. Certainly in the pre-Christian era no great stigma attached either to prostitution or to whore-mongers. Indeed brothel keepers could and did become Roman citizens. As prudent businessmen, too, care had to be taken that the goods offered were as fresh as possible; there are indications that primitive attempts at cleanliness were introduced by compelling the women to bathe affected parts in water or wine.

Despite internal unrest and the ever-increasing Saxon raids as well as Scottish, Pictish and Irish forays, business flourished, and its attendant pleasures likewise – until one dreadful day in 409 when the Emperor Honorius abruptly recalled his legions, with the injunction that henceforward the Romanized Britons must look after themselves and face the raiding Saxons and other savages alone. Thousands of frightened citizens left with the departing troops. Assuredly thousands of the inhabitants of the brothels and their clients went with them. The braver ones enrolled in the feverish preparations to establish some defence forces to try and save their lives and properties.

For about forty years they were able to stave off the final catastrophe, until the last organized Roman-British forces were overwhelmed at the battle of Crecganford (Crayford) in Kent in 457. These troops fled back to Londinium and over London Bridge, abandoning Southwark and its small Bankside row of whorehouses to the oncoming Saxons.

Chapter Two

'Hwilc Weig Horhusweard, Brothur, An Godes Naman?'

For the next two hundred years the Saxons ravaged the entire land, but we do not know whether or when they occupied London, whose stout walls doubtless helped the inhabitants to resist for a while, since the Saxons had no siege trains and they were far outnumbered by the inhabitants of the city, who were by no means disarmed. The Saxons certainly occupied the south side of the river and much of the surrounding country east and west, but there must have been periods when the fighting stopped and normal life was resumed.

The Saxons were seeking a new land to settle in: they could undoubtedly envisage advantages in making deals with the merchants of London: the more so since the Saxons were not town dwellers. They would slaughter when it was necessary: they would eagerly accept bribes and come back for more. In favour of a continued existence for London is the fact that there is no evidence of Saxon sackings, and remains of early Saxon buildings are very few indeed. Whatever the outcome, there are no written records of London's life and certainly nothing about the inhabitants' pleasures. Doubtless the brothels inside the city's north-western perimeter carried on somehow: they may even have increased their business at a time when many were in despair of their lives and took their pleasures quickly, obeying Horace's injunction '. . .*carpe diem quam minimum credula postero* . . . ' (snatch today's chance and put little trust in tomorrow).

The gloomy Scottish chronicler Gildas, in his *De Exidio et Conquestu Britanniae* writing in the year 510 casts a tiny gleam of light on local morals while taking a sideswipe at the local kings of Britain:

'... *they have many wives and all of them adulteresses and prostitutes* ...'

as much as to infer that because of this they failed to co-ordinate their military activities against the Saxons and allowed themselves to be wiped out piecemeal. Gloomy he may have been but he was a brave and martial monk, and his story shows there was at least some military resistance. The morals of the people were even then much looser than Gildas thought proper, discounting his description of these ladies as whores and prostitutes, simply because all non-Christians were *ipso facto* sinners.

It is an indication, nevertheless, that even in such a 'dark' period such women and their profession still existed. If any further evidence is required, Arthurian literature amply demonstrates that, despite the pious king's example and exhortations, many of his knights and their ladies were highly unmoral, when not downright immoral. There are frequent references to their mistresses in the accepted sense as distinct from the chivalrous sense. The saintly king himself was the progeny of a lustful encounter by King Uther Pendragon and the Lady Igraine, wife of the Duke of Tintagel, and the whole episode was cunningly arranged by Merlin at Uther's demand. In its context the action is not thought unworthy nor even unusual. Lancelot and Queen Guinevere, likewise, show little real embarrassment or shame in their famous extra-marital activities.[1]

Little is known of prostitution or brothels amongst the Saxons or Vikings – although the Vikings are alleged by some to have introduced homosexuality into England, which vice they had acquired through constantly being at sea in all-male company. But neither Saxons nor Vikings were immune from basic human failings, and sailors and soldiers everywhere in every age demanded to have their sexual needs slaked.

The Saxons were quite familiar with whores and whore-houses – the very word comes from the Old Teutonic *hore* – so that despite their frequent attacks on whorehouses, it is reasonably certain that the whores would remain. The

[1] Layamon's *Brut.* ed. F.W.D. Brie. Part I, pp.60-67. E E T S Orig. Series. 131. London 1906.

houses could quickly be rebuilt.

The Venerable Bede in his 'History'[2] for the year 604 says that 'London was a trading centre for many nations who visit it by land or sea . . . ' which makes it certain also that it had its quota of brothels and loose ladies like every other large commercial centre.

Although prostitution does not seem to have been organized amongst the Teutonic peoples, they were not averse to selling their blonde beauties, which included their daughters as well as their captives, to the Arab horsetraders, one of whose most profitable sidelines was white-slave trafficking of Nordic blondes, men and women, to the Roman and Near-eastern brothels. That they also got supplies from Britain is evidenced from Pope Gregory's famous remark about the English slaves '*Non Angli sed Angeli*' ('Not Angles but Angels') because they were tall handsome blonde and blue-eyed. Virile fairhaired English male slaves, if bought by passionate Roman matrons could be certain to make their way upwards very quickly.

If there are no records of Saxon brothels in London and Southwark, there certainly were Saxon whores. Some of the very rare Saxon Charters and Laws which have survived make reference to their punishments. Taking into consideration that in general Saxon punishments were of unbelievable barbarity, those prescribed for sexual offences were relatively mild. Thor and Woden (with Freya's influence in the background) were more indulgent and less intolerant than their Christian successors. The first Christianized pagan Saxon kings were still swayed by their very recent pagan *laissez faire* backgrounds.

For example the first Laws are those of King Aethelberht of Kent (560-616) who had married the Christian princess Berhta, daughter of the still pagan King Chariberht of Paris: these laws show a pragmatic cash application based on a social status which would be hard to beat even at the present time.[3]

[2] *Historiam Ecclesiasticam Gentis Anglorum*, Vol. II. p.21. Ed. C. Plummer. London 1906.

[3] All the following extracts are from B. Thorpe's *The Anglo-Saxon Laws and Institutes*, London 1840.

'If a man lies with the king's maiden (maegden-man) let him pay a *bote* (compensation) of 50 shillings.' This payment was, of course, to be made to the king in respect of one of his personal female servants, presumably also a virgin, in which case the fine does not seem excessive even when translated into today's money.

However, if she were the king's grinding slave his *bote* was 25 shillings; but if he were to seduce a female slave of the 'third class' the *bote* was only 12 shillings. Likewise, if he were so misguided as to lie with an earl's *birele* (cupbearing slave), his *bote* was also 12 shillings, but if she were the *birele* of a *ceorl* (churl) the compensation was only 6 shillings. The fine decreased with the status of the seduced girl, being only 50 *sceattas* for a slave girl of the second class and 30 for a third class one. (The Mercian silver pound divided into 250 *sceattas* in those days.) A (Gilbert and Sullivan type) Mikado judgment was reserved for the freeman who seduced another freeman's wife, for he not only had to pay *weregeld* but:

> '. . . *to provide another wife with his own money and bring her to the other man* . . . '

An indication that in fact these were guides rather than laws meant to prevent seduction, is shown by paragraph 64 of Aethelberht's Law that:

> '. . . *if anyone destroy (another man's) penis* (eowende) *let him pay with 3 shillings* leud gelds . . . '[4]

This demonstrates that in those very rough and ready days the aggrieved husband or lover quickly took the law into his own hands to render further assault on his property impossible, and even in King Alfred's laws (para 42) a man was allowed to fight and kill *orwige* (without penalty) ' . . . if he find another man with his lawful wife within closed doors . . . '.

In Saxon times a maiden was usually sold into marriage by her parents, although in Aethelberht's Law (para 77) the girl was protected by the phrase: ' . . . If man buy a maiden with cattle, let the bargain stand if it be without guile . . . '. Much later, the more humane Danish King Cnut was to ordain

[4] This was a *weregeld* normally for manslaughter.

(para 75): '. . . and let no one compel either women or maiden whom she herself dislikes, nor for money sell her . . . '.

Very frequently the marriage ceremony itself would have to wait upon the propitious time or the annual or regular rounds of an officiating priest, much as was happening in South Africa even until the end of the last century when, owing to the vast distances and lack of roads, betrothed people were married in batches when the Dominie was able to get around.

In Saxon times, as in the old Afrikaaner tradition, mid-February was one of the most popular times, and the custom was later incorporated into Christianity by recognizing St. Valentine's Day. 'Trothplight' or betrothal was regarded as valid as marriage and enabled the partners to cohabit without shame or fear of legal consequences. Even the bridal wreath was later taken over from the pagan Saxons as being the garland solemnizing the bethrothal.

King Wihtred of Kent's 'Code of Laws' of 695 legislated that:

> *'. . . men living in illicit union . . . shall repent . . . or be excluded from the communion of the Church . . . '*

This, in a period when the new religion was being forced down the throats of an unwilling but unresisting pagan peasantry, by prelates themselves but one step removed from the same barbarism, was a very serious punishment, and especially in the larger Saxon towns and cities, such as Winchester, the capital, or York or Lincoln or Norwich or Canterbury, to name the most important, where anonymity was impossible.

There is at least one reference to the bankside in the early Anglo-Saxon period in a Charter of sub-King Frithwald of Mercia who was also King of Surrey, 672-674, being a grant:

> *'. . . of the same land however a separate part of 10 hides is by the part of London where ships come to land . . . on the southern side . . . '*[5]

[5] D. Whitelock. *English Historical Documents* 'Charters' B. No.45, p.440. Eyre and Spottiswoode, London 1955.

From this can be inferred that on this quayside were the usual houses of refreshment and prostitution as well as the customary hot baths needed by sailors: and these may very well be the origins of the later Anglo-Saxon stews on that bank, for they were a first necessity for merchants and sailors.

These laws postulate sin at least in the cities and the larger villages: each village certainly had its local whore or group of whores, who were known and recognized and patronized. The existence of the Anglo-Saxon name of *Gropecuntlane* in several towns and cities clearly demonstrates a red light area from pre-Norman times.

The next set of extant laws bear the hallmark of that truly noble and Christian King, Alfred the Great, King of All England, warrior statesman and scholar – and human being. He includes a number of additional offences reflecting his concern at a pastime which had now turned into a sin. For example, fornication between a priest and a nun was regarded as '. . . a serious sin for which the priest will lose his honour . . .' but no penalty was prescribed against either party probably because it was a matter for the ecclesiastical courts. Alfred tempered justice with mercy, for his next paragraph restores monetary penalties, albeit much more expensive than the fines inflicted by the old Kentish King. Of course in the intervening centuries the cost of living and loving had escalated.

Thus, a man who commits adultery with the wife of a 12-hynde man:

> '. . . *carries a* bote *of 120 shillings; with the wife of a 6-hynde man, a* bote *of 100 shillings; and the wife of a churl (ceorlisheman), only 40 shillings* . . .'

The class distinctions were carefully differentiated: the cheaper the quality of the husband, the less the compensation. A *ceorl* by that time was a half-free man under Wessex Law, which Alfred had made into English law.

Further down the scale under Alfred's code comes Article 25:

> '*Rape upon a* ceorl's *female slave,* bote *is 5*

> *shillings . . . (payable to the* ceorl*) . . . and the* wite *shall be 60 shillings . . . '*

being regarded as ample payment for damage to very probably already damaged goods; but:

> ' *. . . if a* theow *(male servant or menial) rape a female* theow *let him make* bote *with his testicles . . . '*

This was clearly because a *theow* had no money to pay any fine and secondly to prevent any further damage to his master's property if randiness should seize him again. This action was in fact regarded as a form of theft: and theft in Anglo-Saxon law required savage punishment.

For example, a slave woman found stealing could be whipped almost to death, or incarcerated, or just thrown over a convenient cliff, or even burnt to death: in the latter case eighty other women slaves were compelled each to contribute a log for the pyre. In the case of a male slave, he could be stoned to death, in which case eighty other male slaves had to supply the stones and the stoning. Unspeakable mutilations were inflicted upon slaves. Occasionally common-sense prevailed, because after all a slave was, to use Aristotle's description, 'only a living tool' and a valuable piece of property, but sometimes it was thought necessary to make an example *pour décourager les autres.*

The lot of women slaves carried the additional burden that they were concubines to the master or the master's sons or the master's guests at any time of the day or night to suit their convenience. They could be hired out to prostitution, or when old and incapable be thrown out to prostitution. The mildest punishments were the 'cucking stole', which often led to suffocation by drowning in dirty stinking water or excrement; or the stocks or the pillory.

A few years later Alfred's son, King Eadward the Elder, made a treaty with the Danish King of the East Anglian territories, Guthrum. They set out an Anglo-Danish code of Laws to be applied mutually to both kingdoms. In addition to a general recapitulation of the laws already mentioned, they legislated:

> ' *. . . re incestuous persons. If two brothers or near*

> *kinsmen commit fornication with the same woman let them make* bote *very strictly . . .* '

Although not explicitly stated, the woman concerned would be a sister or half-sister. Incestuous relationship with a mother was a heinous crime punishable by a most cruel death.

Article No.11 orders that ' . . . witches and whores . . . must be driven from the country . . . '. Some fifty years later this was echoed by King Aethelred the Unready, but slightly amended to:

> ' . . . *witches magicians and whores . . . must be diligently driven out of the country . . . unless they make strict* bote . . . '

which seems to indicate some weakening in resolve.

King Eadmund was more merciful. He was more concerned with backsliding clergy: the wagging of the admonitory finger is to be noticed in his law that ' . . . he who commits fornication with a nun is unworthy of a burial place . . . '. There is no mention of any other penalty, nor of what was to happen to the nun!

Some twenty years later, his kinsman King Edgar,[6] ' . . . a very incontinent man . . . who ravished nuns . . . ' tried to redeem himself by founding some fifty monasteries or other places of worship. This lecherous king, while thus professing Christian piety, nonetheless enacted that an adulterer's punishment should extend over seven years, during which time he must live on bread and water three days a week.[7] Presumably there was an escape clause allowing him freedom to fornicate, on the grounds set out in Juvenal's *Eighth Satire* that ' . . . Blue blood has special licence and gets away with behaviour that would shame a working man!'

It is in King Edgar's day that the first written mention of old London Bridge occurs: although characteristically in a rather horrible setting. In 975 a poor pagan widow was tied up and thrown off Old London Bridge, to drown, for the crime of sticking pins into an effigy of Archbishop Wulfstan's

[6] Thomas Pennant. *Some Account of London, Westminster*, p.83. London 1813.
[7] David Wilkins. *Laws of King Edgar*. 1721.

thieving father, who appears to have helped himself to the small property owned by the poor widow and her son. Since she had no redress by Christian means, she had turned to her tried and trusted pagan witchcraft magic for revenge. Alas! that too, let her down!

During all the years from 886 when King Alfred had captured London from the Danes and restored its walls and had substantially rebuilt the city, the Londoners had been busily making their city once again into the greatest trading conurbation in the kingdom: accumulating great riches and political power. Despite some bad moments during the invasions of King Sweyn and King Cnut, London remained inviolable and grew even richer. Of course the Danes, themselves great businessmen, were clever enough to stop and take a breather occasionally, collecting Danegeld rather than loot. They too were seeking homes as had their Saxon predecessors, and for much the same reasons.

It is about that time, ca. 900 that the hitherto nameless southern suburb of London emerges into written history, and has a name. It is now called the *Suthrige geweorce* which may mean either the 'southern earthworks' or 'fortifications', or the 'defensive works of the men of Surrey (the South Saxons)'. The evidence comes from a collection of ancient documents dealing with the lands and land tenures of the 'hides' belonging to various personages: and the historian Maitland who collated them called them 'The Burghal Hideage'.[8] Hides were an ancient Saxon measure of land, and what is very important is that these were hides in what was now called also the 'Burgh' or 'Borough' of the *Suthrige geweorce.* This description also confirms its continued military character, for a borough was essentially a fortified town or enclosure; and it also infers that round about that time the spit of land known from Roman times had been embanked, most probably in order to protect the Saxons' fortifications from being flooded by the Thames tides. Thereby, the area of utilizable land had been increased greatly until it now encompassed the area called the 'burgh'.

Of even greater importance is the mention in these

[8] *vide* Munic. Guildhall. London. (Rolls Service) ii. 628.

documents of '. . . the head of the bridge . . .' (perhaps a translation of the original Roman *caput pontem*, meaning the southern Gateway to old London Bridge). There is also mention of '. . . a strande . . .' which can be none other than the riverside shore known thereafter as the Bankside. These pieces of land belonged to powerful Anglo-Saxon earls and prelates: and in considerable part also to the kings for the time reigning.

Thus as early as King Edgar's reign there were some substantial buildings since Southwark was the kingdom's only lifeline to the south. From this may stem the legend that some of the original brothels were built of stone, in which case they must originally have been built for wealthy noblemen or prelates, for in those days only the rich could build palaces, monasteries and churches of stone. This infers in turn that the brothels were even then controlled by the church if we take into account that in 1130 the regulations are spoken as being of 'tyme oute of mynde'. This takes us back to the year 950!

Despite the Danish invasions and war and destruction, Southwark was a going concern, for the Danes were entrenched there for some considerable time and doubtless guaranteed business for the shopkeepers and merchants, and certainly would have disported themselves lustily and noisily on the Bankside. (The Danes have been maligned for centuries because their history was written by Christian monks who were not only their religious enemies but also their racial enemies.)

Confirmation of Southwark's status comes from a mention in the Icelandic Saga, the *Heimskringla* dated ca. 1008, extolling the bravery and cleverness of the Norwegian King Olaf (later Saint Olaf) and his help to Aethelred the Unready in a critical period in a battle against the Danes at London Bridge. It states '. . . on the other side of the river there is a large trading place called Sudvirki . . .' and it describes the wooden bridge as a massive turreted structure wide enough for two wagons to pass each other.

The Danes likewise had their full share of lechery. Not only did they regularly extort good English money as Danegeld, but they also exported the captured English maidens as slaves into the Eastern and Roman brothels. In 975 a very well-known Spanish-Arab traveller was travelling all over the Teutonic world buying up blonde female prisoners of war from the Vikings. It was however the Danish King Cnut who abolished the savage penalty of cutting-off adulterers' ears and noses, and substituted exile in its stead. In his youth a truly savage pagan, this king turned out to be a model ruler. It is pertinent to record, however, that his Danish Kingdom was governed by a Regent, who was his English concubine, Ealgifu of Northampton, so the good king found no contradiction in moral principles. It was perhaps one of the reasons which made him a humane and civilized ruler; both kingdoms had peace under his firm and wise guidance.

King Edward the Confessor, the 'holy but imbecile Edward' was an incompetent ruler and for good measure horribly hag-ridden and very probably also of homosexual inclination. Politically he was a disaster for England and the English, but his interest from the viewpoint of lechery's orrible synne was that he owned large tracts of land in Southwark including the Bankside.

His kinsman and vassal, Earl Godwin, likewise owned large tracts in Southwark, wherein he had a palace in which he resided on his visits to London, and also had interests on the Bankside. When in 1062 he confronted his vacillating master with a big fleet, which he moored off the bankside for some weeks, he was very much on his home ground. It is related that during the weeks of haggling with the king, the earl's forces began to melt away, and there are not lacking those who suggest that too much dalliance with the light ladies in the houses facing the docked ships may have weakened the physique and the resolve of the irascible earl's supporters. It is a fact, however, that despite his squabbles with the effete king, the land was at peace and the Cities and their whorehouses grew more prosperous.

King Edward the Confessor was known to have encouraged foreign trade and himself imported costly silks and textiles and objects of vertu 'from all over the world' as a historian observes. While doubtless much of this went to adorn the backs of the Queen and her ladies, a lot of it went into commercial hands. The foreign merchants undoubtedly visited the whorehouses and would encourage their embellishment by giving attentive Madams descriptions and ideas of those establishments in France and Flanders. Since even then many Bawds were Flemish born they were receptive to any ideas that would improve their businesses and thus their profits, so it should not be thought that at such an early date the brothels were still primitive.

This was the period when once again the seeker after sexual pleasures might approach the bridge's custodian and ask, this time in good Anglo-Saxon, 'Which way to the whorehouses, mate?' But not for long; for on the Confessor's death the political and military situation changed, as it were, overnight.

King Harold Godwinsson had the cards stacked against him: in the few months of his reign he had to contend with invasions in the north, insurrections fomented by his brothers, and the aggravation of a bitter argument as to his very kingship with the Norman claimant, William the Bastard, Duke of Normandy, direct descendant of the Vikings; who invaded England while Harold was still fighting at Stamford Bridge. The rest is history. With the death of King Harold at Hastings, the English lands and the English people became the personal property of the new King, William the First, styled the Conqueror.

Chapter Three

Royal Recognition for the Orrible Synne

The Domesday Book, compiled at William the Conqueror's command disclosed that he had by his conquest acquired the lands and messuages of Edward the Confessor consisting amongst other good things of the Lordship of the Manor of 'Sudewerce' which comprised some sixteen houses 'along the strande' bringing in a rental of 18 shillings and two pence per annum.

He also acquired large properties belonging to his hated enemy, Earl Godwin. These in the main lay on the eastern bankside where Tooley Street stands today; but there were also some messuages (lands with sites for houses or with houses already thereon) along the strand, westwards of those owned by King Edward the Confessor, reaching into the area then known as Widflete (Willows by the river) and later as Paris Gardens.

When William came to make his pay-offs for the help rendered by his soldiers and barons, he handed over most of these lands to his courageous but rough and ready brother-in-law Bishop Odo, who had prepared the way for the conquest by diplomacy, besides rendering gallant help as a fighter at the Battle of Hastings. Five years later, about 1090, Bishop Odo passed them over to the Abbot of Bermondsey, and in 1107 the Abbot granted to the Bishop of Winchester at a rental of £8 a year: '... the stretch of lande along the waterside ... to the end of the bankside ...'.

The jump from 18/2d to £8 was extortionately high even for those ruthless days, but it gives the clue to the type of business which was being conducted in the houses on Bankside, since only prostitution could be expected to bring in such an enormous revenue as to enable the Bishop to make a profit and likewise for the Lord of the Manor and his tenants. From this time it becomes known as the Bishop of Winchester's Liberty. The wily Bishop quickly alienated plots of land to various tenants, so avoiding the charge of direct complicity[1] or management of the whorehouses, but since he had already promulgated a set of regulations for the conduct of these 'estuwes' and derived rentals from them, as well as other fees and emoluments, he cannot be exonerated from responsibility. Nor would he really wish to have been: for brothelkeeping was not in disesteem nor even a temporal crime: it was an ecclesiastical sin, or perhaps only an aberration.

In the Pipe Roll for 1130 in the reign of Henry I, Southwark is described as a Borough, but the Liberties of Bankside or the Clink, were seemingly outside its jurisdiction. Both the strand and widflete were even then *hors de la loi*, and this allowed the brothels and even freelance prostitutes and other 'vagabons' to flourish without too much hindrance for another five hundred years, and made both Liberties havens for sexual pleasure for the randy citizens of London as well as a cornucopia of immense profits to the Aldermen and other 'sadde and discreet' worthies of the City.

By this it seems clear that the victorious Normans found, ready-made for them, the sort of pleasure and entertainment which they were accustomed to enjoy at home in Normandy. It is also clear that although William's vanguard rushing up from Hastings to London (being checked at the City's gate by the massed Anglo-Saxon troops who had failed to arrive in time to help King Harold) burnt Southwark to the ground; the whorehouses were very quickly restored to service. There was thus little interruption to the men crossing the bridge although they would now be obliged to ask their way in Norman-French. This enforced change from the uncouth Anglo-Saxon to the more elegant Norman is probably the reason for the creation of the word 'Clink' which was the name borne by the Liberty from about that time.

It must be remembered that by the time these ecclesi-astical property changes were taking place, the morally

[1] L.C.C. Survey *Southwark*, p.45 ff.

correct Conqueror was dead. His son William Rufus ascended the throne in 1807. He was a man of very different character and although he was undoubtedly a vain and effeminate man he was a strong ruler and a man of courage. Rufus has been traduced for centuries, but his detractors were churchmen who resented his mocking atheistic attitude towards the Church. He delighted to indulge in such shameful incidents as staging debates between Rabbis and Bishops and threatening to become a Jew if the Christians lost the debates. In addition, his strong attitude towards his barons excited their animosity. His kinsmen, including his brother, later to be Henry I, also hated him.

His enemies accused Rufus of practising '... the eastern vice ...' and the charge seems to be borne out by the foppish and effeminate attire of the court '... wearing long garments like women ... and pointed shoes ...' which were clearly evidence of '... the outewarde signe of the currupcion withynne ...'. Moreover, the gilded youth spent '... their nyghtes in revelling and dicing and loose talk, and their days in sleeping ...'. Such arsyversy living must therefore be a dreadful vice. A more rational historian adduces sodomy *e silencio*. Rufus had no known mistresses nor bastards, a most rare situation for this lecherous family. Whatever he may have been, he was certainly no killjoy and had little or no interest in interfering with other people's sexual foibles. Rufus had in fact a mordant sense of humour which also must have contributed to his unpopularity. When he was murdered in the New Forest in 1100 he was buried in Winchester Old Minster without religious rites because he was regarded as 'a sodomite'.

He was succeeded by his brother Henry I, and a more sexually profligate character is hard to imagine. He had at least six known mistresses, mostly women of good family and several of them Englishwomen. Those known are Ausfreda, who was drowned when the *White Ship* went down;[2] there was Sybylle Corbett, two women named Ealgifu (Edith),

[2] The *Blanc Nef* was supposed to have been full of court sodomites when it sank '... filthy catamites fit only to perish in the flames, who abandoned themselves to the foulest practices of Sodom ...' William of Malmesbury. *Ord.Vit.Hist.Eccles. viii 10.*

Nest ap Tewdr and a lady named Matilda: and between then they gave him no less than sixteen illegitimate children, nine of whom were girls and not one of whom married any Englishman of any later consequence.[3] The early connection with the House of Tudor is interesting.

This dissolute character took it upon himself to describe his dead brother with loathing as '... obscenitates ...'. In 1102 Henry called a Council at Westminster which stigmatized sodomy, but prudently made the punishment the responsibility of the ecclesiastical authorities.[4]

Notwithstanding, Henry I was a strong and efficient ruler, who established the beginnings of an efficient civil service: so that when his grandson ascended the throne in 1153 he found a smooth working organization.

Henry II was the first of the Norman kings to speak English. He was also an experienced administrator of his huge overseas possessions which he added to his English dominion. He combined his grandfather's intelligence with a strong personality and great organizing ability: and above all had the faculty of choosing the right men for the right places. His personal life was summed up by Iwan Bloch in his *Sexual Life in England* as '... lived in open polygamy ...'.

The main motive for all Henry's reforms was of course financial; and to this end he was astute enough to utilize the intelligence and acumen of the Jews (with himself in the background as the Arch-usurer of the kingdom) by treating them with a general tolerance very unusual for that period, although even so, not such tolerance as that of William Rufus in whose days it was said that '... the Jews of Rouen and London walked erect ... before the princes of the land ...'. French-speaking and with extensive international connections, the Jews fitted in very well with this vital period of transformation of the English economy from barter to feudalism and nascent capitalism, with its concomitant changes in Englishmen's houses from wood to stone. Small wonder then that by 1160 a new stone bridge was proposed, to span the Thames and supersede the old worn-out wooden

[3] Iwan Bloch. *Sexual Life in England.* London 1908.

[4] *Concilium Londinium* 28. xx.col.1152. Ed. Mansi.

bridge that had given such yeoman service and had almost outlasted its physical existence. The Bridge Master, Peter de Colechurche, is usually credited with the idea and its projection and he assuredly got support from the progressively-minded king, who helped in a practical manner by diverting some of his revenue from his wool trade monopoly towards the bridge's construction. That it was also to prove a permanent thoroughfare to the south bank whorehouses was perhaps an unforeseen bonus.

This tidy-minded monarch could also take into his stride a comparatively minor matter, namely the regulation of these whorehouses, which were conveniently in and near his own Bailiwick – the Guildable Manor, of Southwark. In this he was merely officially legislating the ecclesiastical codes laid down some thirty years previously. The Church's attitude was pragmatic; after all it had almost divine sanction through St. Augustine's famous dictum '. . . suppress prostitution and capricious lusts will overthrow society . . .'. Since it was impossible to prevent lechery and prostitution and however abhorrent it was, it was better to regulate it and try and control it. So, like the pagan Greeks and the pagan Romans long before them, the ecclesiastics pronounced it as ostensibly '. . . to prevent the debauching of citizens' wives and daughters . . .'; but they were equally concerned with stopping or controlling '. . . the carnall and unchaste lyves of the preystes . . . whose fornicacions go unpunnysshed . . .'.[5]

A great increase in indigency and prostitution undoubtedly had been caused during the social and economic unrest in the reign of Henry II's predecessor, King Stephen; moreover, there is abundant evidence of priestly immorality in both monasteries and nunneries. The general standard of the priesthood was very low. It was a racket to which many resorted in default of any other outlet; consequently many of the vices attributed to 'preystes' should properly be put down to these unpriestly limitations for most were illiterate or barely literate.

That the incontinence of priests was taken for granted is shown from a touching little anecdote recounted by Guerard

[5] C.G. Coulton. *Five Centuries of Religion*, Vol.II. p. 651. London 1927.

in 1065;[6] where a kindly Abbot had rescued a young servant girl from the lustful attentions of a 'monck' and gave her shelter *pro tem* for the night in the abbey:

> *'. . . la nuit suivante . . . il trouva dans son lit la jeune fille qui l'attendait . . . la pauvre fille s'était imaginé qu'en la delivrait le moine n'avait pu avoir d'autre but que d'à faire sa maîtresse . . . ' ('The following night he found the young girl in his bed . . . the poor child imagining that he had only delivered her from the monk to make her his own mistress . . .').*

And the commentator goes on to say that into this Abbey to which no Queen was allowed to enter, a servant girl had come without any obstacle in the middle of the night straight into a monk's cell.

Coulton gives a number of instances which bear out the priestly lack of morals. For example, in 1157 at Wymondham Abbey, the daughters of one of the 'dairy widows' '. . . come suspiciously to the chamber of the Chamberlain Dom James Blome . . .'. In 1452, of another monastery it is said: ' . . . etiam mulieres in dormitoria petebant quandoque loca secreta naturae . . . ' (' . . . there were women brought into the dormitories and other secret places . . .'); and in 1492, of the Cistercian Abbey at Wardon it was stated ' . . . women of evil fame often enter the monastery . . .'[7]

The famous Abbey of Thorney had a regulation forbidding *inter alia* washerwomen and milkwomen from entering the Monastery because of the lustful nature of the monks.

Nunneries were in a slightly different category. They were for one reason or another, a refuge for distressed ladies, or disregarded widows, or unwanted girls of good family, or even wards whose guardians put them away on one pretext or another. Not many were there because of basic religious devotion, and thus still kept their sophisticated manners and did not especially wish to control their desires. So that it is not really surprising to read that in the 12th century the Nunnery

[6] *Cartulaire de l'abbaye de St. Bertin.* Ed. A.D. 1841, p.52, for the year 1065.

[7] C.G. Coulton. *Five Centuries of Religion*, Vol.II, p.650 *et seq.* London 1927.

14

lis quia non erit impossibile apud
deum omne verbum. Dixit autem
maria. Ecce ancilla dni: fiat mi
chi secundum verbum tuum.
This acte and ordinaunce was
made as here after apperith in this
boke in the parlament holden atte
westm in the viij. yere of the Reig-
ne of kyng henri the secund by
all the assent of ye comons.//And
so confermyd by the kyng & alle ye
lordes, of ye seid parlament. //And
in ye same yere & tyme of parlament
there so holden. Theobaldus, than · mort. 1160.
beyng Archbisshop of Caunter-
bury And Thomas, Beket than

'This Acte and Ordinaunce' 1161 A.D. for the governance of the Bankside Stewhouses, confirmed by Henry II.

at Amesbury was run by an Abbess whose lewd life was notorious and the nuns quickly followed the example of their Mother Superior. St. Brigitte of Sweden could speak about nunneries:

> '. . . *many of them keep their doors open night and day to all who come in . . . where such convents resemble brothels* . . . '[8]

Generally speaking in the Middle Ages prostitution and brothels had, in practice, become tolerated widely by the church, while officially forbidden or restricted to licensed premises.

The row of houses on Bankside, on the highway along the southern river bank, thus licensed by Henry II in 1161, appears to be the very first official recognition and regulation of public synne in Western Europe. The next known official 'red light district' was established in Paris by the 'Ordonnance of 18 September, 1367' – although licensed brothels are evidenced in Avignon as early as 1294. It is amusing and instructive to note that the building of London's stone bridge in 1209 was almost contemporaneous with that of the Pont d'Avignon and both bridges connected their cities with their respective authorized brothels; that is where the resemblance ended.

In 1161 therefore King Henry II promulgated the old rules under the following title '*Ordinaunces touching upon the government of the Stewes in Southwerke under direction of the Bishop of Winchester*'.

The preamble to the original MS is the Bodleian Library in Oxford reads:[9]

> '. . . *This acte and ordinaunce was made as here after apperith in this boke in the p'liament holden atte westm'in the viij yere of the reigne of kyng henri the secund by all the assent of the comons. And so confermyd by the kyng and alle the lordes of the seid p'liament. And in the same yere & time of p'liament there so holden. Theobaldus than beyng Archebisshop*

[8] L. Eckenstein. *Women under Monasticism*, p.205. London 1896.

[9] Bodleian Library MS. e MUS 229, Oxford.

of Caunterabury And Thomas Becket than beyng archideacon of the same . . .'

It goes on to say that the king ordains:

> *'dyuers ordinaunces & constitutions to be kept for evermore within the seid lordeship . . . accordyng to the olde custumes that hath ben usyd . . . oute of tyme of mynde whiche nowe of late are broken to the gret displesuir of god & gret hurte vnto the lorde. And vtter undoyng poore tenantis there dwellyng & also to the gret multiplicacion of orrible synne with the syngle women which oughte to have theur free goyng and comyng atte theur owne libertees as it apperith by old custumes thereof afore made oute of tyme of mynde for th'eschewyng of this inconvenientes . . .'*

Amongst the regulations, each one of which is preceded by a Latin rubric are the following, (somewhat shortened for easier reading):

NO STEWHOLDER or his wife to prevent any single woman from going and coming freely at all times she wishes to.

NO STEWHOLDER to keep any woman to board; she must be allowed to board elsewhere at her leisure.

NO STEWHOLDER to charge her for her room more than fourteen pence a week.

NO STEWHOLDER to keep his doors open on the religious Holy days: the Bailiff to ensure that they were removed from the parish.

NO WOMAN to be detained against her will if she wished to give up whoring: nor must the stewholder receive any married woman nor a nun.

NO WOMAN to take money to lie with any man, but she had to lay with him all night: and no man was to be enticed into the stewhouse; nor could any man be held for non-payment of his debt – he had to be taken to the Lord of the Manor's prison.

The whores were allowed to sit still at the door, but they were forbidden to importune in any way, and were not allowed to 'chide or throw stones' at any of the passers-by.

The women were to leave the lordship during the period that Parliament was sitting at Westminster, or when the king was holding a Privy Council meeting.

Of special interest is the rule:

> '. . . *that noo stueholder kepe noo woman withynne his hows that hath any sikenes of brennynge but that shee be putte out vppon the peyne of makynge vnto the lord a fyne of xxs* . . . '

And when the ordinance was amended sometime later the penalty was increased to the enormous sum of 100 shillings.

The Bailiff was instructed to make weekly visits to see if the women wished to leave; and also to ascertain whether they were diseased or not. There were a number of regulations controlling the activities of the 'gret howsholder' or stewholder, including forbidding him to keep a boat. He was not permitted to make a loan of more than six shillings and eightpence to any woman; if he did so he was fined and the debt was declared null and void. He was not permitted to keep more than one washerwoman and one male ostler (later on the ostler could not be any ex-soldier who had served in the king's wars overseas).

There were two sets of questions which had to be answered respectively by the stewholder and the whore: and the breaking of each rule was met by fines ranging from three shillings and fourpence to much higher penalties in other cases. For example:

If a woman came clandestinely to the brothel and the whoremaster failed to report this to the officers, he was fined 40 shillings: and the woman was fined 20 shillings, and 'bee thries sette vpon de cokyngestoele' and then thrown out of the lordship.

If she kept a paramour 'against the custume of the Manoir' she went to prison for three weeks, was fined 6/8d, set once on the 'cukstole' and then thrown out of the lordship.

If she was foolish enough 'to chide with any man or make a fray' she went to prison for three days and nights and was fined 6/8d into the bargain.

If the brothelkeeper received any woman ' . . . if shee be

knowe with childe after raysonnable warnynge . . . ' he would be fined 20 shillings and the woman 6/8d and of course thrown out of the manor.

The rest of the regulations concerned controls to prevent abuse by the Manorial officials and to ensure that the Lord of the Manor and the King got their own dues without backhanders to Bayliffs and Constables. On the face of it they look very just, but it is to be doubted whether any of these regulations were adhered to; certainly they were never kept in the entirety, for there were no less than seven sets of amendments spread over the years until a Great Court Leet in the time of Henry VI, all designed to tighten up the court arrangements.

It will thus be seen that contrary to continental practice, the English brothels were to be functional and sober: no gaiety was permitted, no refreshments could be served, since the brothelkeeper was forbidden to serve 'any coles, breed, ale, flessh, fyssh, wod or candel nor anie othere vitaill . . . '.

The client had to get full value for his money: the girl had to stay with him all night. This was probably a prophylactic method to cut down casual promiscuity and thereby control disease: and very probably this was the one regulation diligently attended to by the Bailiff on his weekly inspection, for notwithstanding all the hi-falutin reasons given, one prime factor was the (unexpressed) intention to prevent young men, or any man for that matter, from getting venereal disease. This would imply that as early as this time V.D. was beginning to spread more rapidly than usual: and perhaps it was also more virulent, having been brought back by the soldiers from the first two Crusades. Little is known about medical treatment or any methods of contraception; there were very few 'spitals' and these were mainly 'leprosaria' – although certainly 'leprosy' included the *morbus indecens* (the filthy disease), presumably gonorrhoea, as well as the 'perilous disease of burning' which was syphilis, as yet not separately identified nor named.

Behind all this camouflage about concern for the public weal and morals was the unspoken fact that these brothels were very lucrative and a source of great revenue both to the Bishops of Winchester and the Kings. The Monarch had a further bonus in that all clients coming over the bridge had to pass through his own 'Guildable Manor' and at least spend some money in so doing. The third beneficiaries were the worthy Aldermen and Burgesses of the City of London who owned many such houses which they farmed out to 'Froes of Flaunders' (who performed the functions of Madams as well as whores).

There were apparently about eighteen of these brothels originally, according to John Stow's *Surveigh*. Their names were to be painted flat against their walls and (very probably) the outsides were painted white to '. . . make them known for what they were . . .'. In this way they would be distinguishable from taverns, for most of them had names similar to those borne by inns. The only distinction was that inn signs as well as shop signs, were allowed to swing at right angles over the street. Moreover, being painted white and flat, they were easily visible from across the river, whence most of their clients came in small wherries, which ran fast and frequent shuttle services and helped the watermen to make money too.

From the ancient records the names of very many of them are known, although not the exact locations on the bankside. There were in Stow's time 'Ye Boar's Hedde', 'The Cross Keyes', 'The Castle', 'The Gun', 'The Crane', 'The Cardinal's Hatte', and 'The Swan': but others were 'The Bell', 'The Cock', 'The Barge', 'The Unicorn', 'The Blew Meade' (Blue Maid), 'The Half Moon', 'The Elephant' or Olifant, and 'The Bull'. There also was another 'Cardinal's Cap'. This last was a popular name, since as early as 1300 there were no less than four inns of that name inside the City of London, but its precise connection with any particular Cardinal is hard to establish.

The name however may be of much more earthy origin, as it may refer to some vulgar reference to the redness of the prepuce. This allusion is very old and found in many lands, and many even stem back to the Temple of Lampsacus in Phrygia in Roman-Greek times, which was the great centre of the cult of the god Priapus. The Phrygian cap, bright red with its folds in the shape of the rounded prepuce always had a great vogue. Indeed craftsmen in various London trades wore them in mediaeval London. There would thus be many such a cardinal's cap to be found in any brothel: and our rough forefathers would not flinch for dubbing a whorehouse in such a suitable term.

Within a few years hundreds more 'illicit' stewhouses sprang up all over Southwark, as well as inside the august City of London itself, as will presently be seen. It is not known whether these royal rules applied to them then, or indeed at any other time, although 'regular' brothels were known on Queenhithe and in Blackfriars.

Chapter Four

Over the New Bridge to the Old Stews

Henry II having now placed prostitution (at least in one small part of his kingdom) on a legal footing apparently gave the matter no further thought; yet during the closing years of his reign a judgement was given by his own Chief Justiciar, the great Ranulf Glanvill which was to establish legally also the rights of the Borough of Southwark. In 1181 he laid it down that:

> '. . . *a Borough was originally a walled town or place of safety, a sanctuary for escaped serfs . . . residence for one year and one day in a borough giveth a thrall his freedom . . .* '

The repercussions of that judgement were remarkable. In this way, Southwark Sokes, wherein every petty lord was his own judge, disappeared, and Southwark became a legal sanctuary not only for escaped thralls but for felons and misdoers in the City of London. A fugitive had but to get across the river to safety, stay a year and a day (this presented no difficulty for there was no overall temporal control and they had nothing to fear from ecclesiastical control) and be free. The *de facto* refuge in the marshes from ancient times now became properly established: and it enabled *inter alia* the Bankside houses of prostitution to continue without interference, albeit they stood in the Lord Bishop of Winchester's liberty and could not be interfered with anyway! It enabled the denizens of Southwark to cock innumerable snooks at the City authorities.

Henry II died in 1189 and was succeeded by Richard I 'The Lion Heart', the most popular king in the Plantagenet line. All the kings of this line were sensual, cruel and

Richard Coeur de Lion's arrest in a Parisian Brothel.

unprincipled to a degree unusual even in those brutal times: and Richard basically was no different. Indeed according to Sismondi he was '. . . a bad son, a bad husband, a bad brother and a bad king . . . '. Since he spent most of his short reign abroad, and his own amorous adventures were amply publicized (indeed the frontispiece to Dufour's *History of Prostitution* Volume V shows Richard I in a House of Ill-fame) it is not to be expected that he interfered with brothels and whores at home. The few occasions that the king did come home to England were for the purpose of raising more and more money for his warring and whoring. He also almost bankrupted the kingdom to pay his enormous ransom.

His reign started off inauspiciously with the dreadful massacre of Jews who had actually come to give him a gift at his coronation, and when the mob had finished slaughtering them, they turned on the Flemings as being their next most unfavourite foreigners. Despite the king's demand, the perpetrators were never brought to justice. There had been Flemish and Breton soldiers in William the Conqueror's army, who had settled in England but had never become anglicised completely. They were great traders and merchants, and it is not unlikely that amongst their imports were Flemish (which would include German and Scandinavian) women. According to Ploss and Bartel 's *Women*, Vol.II, p. 100:

> '. . . *Flemish women were taken to London (by white slavers and merchants) and considered good examples of (whores) in that City* . . . '

These Flemish woollen merchants were known from the Confessor's times. They had their own 'House of Flemings' on the east side of Old London Bridge. Thus from very early times Flemish Bawds and Flemish whores were part of the London scene, and as 'Froes of Flanders' we shall meet them again in Wat Tyler's time. After the expulsion of the Jews in 1290 the Flemings became the substitute for that unhappy people. The Flemings' unpopularity stemmed partly from the jealousy of their English commercial rivals, partly from native English xenophobia exemplified by the wry joke: ''ere Bill! 'ere's a foreigner. Let's 'eave 'alf a brick at 'im!'. The English whores too would show opposition to their Flemish competitors who were probably more skilled in their art as well as being more efficient as Madams.

Prince John, who all this while under pretence of managing the kingdom had been systematically milking it, became King in 1198. He was to prove the worst king that ever afflicted this country. He did however leave two lasting monuments. The first was the new stone bridge of London which he opened in 1209. Within three years the bridge was to suffer the first of its disastrous fires: *vide* Fabyan's *Chronica Major* for 1212:

> '. . . *and also vpon seynte Bennettes Day Suthwerk and London brigge and the mooste parte of London was brente* . . . '

Three arches collapsed. A change in wind started fires at both ends, trapping hundreds of men, women and children in the middle. Many jumped over the parapet and were drowned when some of the small boats overturned in the millrace under the bridge. The death roll, says Stow, was three thousand.

In the destruction of Southwark some of the old wooden brothels must have perished too. Fire services were non-existent; the streets were unpaved and when it rained they were inches deep in mud and almost impassable. They were however very quickly rebuilt and soon were back in business. Such is the resilience of human beings and of their sexual ebullience after disaster.

John's other lasting achievement was thrust upon him by his Barons, aided by the citizens of London. In 1215 on Runnymede they extorted the Magna Carta from him and laid the basis of England's democracy. Since he had no intention of submitting to its terms, civil war broke out the following year. The barons deposed the king and called on Louis the Dauphin of France to accept the Crown of England. Louis was welcomed by great crowds of inhabitants of Southwark and London with acclamation.

In the usual mediaeval tradition amongst the throng would have been hundreds of the 'daughters of the City' ready and willing to engage the gallant French soldiers and make them feel at home in the Southwark *Maisons de Débauche.* When, after John's death five months later, the Frenchmen left by the same route they doubtless enjoyed the same hospitality again.

Needless to say King John's personal morals did not differ from those of his family predecessors.

When he died his nine-year old son succeeded him as Henry III. This boy grew up to be a violent-tempered and cruel and rapacious scoundrel, who in a long reign of more than 50 years, ably aided and abetted by his equally avaricious Queen, managed in turn to antagonise every section of the English people. While Henry was so sexually profligate as to be branded as 'living in a state of polygamy . . . ', Eleanor la Belle was avidly concerned with money and property, and both used every device open to them to extort by force or persuasion more and more money from every section of the population. Strangely enough, they left one lucrative source of revenue untapped. There are no records of this reign concerning the stews, although they were flourishing all the time; the new stone bridge was a very commodious highway.

It was also the scene for very spirited protests against La Belle Eleanor's closefistedness. The Harley MS.565 in the British Museum chronicles that in 1263:

> *' . . . in that discord Elianore the quene was foule repreved and almost sclayne uppon London Brigge . . . '*

the bridge being crowded with the commons lining the parapets, and when she tried to get away under the bridge, they threw stones and dung on to her barge crying the whiles 'Drown the Witch, drown the witch!'. It was more probably 'drown the bitch', since mediaeval Londoners were not mealy-mouthed. But old chroniclers had to be careful too!

It is quite certain that the Southwark commons and the local strumpettes joined in this defiance of royal authority. They had already once shown it when welcoming Simon de Montfort and his army. When the King later gained control he never forgave the insult. His enmity towards London and the Londoners was shown on many occasions. He deprived the City of its Charter: he gave the bridge and its revenues to his Queen: he mulcted the merchants and leaders with fines – alternately pleading with them for money when they dug in their heels.

On one memorable occasion this hot-tempered irascible King, convinced that once again the London merchants had given him a bad bargain when he had compelled them reluctantly to buy (or pawn) his jewels to raise money, was overheard by Matthew de Paris (his faithful lackey and chronicler)[1] to mutter *sotto voce* that he was completely fed up with this city of inexhaustable whores and that he had made his mind ' . . . to squeeze them with tallages that would break a Jew . . . '.

[1] *English History*. Ed. J.A. Giles. London 1852-54.

Chapter Five

Of Thieves and Whores and Boatmen

The lack of documentation of the lives and loves of the English people during Henry III's long reign should not be taken to mean that they ceased their aberrations. Far from it. It was however only during the reign of Edward I that records became more copious.

When Edward I ascended the throne in 1272, he quickly made it clear that he was determined to rule autocratically and firmly. His task was simplified by the fact that in those days the levels of townspeople were nicely stratified into three social categories. These are succintly described in the Tax Returns for 1292 as '*potentiares, mediocres* and *populares*' ('The rich and powerful, the middle-class and the plebeians')[1]. People knew their places and stayed in them.

Edward had got to know his people well and in the main was congenial to them, although his avarice and ambition laid the ground for disaster in his last years. He was deeply involved in the Crusades and needed ever more money for his campaigns. His father, Henry III had squeezed the Jews dry and impoverished them and they were now useless as king's usurers, so he took the opportunity to expel the remnant of this unhappy people from England in 1290. When they were gone, he relied for loans on the Florentine bankers who now swarmed into England, together with the hated Cahorsin usurers, whose exactions far outdid anything done by the Jews previously.

The turn of the prostitutes and brothels soon came. The City Fathers of London were emboldened to follow the king's lead, so it is not surprising to find that in 1285, within

[1] G.A. Williams. *Mediaeval London from Commune to Capital,* p. 24. Athlone Press. London 1963.

the framework of an ordinance *De Vicis et Venellis Mundandis* ('Regarding the Cleansing of Streets and Lanes') appears the injunction:

> '. . . *and that no courtezans nor common brothel keepers shall reside within the walls of the City, under pain of imprisonment . . .*'[2]

and the reasons were spelt out in the next ordinance from the king himself entitled *De Larouns et Puteyns* ('Of Thieves and Whores'):

> '. . . *and whereas thieves and other . . . light persons of bad repute are . . . more commonly harboured in the houses of women of evil life within the City than elsewhere, through whom evil deeds and murders . . . and great evils and scandals . . . the King doth command that from henceforth no common woman shall dwell within the walls of the City and if such be found they shall be imprisoned for 40 days . . . and where found . . . let their limits be assigned unto them . . .*'

It will thus be seen that despite the special measures taken just over one hundred years earlier to confine the orrible synne to the south bank it had persisted and indeed alarmingly spread within the City itself. The 'limits assigned to them' were still the Bankside, so that another ordinance followed almost immediately to the boatmen who ferried across those randy ones who eschewed the crowded crossing and jostling on the Bridge. The synne could not be abolished, so it had to be shifted back again across the water. Hence under the ordinance *De Batellaria* ('Concerning Boatmen') the king ordered in 1285:

> '. . . *boatmen shall keep their boats moored on (the city) side of the water after sunset . . . nor may they carry any man nor woman neither denizens nor strangers into the Stewes except in the day time, on pain of punishment . . .*'

Since the Ordinance of 1161 demanded that the whore

[2] This and the next two excerpts from *Liber Albus*. trans. T.H. Riley. 1862.

keep the client company all night, this was no inconvenience, but the real reason may have been to stop malefactors or disaffected persons from slipping across the river at night to be 'harboured' in the stews, there to hatch their treasonable plots.

The hypocritical part of the matter is that the king, through his hidden nominees, the Jews, owned brothel properties in Southwark. For example, in the Calendar of Patent Rolls for 1280/81 the King had issued a licence to:

> '. . . *Isaac de Suthwerk, Jew of Suthwerk, to sell his houses in Suthwerk but not to put them in mortmain* . . . '

(that is, not to let them out of the king's hands permanently).

Subsequent reference in the same Rolls show that these tenements were situated on land called 'Bordych' or 'Bordich'. It was finally discovered many years later that in fact the lands belonged to the Prior of Bermondsey Abbey who was entitled to the annual rent of one penny. Isaac de Suthwerk, also described as Isaac 'Jew of London' was in his heyday one of the richest Jews in England. The Bordych[3] was most probably within the Great Liberty Manor on the east side of the Borough High Street on the riverside road leading to Bermondsey, formerly part of Earl Godwin's estates.

Hence Bordich may mean an area enclosing several brothels. Isaac may well have leased out these properties for this purpose, since the neighbourhood was full of brothels, and the revenue went into the King's exchequer. This raises the speculation whether one might have been a special house for young Jews to visit, since 'Jews and Turks' were forbidden entry into Christian (sic) brothels. After the 'disappearance' of old Isaac in about 1290, when he was said to be dead, these properties fell into other hands, but some part of them appear to have been granted to the *Domus Conversarium* (The House of Converts for the proselytising of

[3] From O.E. 'bord' and 'wic' – meaning either dwelling or hamlet, or small townlet, or a street in a town, from Latin *vicus*. E. Ekwall *English Place Names*. OUP.1959. 4th ed.

the few remaining Jews into Christianity) for it much later transpires that the *Domus* also owned brothels on the Bankside which they had leased to the nuns of Stratford-at-Bow.

In the same year the pious king enacted:

> '. . . *Those who have deals with Jews and Jewesses and those who commit bestiality and sodomy are to be burned alive after legal proof that they were taken in the act and publicly convicted* . . .'[4]

Shortly afterwards, it appears that the 'places assigned' had been extended to give recognition to part of the 'red light' area round West Smithfield, particularly Cocks Lane just outside Newgate, so that the Bankside now had a partner in popular prostitution. Meanwhile there are many instances in the records of joyful goings-on in the City.

The ever chatty Fabyan[5] tells us that imprisonment for '. . . nyghtewalkeres . . .' was now to be in '. . . ye tonne (The Tun) in cornhyll . . . a pryson for nyghtewalkeres bylded Anno 1296 . . .' after which they were to be carted, whipped and put outside the New Gate as hitherto. The Guildhall records also show high spirits: drunken revellers rolled barrels through the streets and on to London Bridge, what time one Willyam de Benyngtone was called on to give the sordid details of his wild night at the Brewhouse on the south side of London Bridge. Brewers, ale-wives and ale-hucksters were little esteemed in those far-off days. They were frequently in trouble and almost as frequently legislated against as whores. Indeed brewhouses were often synonymous with brothels and were certainly places of assignation in which all sorts of amusements took place as witness the following vignette:

> '. . . *dysinge and cardynge till past midnyghte* . . . *and ther one pyckethe an other purse* . . . *and (the felon) doth resort them (the strumpets and their clients) in and owte atta a backe dore* . . .'

[4] William of Malmesbury. *Hist.Mod.I.Ord.Vit.Hist.Eccle.* viii 10. 10.

[5] Fabyan. *Chronica Major.* Ed. A.H. Thomas. 1938.

The reference to card playing is very interesting, for it was originally a game reserved for royalty and aristocrats. By now it had descended to the gentry and the plebs, although played more or less clandestinely in brothels and secret gambling houses where the Bailiffs could not so easily reach them.

These pastimes, together with bear-baiting and bull-baiting, created an abundance of criminal talent and there was little or nothing to restrain malefactors. The spiritual power had no criminal jurisdiction and was, in any case, more concerned with fornication amongst the clergy. Moreover, to the Church, fornication and whoredom were 'necessary evils' as pointed out by St. Thomas Aquinas himself ' . . .like unto a cesspool in the palace: take away the cesspool and the palace becomes an unclean evil-smelling place . . . '. Spiritual sanctions weighed very lightly on the amoral ponces, pimps, panders, whores and brothelkeepers, who moreover now had the protection of the Bishop's own Regulations confirmed by His Majesty.

Likewise the necessary temporal power hardly existed. The King's Bailiff of Southwark had little or no forces to exert authority. More than likely he had a vested interest – even part-shares – in the proceeds, which naturally inhibited him from being too captiously inclined to keep good order, and so interfere with his own venal interests.

Other types of skullduggery were also rife as evidenced by the episode of September 1306 when one William de Prestone, who owed money to John le Spenser complained to the magistrates that although the said William had promised to pay, John had told his servant to follow him:

> ' . . . *the whiche he dyd thorough divers stretes untill they came to London Bridge where he (William) told the servant to wait for him while he went to the privie ther . . . and then left the prevy by an other entrance . . .* '

thereby eluding the sleuth and escaping into Southwark, although obviously eventually he found himself in the Mayor's Court.

Southwark's loose local government and the concentration of people of very uncertain status and dubious morals was aggravated by the presence of the bawdy houses. Because more and more clients passed through the king's own Guildable Manor, more and more shops and taverns sprang up all along the High Street and overspilled onto the eastern side and all the little alleys, interspersed with brothels. Everything conduced to tempting the gulls' money out of their pockets. Of course robbery and murder, brawls and mayhem were daily and nightly concomitants. Criminal gangs, up to 200 men strong, would invade the City, rob and disturb the peace and slip back across the river to sanctuary in Southwark. The law originally designed to protect runaway slaves and serfs trying to escape from bondage or injustice, now protected all criminals. That was the essential value of the Borough, and unless the King's henchmen or the Bishop's Beadles were very determined, no law enforcement agency was interested to find the wanted felons. The King's servants would diligently seek out political enemies but were otherwise not really interested. Maintaining law and order was in any case too expensive for a constantly hard-up monarchy. Moreover there were perks for keeping one's eyes averted.

Partly in self-protection the Mayor and Corporation had for many many years sought jurisdiction over Southwark, but their petitions to the kings were always refused on one or other pretext. Many City potentates owned brothel property, and records show that all this time tenements were changing hands in Gropecuntlane and Bordhawe within the City's walls. Perhaps these brothels were run a little more discreetly since, despite the high-minded moral principles expressed for public consumption, the properties which were used for 'harbouring' belonged to burgesses, Aldermen and even upon occasion, to a Mayor!

We now learn from the records of the existence of a maze of small streets in Moorgate and Cripplegate (near today's Coleman Street and Guildhall) full of brothels. The crude name of one of them not only describes what went on in it but also demonstrates that our forefathers called a spade a spade. Gropecuntlane first appears in 1276 as a property belonging to one Henri de Edelmonton.[6]

[6] Cal. Wills. Court of Hustings. Vol. I Roll 10, (50) 1276.

> '. . . *in Gropecuntelane in St. Mary Colechurche parrish near the Bordhawe leased from St. Pauls Cathedral . . .* '

The Bordhawe is already mentioned in 1275 as ' . . . le Bordhaw in St. Marie de Colechurche . . . ';[7] in 1305 it is called 'bordehawelande' and in 1405 'Burdellane', that is 'Brothel Lane'.[8] It is last heard of in 1557 when it is still 'Brodhawlane'.[9]

The word 'bord' is derived from a root meaning a house or tenement or enclosure used as a bordel or bordels, plus the O.E. 'haga' later 'hawe'. While 'bord' means timber it is also 'boarding' in the sense of an inn or brothel. The latter meaning is confirmed by the entry in the Calendar of Wills, Roll 51. for 1323 when:

> ' . . . *Richard de Gloucestre left to his daughter . . . (certain rents) . . . of a tenement in St. Mary de Colechurche and St. Pancras betwene a lane called Bordhawe and Gropecuntlane . . .* '

The Anglo-Saxon Gropecuntlane appears also in several other towns and cities, in all cases in their 'red light' districts.[10]

It signifies an area of the lowest type of prostitution, that is to say old worn-out prostitutes who catered for the poorest clientele who could not afford to pay for the full treatment, and so were charged à tiny sum just to put their hands up the old woman's skirts and grope. The same activities were carried on until fairly recently in Marseilles and Rotterdam, where every lowest foible of mankind was permitted and no sum of money, however ridiculous, would be passed up.

Ekwall also lists Love Lane and Maiden Lane, wherever appearing, as referring to former places of assignation or prostitution. Maiden Lane was hard by Gropecuntlane and Coleman Street. So was Love Lane, sourly described by John Stow three hundred years later as being a 'street of wantons'. Love Lane and Maiden Lane in Southwark likewise made no pretence of their activities, which had nothing to do with

[7] Cal. Wills. ct. Hust. Vol. I. Roll 25, 1275.

[8] Cal Wills. ct. Hust. Vol. II Roll 133, (44) 1405.

[9] *Inquests.* p.m. London i.159, 1557.

[10] E. Ekwall. *Early London Street Names* OUP, 1954.

true love nor could many maidens be found there. Gropecuntlane is universal. In Paris at this time there was the Rue Grattecon. In Paris Mary Stuart used to faint when going through the Rue Trousse Puteyne (literally 'the whore's slit') which is a rough translation of 'slut's hole'. Eventually it was shortened and 'refained' into Grape Street, and the northern extra-mural part transmogrified into Grub Street, which had the same salacious tenantry and reputation till last century. Codpiece Lane eventually became Coppice Lane: Shiteburnelane became Sherborne Lane. Sluts' Hole became Sluts' Well before it disappeared for ever in Mr. Elleron's Tenter Ground in 1700.

On 7 July, 1307 at the age of 68, Edward I, that formidable man 'fell back dead in his bed . . . ' after a blazing row with his son over the latter's homosexual behaviour with Piers Gaveston. Edward II was then 23 years old, strong and handsome, much given to the company of base-born people like carters, diggers and blacksmiths, and despite his homosexual leanings, he was also partial to harlots. His kingdom was heavily in debt because of the incessant drain of his father's wars, and the revenue was in pawn to the detested Florentine money-lenders, the Frescobaldi and the Bardi. A war with the Scots was also in the offing.

His exiled friend, Piers Gaveston, was recalled to the kingdom and made Earl of Cornwall. He seems to have been quite a civilized person for that rough and tough age, as well as being quite a capable warrior and diplomat. His besetting sin was a complete lack of respect for the rude and uncouth English barons, for whom he had utter contempt. This was to be his undoing, for within the year he was stripped of his titles and honours and forced to quit the country.

It was a difficult time for Edward II. Not only was there trouble with money and the barons, but the condition of the people was dire. In Merrie England of that time most of the people 'owned nothing but their bellies . . . ' in the rural areas although the townsfolk were somewhat better off.

Because of the King's lack of money the City magnates were now able to press him into granting them the control over Southwark which they had so long sought from previous rulers. Thus, in 1307 he granted a Charter to the City of

London, which included a chapter headed *Pro Meretrabus et Pronubes* ('Concerning Whores and Scolds') *vide* Liber Albus B.III page 322:[11]

> '. . . *NO WOMAN OF EVIL LIFE, whore or bawd nor common scold shall reside in the city but shall be removed immediately by the Aldermen and escorted out of the City either by the constables or the Beadles and taken to the Compter (the city prison) . . . and there kept according to the terms of keeping the peace . . .* '

The Church's pragmatic attitude towards prostitution is evidenced by a record dated 1321 under the sonorous title '*SUPER VENDITIONE DOMUS FACTA GULLIELMO CARDINALI QUAE LUPANAR VILIUM MULIERUM EXISTEBAT*' (regarding the sale to Cardinal William of a house, which is a brothel of vile women). The name of the house was *Aula Comitis* (The Social Club), and the owner, the Noble Lord Almaricus of Creda, wished to dispose of it because it was in a rather ruinous condition. He asked for 'a price of 300 Bordeaux pounds and a further 200 pounds to include the surrounding land and the ovens'. The extra *douceur* was twelve requiem masses for the souls of the poor in the King's name. It was signed on his behalf by Roger de Baldock on May 12 of that year at Westminister.[12] The Cardinal was William de Testa, papal representative sent to reorganise the parlous finances of the English church. The brothel may well have been on Bankside, since the Archbishop of Canterbury was then Walter Reynolds '. . . an evil-living secular-minded man, son of a Windsor baker . . .' and a pander for King Edward II's licentious requirements.

Notwithstanding all the troubles of the kingdom, there seems, at least towards the end of King Edward's reign, some

[11] In Norman-French it reads quaintly as: ' . . . qe nulle femme de fole vye baude putere ne comune tenseresse ne soit resident en la Cite mez tantosit soit remove par Lauderman et enchace hors de la cite ou par les conestables et bedelle amesnes al Contour et illoques a demurere salonc ces qest contenue en larticle de la peas . . . '

[12] Thos. Rymer. *Foedera.* Anno 14 Edw.II. Pat.14. fol.880. London 1704-35.

THE CHAPEL OF THE HOSPITAL FOR LEPERS IN KENT STREET, SOUTHWARK, CALLED LE LOCK, *dedicated to St. Mary and St. Leonard,* Founded prior to the XIVth of Edw. II.

M B
This Chapel Was Built
To the Honour of God and for the Use of
the Poor Infirm and Impotent People
Harbourd Within this Hospital
May' Mar' Bond Esq' Treasurer
Annó 1636
Inscription over the Door

LONDON, Published 1st January 1813, by ROBERT WILKINSON, No. 58 Cornhill.

Le Lock.

social and economic advancement and a march towards a better life for many of the people. There was a little more ease and even some steps towards certain elementary graciousness. Amongst the nobility this mediaeval time was characterized by the glorification of virtuous and chaste womanhood, but by the end of his reign chivalry had vanished, to be replaced by a general vulgarity and boorishness towards women of all walks of life, and of unbelievable harshness towards 'Venus's handmaids'.

However, if for nothing else Edward II will be remembered with gratitude by generations of sufferers from venereal disease. In 1321 he founded the Lock Hospital in Southwark, originally as a Leprosarium: but since many so-called lepers were in fact suffering from gonorrhoea or syphilis,[13] they were the ones to receive the most benefit, and ensured that after many centuries, the later 'Lock' hospitals concentrated on and specialized in venereal diseases.

The king's own family life and his sex life were in a parlous state. His wife, Queen Isabella and her lover, Roger Mortimer, Baron of the Marches, were exiled and openly living in adultery in Paris, with their son, who was to be the future Edward III. In fact so great was the scandal that the French king compelled them to leave Paris. Meanwhile, their faction in England had prepared the ground for their return, which they did in 1326. So weary were the English people of their unstable and unprofitable king, that they gave the Baron and his royal leman almost universal support, the Londoners in particular rioting in the Queen's favour, and murdering one of Edward II's most unpopular Ministers, Bishop Stapledon, the Lord Treasurer. Edward II abdicated and was imprisoned, his son being proclaimed as King Edward III, under the Regency of his mother and Mortimer.

A few months later, King Edward III '... borne in Wallys and coulde never speake a worde of Englishe ...' to quote one of his contemporary detractor's slanders, was most atrociously murdered in Kerkelsey Castle, by being smothered and '... with a hotte broche putte thro the secret

[13] C.G. Creighton in his *History of Epidemics in Britain* says that syphilis had already reached this country 'early in the 14th century'.

place posterialle . . . ' – in other words having a red-hot poker thrust up his anus, as a savage reminder of his homosexual relationship with Piers Gaveston.[14] A later medical investigation says that no trace of such torture was discovered on the body, but the matter is open to doubt.

The adulterous Queen and her brutal paramour were, naturally, no better than the previous royal gangsters, and the boy king had been biding his time for revenge for the brutal killing of his father. In 1330, Edward, now an adult, and with a son and heir of his own, seized power, killed Mortimer, reduced his mother's power, and began to rule himself.

With such a highly immoral background as well as an international upbringing in his early years, Edward III's bonhomie never failed him in his statecraft. His boyish attitude gave him popularity with the common people, and he was even in harmony with his nobles. He was a very able and astute king politically, inheriting too the strong will of the Plantagenets. Although war and hunting were his passions, and wenching one of his favourite pastimes, he never developed into a tyrant. The prestige earned by his military victories stood him in good stead when it came to solving the nation's domestic problems.

On his accession in 1327 he had at last granted the Mayor and Sheriffs of London permission to 'farm' Southwark and was undoubtedly swayed in this decision by the great support Londoners had given him. But he was astute enough not to give them all they wanted and had restricted the City's jurisdiction in certain spheres by the powers of his own Bayliffe.[15] This office of King's Bailiff for Southwark continued till Henry VIII's time.

With flagrant immorality openly and shamelessly manifested in royal and aristocratic circles, small wonder that the rest of the people took their cue; but while the rich were allowed to indulge their sexual proclivities to the full, the poorer and less important citizens were harassed and the puteyn at the lowest end was unmercifully treated. A

[14] The murder of Edward II is described in Higden *Polychronicon* (Rolls series), Vol.VIII. pub.1882. In the Middle Ages sodomy seems to have been equated often with sorcery.

[15] Cal.Pat.Rolls.Edw.III 1327, p.337;1340, p.447.

contemporary, more intelligent and merciful nobleman summed up the situation: '... those that were rich were hangid by the purse, and those that were poor were hangid by the necke!'

As if to demonstrate that these constant proscriptions were without effect, the Calendar of Plea and Memoranda Rolls of the City of London for the years 1338 to 1340 gives many vivid examples.

In June 1338 a Spicer, William de Dalton, was charged with keeping a House of Ill-fame in the City to which married women and their paramours resorted. This is a clear indication of another type of loose living, whereby the sexually unsatisfied wives and daughters of respectable citizens repaired to special houses of assignation, either merely to satisfy their sexual appetites or to add to their incomes by a little judicious and discreet prostitution. It was to some extent an offset to the private infidelity of their own husbands who often had recourse to the convenient stews and doubtless gave business reasons for their absences, then as now. This particular bawdy-house keeper was sent to prison but his influential friends secured his release after two months, presumably to start up elsewhere, since his special services were obviously greatly in demand.

During the next month Robert de Stratford, a Cordwainer and thus a member of a highly respectable Guild, was attached on a charge before the Mayor and Aldermen for harbouring Alice Donbelly and Alice Tredewedowe and other prostitutes. He elected to be tried by a jury and was found guilty and fined 6/8d; a comparatively small fine for those days and doubtless influenced by the fact that other members of the Guilds who sat on the jury were a little apprehensive. The normal punishment of pillory and carting would doubtless have caused some unpleasant repercussions.

At Christmas 1339, there were the usual junketings in the houses and the streets with their aftermath of appearances before the Law. Ellen de Evesham, who lived in a mews off Fleet Street:

> '... *keeps a Disorderly House and harbours theeves and prostitutes ... and that in Christmas week certain*

foreigners from her house attacked a man who was passing along the highway with a light . . . bound and beat him up . . . and carried him to the said Ellen's house while she was present . . . with a lighted candle in her hand . . .'

Fleet Street and environs were areas of *quasi* tolerated prostitution, being immediately 'without' the City walls and gates but still 'within the Liberties' of the City and thus within the jurisdiction of the Mayor and Aldermen. A picture thus builds up of a girdle of 'red light' districts to the north and north-west just outside the City walls including Moorgate and Cripplegate, then westerly to Holborn, Shoe Lane, Fleet Street and Chancery Lane.

In January 1340:

'. . . Gilbert le Strengmakere, living in the hospital rents in Fleet Street, and Margery de Wantynge and Isabella de Actone (living) opposite Chaunceleres Lane; Joseph Sewy and his concubine Salerna Livynge in Fayterslane in the rents of the Prior of St. Mary of Southwark . . . keep common Disorderly Houses and harbour Prostitutes & Men of ill-fame . . .'

The same charge sheet continues:

'. . . also two sisters Agnes and Juliana, living in . . . Holbourne as prostitutes & harbourers of men of ill-fame: Agnes widowe of robert-atte-Hale for lettyng a house in Sholane to a woman of bad character . . . and Juliana-atte-Celere of Cokkeslane (and) Alice de Lincoln . . . keeping a Disorderly House in Hosierlane . . .'

The 'hospital' rents were in fact mews or alleys rented out by one of the churches and it is noteworthy that the ever-enterprising managers at St. Mary Overie in Southwark also winked an eye at the sinful competition with their own stews of Bankside.

The women were recruited from suburbs, like Acton in West London, to the City of Lincoln, far away. Agnes and Juliana were assuredly 'noms de plume' for Flemish or German whores. It was the custom for prostitutes to adopt fancy names like Petronella (Peronelle in Old French means 'hussy'), Julia, Clarice and so on. Piers Plowman[16] refers to 'Purnell'(Petronella) of Cokkeslane' and 'Pernel the Flemish whore' as well as 'Ionette (Janet) of the Stewes' in Southwark. Of special interest is Juliana operating from a cellar in Cock's Lane which seems to have been a designated 'red light area' as early as 1241; and the presence of whorehouses under the very noses of the judiciary in Fetter Lane and Chancery Lane shows that the same men who punished sin let it flourish openly on their doorstep, for the ease and convenience of the same lawyers who would later prosecute – rarely defend – the objects of their lust.

Nevertheless the situation was getting the City Fathers down, because crime was increasing, and the houses of prostitution both harboured criminals and aided and abetted them. They decided to make a great round-up over several nights at the end of June 1340 in all the wards and suburbs of London, and empanelled a jury of twenty persons in each ward, sitting under the Mayor and the Sheriffs in 'An Inquest as to Evildoers and Disturbers of the King's Peace', and in July all the malefactors so rounded up appeared foı judgement. The original report gives the full flavour of the exercise:

> *'. . . as regards Cripplegate Without . . . John Mazerer, Walter Kyng. Thomas 'consanguineus Litelwatte' (literally a blood relation, perhaps a cousin), Thomas fitzSimon, Nicholas de Westsmythfielde, Walter le Tyretener and John Wantynge, are evildoers, nightwalkers and disturbers of the peace (and) that John de Catton keeps a common bawdy-house, and that John le Clerk is a receiver of bawds.'*

The authorities had now caught up with Margery de Wantynge's husband operating quite a way from Fleet Street, and in the bag there was now a cleric, John, as a known receiver of bawds.

Then the jury for four other wards considered their problems. Firstly, they charged Henry de Pountoys (perhaps originally from Pontoise in France), and a brewer, Nicholas

[16] Piers Plowman also mentions '(Sloth) wedded on Wanhope (Despair) a wench of the stewes . . . ' and elsewhere ' . . . Denote the Baude . . . '

de Kent, as being receivers of men of ill-fame in Aldersgate Ward.

This is a most important item. There was great peasant unrest throughout England at this period caused by the exactions of King Edward's many wars and campaigns, and the extortions of the barons in this time of changeover from feudalism. The various factions of the barons utilized the whorehouses for their discussions or machinations and the recruiting of their mercenaries. Brothels and taverns, and in some cases even church crypts, were also the meeting places of the dissidents, downtrodden workmen and peasantry, where they exchanged news and ideas and instructions for organization. Since they were in the main illiterate, although helped by worker priests like John Ball, frequent discussions and memorizing of plans must have been necessary in these purlieus.

The stark realities of the 100 years' war lay heavy on the masses of the poor; Chaucer's graphic description cannot be beaten:

> '. . . *The carraine (carrion corpses) in the bushe, with throte ycaerven, a thousand slayne and not of qualm ystorven (not dead of plague).*
> *The tirant, with the prey by force yraft the toun destroied, there was nothynge left . . .* '

More dangerous to the Establishment was the fact that many thousands of the common folk had arms in their cottages which they knew how to use; and those who had been soldiers knew also the value of discipline.

This fact was not forgotten by the King nor his barons; and the agitators, the trouble-makers, the popular representatives, the vagabonds were the 'men of ill-fame' thus meant.

William Langland's poems must have been sung, and slogans worked out. 'Whanne Adam dalf and Evë span, wo was thanne the Gentilman' must certainly have been repeated in secret for many years before it is blazoned forth as the slogan of the English peasantry and artisans seeking a new square deal. The slogan in fact was composed much earlier in the century by Richard Rolle de Hampol in a religious poem:

> '. . . *When Adam dalfe an Evë spane*
> *so spire if thou may spede:*
> *whare was than the pride of man*
> *thatte now merres hys mede . . .*'[17]

Meanwhile back in the Mayor's Court more vice was being uncovered. Andrew and Beatrice Wrenne were declared common evil-doers who had once wounded Alice le Shepstere in the nearby street: William le Chapman, an itinerant pedlar, received both evil men and disorderly women, and Hugh de Staunton is exposed as frequenting Alice de Stanewell's house of ill-fame.

Next day it is the turn of the wards of the Bridge, Billingsgate and the Tower. All nightwalkers are objects of suspicion even if they are only insomniacs, but Richard le Wayte from Essex is also armed with sword and buckler and is an associate of bad characters. Alice la Jueler keeps a disorderly house, and Henry, late Keeper of Henry Combemartyn's wharf, has robbed the potter, William de Satnes, of 22 pieces of brass worth 40 shillings.

Next comes an anonymous Chirurgeon, who is a receiver of bad characters: and also Agnes de Chedyngefeld and Clarice la Claterballock, who are in addition common whores! There is also a French nobleman, Sayer de Valoyns (Sieur de Valence) who 'prefers bad companie to goode' – but as this is not an offence (and perhaps because he is a foreign dignitary) the jury dismisses him.

It would not be strange to find a jeweller's lady mentioned in these bawdy goings-ons but actually Alice is a 'player' and what she plays with needs little imagination, but as for Clarice, whose speciality as a whore is to clatter her clients' 'ballocks' – a delightful phrase which must excite some curiosity about the *modus operandi*, she is sentenced, but exactly to what is unclear, because the jurors made 'no presentment'. Perhaps some had enjoyed her particular ministrations, while the others wished to experiment and did not want to forswear future pleasure.

The surgeon has the wit to keep his mouth shut and refuses to give his name. He is very likely well-known in

[17] E.E.T.S. 0 Series No.26 *Religious Verses* vii.

respectable City circles for his services, which may include convenient abortions or treatment for unfortunate diseases: it is certainly not expedient to have his name mentioned in open Court.

The explanation may be much more prosaic. It was the custom in those times when nobody had nor needed a surname, for the authorities on such occasions to assign a description. So one was made up for them. Often the surname would be the place of birth or residence, or the occupation; and there are many instances of one Alice, for example, being distinguished from a host of other Alices by being dubbed then – and presumably thereafter – as Alice Strumpette. There were many names which were so disgusting and vulgar that the learned historians refused to translate them into modern parlance, but recalling the essential simplicity and vulgarity of the times they were probably not cavilled at by the recipient.

The same day the jurors of Broad Street and nearby wards presented Thomas Whitheved (Whitehead), Joan la Tapstere and William atte Pond as persons of ill-fame. Their House in Apcherche Lane 'Atte the pye on the hope' and the neighbouring brewhouses were the resort of bad characters. Joan la Tapstere was most probably an ale-wife or a huckster of ales, and anyone connected with the brewing industry was suspect. The House 'atte the pye on the hope' was a brothel, and is linked with the next two items stating that not only are John le Leche and John Albon thieves, but that their friend Thomas le Keu, a 'herberger' (harbourer) dwelling in the rents of the Abbot of St. Albans, is a receiver of evil-doers, while Sarra le Mareschal keeps a disorderly house in the rents of the Archdeacon of Colchester.

The next three malefactors strike a very modern chord; they are described as nightwalkers, well-dressed and 'lavish of their money though none knows how they get their living'.

Several were 'armed nightwalkers' and included one John le Keu. He must have been a real desperado because he and his servants had 'threatened the Beadle of Algate Ward' who had refused to open the City Gate for them at midnight. The jury noted that there were some brothels, one called 'Le Breggehouse' to which prostitutes resorted, on or very near

London Bridge, the other being John le Hosteler's house and that belonging to Hugh le Peleter. One of the men caught in the net was Master Gerard le Armourer, an honourable member of a most honourable Guild, but he was a member of le Keu's gang and probably supplied their swords and weapons.

The tally of crime was completed by the jury in Farringdon Ward Without; at a Wardmote – a meeting of all eligible citizens assembled as a sort of People's Court. Thomas de Hundesmor living in the rents of the Church of St. John of Clerkenwell was indicted as an armed bully and manager of a group of prostitutes. They wound up with sentencing a job lot of 'male and female, keeping disorderly houses, committing assaults . . . in consequence of which the neighbours did not dare to come out of doors at night . . .'.

Municipal authorities had quickly realized that official brothels were a very good investment. As soon as citizens knew there were places where they could go and sin openly, or at least officially, the way was open for expansion. Private whorehouses had sprung up all over the place to cater for the increased demand: and the municipality had to take stern measures to ensure that such free-lance, even 'black-market' operations be stopped, so that their profits and their monopoly could be protected. The private sector possibly offered not only lower prices but better amenities; one hesitates to say quicker services and more choice of goods, and less regulation, but these were certainly part of their attraction. How great was the demand may be gauged by the fact that the City Fathers had already been constrained before 1250 to 'assign' the age-old 'unofficial' brothel belt around Smithfield as a place to which offending whores could be consigned, in addition to the Bankside.

Strangely enough there is no record of any City Regulations for the Cokkeslane area. Presumably the Bishop's Regulations of 1161 would be the basis. It is difficult to see how the Mayor could make any official controls for what was a punishable crime. It was expedient, therefore, to designate the district and turn a blind eye to what was going on, unless some serious breach of the peace or threat to established order supervened.

In a certain way, brothels served to solve some other municipal problems. There were frequent visits of provincial or foreign dignitaries with their retinues and it was the custom to greet them at the City Gates, and lay on a lavish and noisy welcome, in which the Mayor and all civic dignitaries and of course, their wives and daughters would participate. If they entered from the south, they would be welcomed at the Great Gate on Old London Bridge. While the taverns could supply food and drink, the billeting of large numbers of unattached men posed a different problem. The whorehouses provided a partial and practical, and doubtless very welcome solution, as may be seen in the contemporary engraving beneath:

A mediaeval brothel. Engraving by the Master of the Banderoles.

The handsome young nobleman is attended even in the act by his Jester, who feigns horror at the proceedings while slyly peeping through his fingers. The bed seems rather hard although the refreshments are adequate. Both whores look rather coy, but the banner draping the second girl encourages enticement to sin, to overcome the power of the cross worn by the young lecher during the sexual stimulation being performed on him by the first girl.

The brothels also supplied the 'daughters of the city' to

supplement the crowds assembled to welcome the most distinguished visitors, often in suitably diaphanous raiment, for it was not considered seemly that the burgesses' wives and daughters should be exposed to the possibilities of lewd approach or suggestive insult – however much they might have welcomed such an opportunity. There is, alas, no record that the City followed the continental practice of paying for the hire of such scantily-clad alleged maidens.

Likewise there is little or no contemporary account of the internal state or amenities or organization of English brothels: but there is enough comparison from Flemish and Italian sources to allow us to assume that some of the 'London Houses' must have been of considerable comfort, perhaps even of a degree of luxury. Some would of necessity have been of substantial construction following upon the Royal Ordinance of 1198 governing new structures, insisting that they be of brick or stone up to the first storey, with tiled roofs. There always was contact between British and Continental whoremasters, especially, as we have seen, with Flanders, with exchanges not only of information but also of selected wenches. Both would keep wary eyes on the various manifestations of local or royal tolerance or intolerance, as well as the content of new ordinances which affected them.

The wenches themselves would be exchanging information about new fashion in clothes, and in time these same fashions would be avidly aped, or at least jealously observed by the respectable matrons and damsels, as witness the rather disgusted remark in *The Brut* about 1345 (ed.Brie. Vol.II, page 296 ff) '. . . ladies . . . waering foxetayles sewed withinne to hide their arse . . .'.

Another chronicler, Knighton, in his *Chronicle of St. Albans*, page 57, H.M.S.O. London 1889 takes a swipe at the knights and retainers and other types of people flocking to the tournaments, which by this time had degenerated into circuses and booze-ups and for picking-up prostitutes as well as securing the favours of easy-going respectable ladies. The Latin quotation is rather long but can be summarized in the following words:

> *'... they dressed in a lascivious, scurrilous and lubricious fashion, with their breasts and bellies exposed to the umbilicus ...'*

adding rather wittily that they were '... ladies from the more handsome and more beautiful class, but not the better ones ...'.

Then, in the midst of all this carefree junketing the dreadful Black Death struck, with fearful impact on all classes. First it inspired terror and then, when all were dying in shoals around them, a reckless abandon amongst the survivors. Knighton gives a most detailed and moving account of the disaster, recording the general coarseness of the age, the flagrant cowardice of the rulers, the sexual immorality of king and nobility, the terrible uncertainty and sense of imminent death and damnation, which engendered the feeling that:

> *'... if thei were to be depreved of lyffe it mattereth not what thei did in the tyme left to theym ...'*

From the highest to the lowest, all abandoned themselves to sexual profligacy, ignorant or careless of the fact that the very crowding into the taverns and whorehouses was the best and quickest means to spread the plague. Many believed that those suffering from venereal disease could not catch the plague, others that sexual intercourse could prevent it. A marrying mania developed, since the rapidly increasing numbers of widows and widowers rushed to replace partners while life lasted.

It was perhaps with some rudimentary premonition that already in 1345 Edward III thought it opportune to re-enact and confirm the original Ordinance of the Stews of 1161, adding also that the whores must wear a badge of distinction (very probably a red rosette or ribbon) which had not up till then been the rule.

In passing it may be said that the Bordhawe was still flourishing at this time, as was Gropecuntlane; the latter appears in the records for the last time in 1349, under this name.

As the Plague waned and waxed intermittently for the

next fifteen years, so did the sense of futility expand, and one of its manifestations was extravagance in men's dress. So much so that in 1362 the good old monks of Malmesbury in their *Eulagium Historiacum* III. page 230 had a special chapter headed *MEN! Lions in the Hall: Hares in the Field!* in which appears the following objurgation:

> '. . . *in this yere . . . Englishmen have gone stark mad over fashions in dress . . . so that when their backs are turned you think they are women . . . they wear small hoods fastened at the chin in women's fashion . . . and a latchet (to their jackets) called a 'harlotte'* . . . '

As a break from this welter of sexual satiety there occurred in this same year of 1362 the momentous event that Parliament was for the first time opened by a speech in the English tongue. A few years afterwards William Massingham was to write proudly:

> '. . . *but lerid and lewed (learned and illiterate)*
> *olde and yonge*
> *Al understanden Englishe tongue* . . . '

and Parliament was to enact that all legal pleadings and judgements must be done in English:

> '. . . *menne of lawe fro thatte tyme sholde plede in her moder tunge* . . . '

The spelling might be a bit capricious but the sentiments were quite unexceptionable!

However, despite such important interruptions we are never far away from the attempts to defend morality: and the City's *Calendar of Pleas and Memoranda Rolls* for 1364-1366 return to the recital of Authority in action.

On 2 November, 1364 Joan, the wife of Williame-atte-Green, swore on oath that she would not keep her house as a brothel, and to ensure her *bona fides* she was mainprised (released from custody under bond) by John Chaundeler, Citizen and Cordwainer and a respectable householder.

A very rare case comes up in March 1366 before the Mayor and Aldermen. A man named John Bunny had been sold together with his master's estate, to one 'Joan Hunt, who kept a stewes on the far side of London brigge . . . '. She had set him to all sorts of hard labour, ill-treated him and starved him, and through carrying heavy loads he had sustained some physical injuries, very probably a rupture. When, understandably, he complained she rounded on him and got her paramour, a certain Bernard to beat and otherwise ill-treat him. When Bunny fell ill through all this usage, she turned him out to starve. His plight was brought before the Mayor's Court, who released him from his servitude and made some scathing remarks about Joan and her lover: but it is not stated what punishment, if any, was levied on her. She probably got off scot free because of the anomalous situation of the Clink Liberty, over which the Mayoral writ did not run.

Lastly, in the same month and in the same Court, the magistrates condemned ' . . . one Zenobius Martyn for being a Common Bawd and an associate of prostitutes . . . '. His crime was that, not being a freeman of the City of London he had kept a ' . . . lodging house for aliens to which he admitted prostitutes . . . '. He was most likely a Fleming who allowed other Flemings to resort there. This hospitality cost Zenobius a spell in prison. There are a number of cases of aliens keeping lodgings for their own confrères, and this was probably a measure for safety and social solidarity, for xenophobia was always rife in the City and could always be whipped up swiftly in times of stress.

So much for the troubles of some of his Majesty's subjects. The King's own affairs were also in a tangle, for when a widower and senile, he had become besotted with his mistress Alice Perrers, Lady Windsor, a very strong-minded woman who interfered much in public affairs and was profligate with power and money. As the king lay dying, she stripped the rings off his fingers, such was her degree of affection for the old lecher. However, she had made so many enemies that she was banned from the Court in 1376, stripped of all her property and barely escaped with her life.

Even in the last days of his life the old king was to be nagged about the wickedness of the Southward stews, for the Mayor petitioned in 1377 for London to have the right to punish all misdemeanours there, but the king still had strength enough to refuse, on the grounds that it would discriminate against others. On his death he left to his young grandchild, Richard II, an exhausting and hopeless war, a group of rancorous barons jockeying for power, and a resentful and rebellious people ground down by extortionate taxes and unbelievably harsh feudal restrictions still rife even though the ravages of the Black Death should have lightened their burdens.

King Edward's body was hardly cold when the pertinacious Londoners were nagging the boy-king to give them jurisdiction over Southwark, as well as, for good measure, an undertaking that the King's Marshal, Governor of the Marshalsea Prison (which was outside the City's jurisdiction) should not interfere with the City's Manor in Southwark. Moreover they wanted both the Magistracy and the Bailiwick of Southwark. All these requests were turned down. The 'mislivers' of the Bankside could breathe again.

Within three years there was to be something more serious to worry the burghers of London, the evil-livers of Southwark and the King. The pent-up resentments of the peasantry and commons of half England were to burst into flame under the inspired moral leadership of John Ball, and the equally inspired and excellent organizer, Walter the Tighlar of Kent, better known to history as Wat Tyler.

Chapter Six

Wo Was Thanne a Gentilman?

English history is a bitter story of movements led by kings and barons who knew what they wanted and were determined to get it by manipulating the ignorant and the poor. But every now and again their plans would go awry because there arose men who knew what they were after and who could organize the victims to resist. Such a man was John Ball; such a man was Wat Tyler.

John Ball was a priest of York, who moved later into Wessex, a follower of John Wyclife who preached equality of all men under the slogan 'When Adam dalf and Evë span, Wo was thanne a gentilman?'. For several years he had preached up and down the country to the peasants and poor working people in a tongue and with parables that they could easily understand – a forerunner of Karl Marx preaching a very early social democracy. He had been forbidden to preach and was defrocked in 1366 but nevertheless had continued with his proselytising, while training dedicated local organizers in some 28 counties, who persevered amid difficulties until the time was ripe.

Some idea of John Ball's method of organizing can be seen from the following 'advice', most probably inspired by Langland's *Piers Plowman*:[1]

> '. . . *John Schepe . . . greteth wel Jon Namles, and Jon the mellere and Jon Karter and biddeth hem that thei be ware of gyle in burghe and standeth to gidr in Godes name and biddeth Piers Ploghman to go to hys work and chastise wel Hob the Robbere and takith with you Jon Treweman and al hys felowes and no mo and loke ye*

[1] Froissart. *Chron. Anglorum*, 322. Ed. Jones. London 1862.

shape you to oon hede and no mo . . .' ('John the shepherd greets John Nameless and John the carter (i.e. all men of whatever type of work), and bids them beware of guile of the city swindlers and stand together in God's name and bids Piers the Ploughman (all field workers) to carry on working, but to chastise Hob the Robber (the tax collectors of Robert Hales, the Prior in charge of the Poll Tax), and to take with you John Trueman (only trusty men) and none other; and take care to have one leader only . . .)'

These injunctions would have been repeated everywhere where the peasants and workers foregathered, in inns and ale houses and also in the brothels. Small wonder, therefore, when the insurrection broke it was organized with great speed throughout the Home counties.

Their Lenin was to be Wat Tyler of Kent, and their Trotsky the organizer, Jack Straw of Essex. Wat the Tyler, son of a respectable worker, born in Deptford but forced to seek work in Maidstone in Kent, in a fit of angry exasperation beat out the brains of a Poll Tax collector. This incident sparked off rebellion in half the counties of England. The men of Kent, a motley collection of serfs, poor peasants, dispossessed small tradesmen, unemployed ex-archers and soldiers, first released John Ball from Maidstone Jail, then marched on London to seek the aid of the young King against the, by now, unbearable extortions of the barons.

They were welcomed with open arms by the 'comons' of Southwark as liberators from feudal oppression; and they were also welcomed by the 'comons' of London.

No better testimony can be given than to quote old Froissart:

'Many in the City of London heard John Ball preach and said' "they considered the country was badly governed" . . . the wicked Londoners began to assemble and show signs of rebellion and invited all those who held like opinions to come to London . . . and the town was opened to them . . . and they would so press the king they would be no longer as slaves in England . . . By this means the men of Kent, Essex and Sussex and

Bedford, to the number of 60,000, were brought to London under Wat Tyler the leader, Jack Straw and John Ball . . . Wat Tyler was a bad man and a great enemy to the nobility . . .'

While they were encamped in Southwark overnight they maintained perfect order but they '. . . despoyled the brothels . . . ', first turning out the women, many of whom were doubtless their own kith and kin forced into whoredom by the cruel system. Many of them would certainly have joined the rebel host in their hope of liberation from the shackles of prostitution, much as the whores followed the French Revolutionaries and the Russian Revolutionaries hundreds of years later.

The destruction of these brothels is mentioned in a contemporary manuscript the *Anonimalle Chronicle* which is worth quoting because of the important incidental information which appears nowhere else, neither before nor after:

'Mesme le iour de Corpore Christi en le matyne les ditz comunes de Kent abaterount une maison destwes pres le pount de loundres qe fuist en mayns del frows de Flaundres et avoient a ferme la dite measone del meare de Loundres . . . '
('The same day being Corpus Christi day in the morning these commons of Kent despoiled a house near London Bridge which was in the hands of Flemish women who farmed out the said house from the Mayor of London . . . ')

The Mayor was none other than William Walworth, Citizen and Fishmonger, head of the Guild of Fishmongers, former Sheriff, and then Mayor for the second time.

It was another Fishmonger, Alderman John Sybyle aided by Alderman John Horne who opened the gates to the rebels, who were then joined by the commons of London: and together they passed over the Bridge into London City, doing no harm and molesting nobody, until they came to Fleet Street and the Savoy where they opened the prisons and released the prisoners, by which time the commons of London had fired the palace of Savoy 'before the arrival of the men from the country'.

The rest is history. Richard II met the rebels, promised them pardons and Charters of Liberty, arranged to meet them the next day at Smithfield and, when Tyler came up to the King to receive the first charter, he was set on and stabbed to death by Mayor Walworth, and the barons' troops who had been gathered in the meantime then took a dreadful revenge on the rebel host. William Walworth, Fishmonger and Whoremonger, was knighted for this gallant deed, but there are historians who believe that his reason for stabbing Wat Tyler was not because of fervent loyalty to the King but rather because of the despoiling of his brothels.

Later in the same year, Walworth was succeeded as Mayor (1381-1382) by John de Northampton, Citizen and Draper, who made a great drive for purity in public morals. This Mayor was probably one of the 'liberals' who covertly favoured the 'comons' in that dreadful time. Nevertheless he had his spies and constables in every street to apprehend strollers:

> '. . . *and such women as were neither handsome nor rich enough to bribe his officers, were carted through the streets in great pomp with their hair shorn and trumpets and pipes playing . . . (although) . . . this was contrary to the bishop's express command . . .* '[2]

The incident which had spurred off the trouble with the ecclesiastical authorities was the arrest of John Kempe and Isabelle Smythe in 1381, being found in adultery and taken to the Mayor's Court and punished by a heavy fine. Such offences were normally punishable by the Ecclesiastical court, but the courageous Mayor was insisting that from now on sexual crimes in the City must be dealt with by the City's Magistracy. Although the Bishop of London resented this infringement on his rights, he refrained from pressing the matter owing to the still very dangerous situation. This was not a good time for prelates; they had come off very badly during the peasant troubles. Having eventually antagonized

[2] M. Concanen and A. Morgan. *History and Antiquities of Southwark*, p. 242. London 1795.

Church and King, it is not surprising to learn that the brave Mayor was committed in 1383 '. . . perpetually to prison, and his goods confiscated . . . '.

It was about this time, in 1384, that Robert de Parys, this 'Cittizen and Grocer of London', was appointed as the King's Marshal of the Marshalsea Prison nearby the Clink on the Bankside, which post he held until 1392. Meantime he acquired a plot of land further along the Bankside which was known as a laystall for refuse of all kinds into which '. . . butchers offal and entrails were throwen . . . ' and in later years this was to be known as Paris Garden and to stink even worse when next mentioned in 1542, when it had also acquired the stench of immorality.

In yet a further endeavour to contain synne, the City Fathers had issued a Proclamation in 1351 *AS TO THE DRESS OF COMMON WOMEN WITHIN THE CITY; AND AS TO THE SALE OF FISH*, a mixture as curiously worded as many in earlier times. The idea was now to identify ladies from women, a kind of early apartheid.

> *'WHEREAS the common lewd women who dwell in the city of London . . . have now of late . . . assumed the fashion of being clad and attired in the manner and dress of good and noble dames and damsels of the realm in unreasonable manner, it is Ordered by the Mayor Alderman and Commons that no such lewd woman shall be so daring as to be attired either by day or night in any kind of vesture trimmed with fur such as miniver, grey work (badger), squirrel . . . or any other manner of noble budge (fur) or lined with sendale, bokerames, samytes (rich silk) or any other noble lining nor yet to be clothed either in coat, surcoat or hood relieved with fur or lining, on pain of forfeting the said vestments; But to go openly with a hood of ray (striped) cloth, single (unlined); and with vestment neither trimmed with fur nor yet with lining, and without any manner of relief, that all folks native and strangers may have knowledge of what rank they are . . . '*

The word 'lewd' in that period referred to all who were not of noble birth, who would be known nowadays as ordinary people with whom, in the paternalistic upper class attitudes still prevalent even today, all prostitutes were also lumped. But the special sense which makes this ordinance pertain to prostitutes is that the hood or kerchief must be of striped cloth which was a distinguishing mark of a prostitute; the hoods usually had red and white alternating stripes.

In Avignon each wench had to wear a red rosette as the distinguishing mark, which at least gave her a wider option as to her general dress. In Switzerland, harlots had to wear little red caps. The ordinance was designed also to ensure that fashion should be exclusive to the ladies – the Dames and Damsels; but feminine reactions being what they have been for centuries before then and centuries after then, meant that women of every sort would seek to adorn themselves in the latest fashion and in the best materials they could afford. Another and sadder reason was that many a prostitute might take to finer plumage in the endeavour to protect herself from persecution by the beadles and constables, then as now, less liable to approach or arrest a respectably well-dressed woman.

In 1437 they were back again on the subject of dress. The Harley Manuscript 565 in the British Museum states:

> '*. . . it was this yere ordeyned that strumpettes shuld were rede (red) hoddes (hoods) and white roddes in their handes . . .*'

The punishment for wearing the incorrect dress was imprisonment, which showed the degree of importance the authorities attached to the crime. Needless to say, it was an ordinance impossible to maintain and was honoured more in the breach than in the observance, as witness the fact that it was rather wearily repeated from time to time until it was allowed to peter out. The improvement in living standards which had gradually percolated over the centuries down to the lower classes, doubtless hastened by the work opportunities available to them as a result of the Black Death, intensified this process. Hence the anguished protests by the nobility at the usurpation of this great dress privilege by charwomen, washerwomen and all manner of working class girls and women who, in the eyes of the adulterous gentry, were all harlots anyway. The great middle classes, typified by the wealthy and comfortable citizenesses, also wished to ape their betters, and eventually the obstinate males had to throw in their hand – not, however, before many a poor woman had been cruelly punished for such normal, harmless feminine traits.

That this is no flight of imagination or exaggeration is shown by the 'warning' given in *Le Menagier de Paris*[3] about choosing servants.

> '*. . . such women from distant parts have a reputation for vice which brings them to come away from service in their own districts . . .*'

a theme which can be heard today in many a respectable middle class household.

It was rather hard lines on the boy-king to be confronted with this problem at an age when he could hardly have been expert on the subject. Nevertheless in 1394, and in his name, the Mayor and Corporation returned to the fray, in an ordinance with the grim title of *REGULATIONS AS TO STREET WALKERS BY NYGHT AND WOMEN OF BAD REPUTE.*

The first part ordered that nobody, whether a freeman (a citizen of London) or a foreigner or alien (any stranger, whether provincial or alien):

> '*. . . shall be so bold as to go about by night . . . after nine p.m. or the suburbs (the adjacent Liberties including Southwark) . . . on pain of imprisonment, unless he is a lawful citizen of good repute or a lawful man's servant on some real errand . . . and also with a light . . .*'

An 'alien' could not be abroad after 8 p.m. But the crux of the matter then comes, after the usual preamble about broils and affrays and murderers caused by '. . . consorting with common harlots at taverns . . . and other places of ill-repute . . . and more especially through Flemish women who profess and follow such shameful and dolorous life . . .' who are to keep themselves in the assigned places, that is to say the stews on the other side of the Thames and Cokkeslane:

[3] J.F. Pichon. Ed. II, p. 57, Paris 1846.

'. . . on the peyne of losing and forfeiting the upper garment which she shall be wearing, together with her hood, every time any one of them shall be found . . . and every officer and serjeant of the City shall have the power to take such garments . . . to the Guildhall and shall have the lower half for their trouble . . . '[4]

Only ten years before, in 1382 the Mayor and Aldermen had proclaimed:

'. . . that all common harlots and all women commonly reputed to be such, should have and use hoods of ray (stripes) only and should not wear any manner of budge (fur) . . . within the franchise of the City . . . and if found doing so to be taken to the Compter and the Sheriffs were to have the coloured hoods and furs etc., found on her . . . '[5]

What the sheriffs were supposed to do with these old clothes is not stated either: perhaps they were to sell them on the old clothes market whence they would most certainly be bought by another '. . . comon or lewd woman . . .' for certainly no Lady, Dame or Damsel would be found dead in them. But the sheriff usually (and illegally) took their jewellery.

Such 'sumptuary laws' were to be a feature of much legislation for another couple of centuries, designed to safeguard the privileges of the nobility by prescribing minutely what they and their ladies could and could not wear, so that each class distinction even among nobility, was to be strictly observed as a protocol.

In 1383, the seventh year of Richard II's reign, a long ordinance was issued *OF COURTEZANS AND OTHERS TAKEN IN ADULTERY* in which there is a special section detailing the punishments of whores and Bawds, in a tone rather of exasperation. For the first time, the Alderman of each Ward is made responsible for offenders being taken before his own Wardmote, possible because sin had become so widespread that the Mayor's Court was overloaded, and the cases had to be sieved out to save time:

[4] Letter Book 'H' fol.287. Guildhall.
[5] Letter Book 'H' fol.139. Guildhall.

'WHEREAS, in divers wardmotes . . . are indited . . . certain men as common whoremongers, common adulterers, common bawds as also certain women as common courtezans . . . common bawds, and common scolds . . .'[6]

and to clear them out of the city because ' . . . no correction has hitherto been made . . . ', the Aldermen will make an Inquest (enquiry) in preparation for bringing them before the Mayor's Court if necessary, ' . . . within the next two days . . . ' because they wanted to make a quick cleansing. That was in 1383.

Within a few weeks yet another proclamation was made *OF MEN FOUND TO BE WHOREMONGERS OR BAWDS* with exact details of the punishments to be meted out, so as to avoid any loopholes.

Briefly, if a man were found guilty of being a Whoremonger or a Bawd, his head and beard were to be shaved except for a two-inch fringe on the head. He was then to be conveyed to the pillory '. . . with mynstrels . . .'. If he were attainted a second time, he was to get the same plus ten days imprisonment without the option: ' . . . withoute ransom . . . '; but if he offended a third time he got the pillory, jail and was then put outside the City gates ' . . . to forswear the City for ever . . . '. This was a terrible punishment, because for a Citizen to be shamed before the whole community was hard to live down: but to be exiled from his City was a fate almost worse than death. It was, after all, not treason nor theft nor murder: just a simple business misdemeanour, so to speak, the more galling because among the judges were malefactors like himself.

The punishments for women were traditional and follow closely on the old Anglo-Saxon precedents, with some Norman-French refinements added.

A female whoremonger or bawd, was brought 'opynly' (in an open cart) from the prison 'with minstrels' ' . . . unto the thew . . . ' (a special kind of pillory for women), pinned there for a certain time, and while there her hair would be cut ' . . . round about her head . . . ': For the second and third

[6] *Liber Albus* 7. Rich.II. Fol.239 b. Ed. Riley.

offence, the same punishments plus ten days in prison and eventual exile 'forever' from the City.

'Minstrelsy' was a vestigial remnant of something very much older. It was designed to bring maximum publicity to the offender and the offence: but in Roman times the sistrums were used to celebrate the '. . . lascivious festivals . . .' of Isis (Ceres in the Roman canon) which were avidly attended by women from every walk of life, and during which nothing sexually lewd or indecent was barred. The function seems to have become inverted during the ages, when the 'music' condemned the offence rather than lauded it. Minstrelsy ensured that large crowds would follow, banging drums and making all sorts of noises. Cartings were occasions for amusement and entertainment, much as a visit to the cinema is today. It was (except for the unlucky victim) an occasion for mirth.

For a 'comon courtezane' the punishment differed. She was taken from the prison to Aldgate, dressed in 'ray hood' (red and white stripes) with a white wand in her hand; thence 'with minstrels to the thew', where a 'Cause' (a piece of paper setting out her offence) was proclaimed at large, and the bit of paper stuck on her head. After the carting, she was led through Cheapside to Newgate and thrust out of the Gate unceremoniously to nearby 'Cokkeslane', there to 'take up her abode'. The punishment for a second offence was the same; but for the third offence, in addition, her hair was shorn while on the thew and she was ejected from the City 'for ever'.

Then there is a section dealing with priestly misdemeanours. 'ITEM: si ascun prestre soit trove ove ascun femme . . .' if any priest is found with any woman, he was taken to the Tun (a prison shaped like a barrel) on Cornhyll with minstrels. If he did it a third time he was exiled from the City forever.

If an adulteress be found with a priest (or a married man) both were taken to the Compter (prison) of the relevant Sheriff or to Newgate. Then they were arraigned at the Guildhall before the Mayor and Aldermen, then taken to Newgate and shaved bald and then carted with minstrels through Cheapside to the Tun, there to remain 'at the discretion of the Mayor'.

A single woman found with a priest got off more lightly; both were taken to the Compter, thence to the Tun where they sat until released at the discretion of the Mayor. An adulterer or an adulteress were taken to Newgate with minstrels through Cheapside to the Tun, and left there 'in the discretion of the Alderman'.

For a prostitute, such punishments meant little more than a trade risk, and as can be seen, even those exiled 'forever' came back again and again. On the Continent the punishments were much more severe. Ducking to death, or exhibition in small cages and then ducking and/or mutilation for *mulieres rixosas* were quite common. The victim was shut into an iron cage, which was then plunged into the water and frequently not withdrawn until the victim was asphyxiated. Such practices were common in the Plantagenet period when the kings of England were also rulers of large tracts of France. At an earlier date in England there was a savage law *MERETRICES ET IMPUDICAS SUBNERVARE* (*vide* Jacob's *Law Dictionary*, section, *Subnervare*) that if guilty, a whore should be hamstrung by cutting the sinews of her legs and thighs. No cases are quoted but certainly some unlucky women suffered this horrible mutilation at some time.

The effect of this ordinance was as futile as all the previous ones, for on 25 July, 1385 Elizabeth Moring was up before the Mayor on the grounds that under the guise of carrying on the '. . . craft of broidery . . .' and allegedly employing several women and girls as 'apprentices':

> *'. . . whereas the truth of the matter is that she did not follow that craft but incited Johanna and certayne other women to live in a lewd life . . . and to consort with friars and chaplains and all such men as desired to have their company . . .'*

As well as using her own house for the purpose, she also hired the women out to the same friars and chaplains for stipulated sums as were agreed upon . . . '. . . she retaining in her possession the sums so agreed upon . . .'

However, on 4 May, 1385 she had sent Johanna to accompany the chaplain (unnamed, but obviously a regular

A naked harlot about to undergo punishment in the Ducking Cage at Toulouse.

customer) and stay with him all night, which she did; but when she returned in the morning Mrs. Moring asked her whether she had brought back anything with her for her trouble that night. When Johanna said that she had not:

> '. . . *the same Elizabeth used words of reproof to her and ordered her to go back to the chaplain again on the following night, and whatever she should be able to lay hands on to take the same for her trouble and bring it back to her (Elizabeth).*'

Accordingly, Johanna trotted back and spent the night with the chaplain and rose very early, and '. . . bearing in mind the words of her mistress . . . ' and being afraid to go back without '. . . carrying something to hyr . . . ', she took a Portifory (breviary) that belonged to the chaplain and gave it to Elizabeth – the chaplain knowing nothing about it – and she '. . . although knowing quite well how Johanna had acquired it, pledged it for eight pence to a man whose name was unknown . . . '

> '. . . *And many other times* (continues the indictment) . . . *this Elizabeth received the like base gains from the same Johanna and her other sewing women . . . thus living abominably and damnably, inciting other women to live in like manner, she being herself a common harlot and procuress . . .* '

The jury found her 'guilty' and committed her to prison.

What is very interesting about all this is that the chaplain, who was obviously well-known to all and a regular customer of the crew, was not indicted by name nor even punished, despite the Law of the City or the ecclesiastical law, although he must have instigated the prosecution about his Portifory which was sold for 8d and which he never got back.

Equally interesting is the fact that Elizabeth Moring was otherwise allowed to carry on a craft and to employ apprentices. She must therefore have been a Guildsman's widow, or the legatee of a Guildsman. Her crime was that she used her servants for immoral purposes; but clearly, had she not incited them to thievery she could still have carried on unhindered her very lucrative sideline.

It also shed light on the non-religious habit of friars and other clergy. Possibly one of the reasons for not dragging in the chaplain was because the Mayor and Sheriffs were at feud with the Bishop of London over jurisdiction in crimes committed by priests and commoners in the City and did not want to hand him over.

About the same time another ordinance had tightened up the regulations for street markets which tended to carry on trading long after their permitted daylight hours. Hence evening markets encroaching upon daytime were forbidden because *inter alia* '... they are vsed as a cover for the synne of harlottry ...'.

Before the century ends there is in 1394 a reference to Bankside, when John Radyngtone, Prior of the Knights Hospitaller:

> '... *granted all ther waste lands and marshy lands opposite to London to Stephen Spelemen Cittizen and Mercer of London ... lying between the road runnyng from les Stywes to Lambeth* ...'

which land comprised part of the Paris Garden Manor already mentioned in 1383.[7]

Then in December 1399 at a critical juncture in the King's reign, his faithful and loyal old uncle, John of Gaunt, died. It was a disaster for the young man. It is perhaps of some interest that the ravages of royal syphilis seem to have persisted, since this son of King Edward III '... died of a putrefaction of the genitalls ... due to carnall copulation ... whiche mortification he showed (before he died) to his nephew King Richard II ...'[8]

After the deposition of Richard II in 1399, Henry IV came to the throne, and within three years Parliament was asked to deal with the *REMOVAL OF NUISANCES FROM THE BOROUGH OF SOUTHWARK*[9]. In the seventh year of his reign the King issued a Patent against Robbers in Southwark

[7] L.C.C. Survey. *Southwark-Bankside.*

[8] Thos. Gascoigne. *Liber Veritatum.* Lincoln College MS, Oxford EETS Extra 15, London.

[9] Rotuli Parliament. p. 111 669A. 1402.

Barton Maire John Barton Recordatore Ric Merlawe Robt Chichele Will Crowmer Th Fauconer
Nich Wotton William Louth Will Norton Will Chichele Joh Penne Will Sevenoke John Michell Th
Pyke Th Aleyn Alan Everard Will Cambrigge Joh Reynwell Rich Bartone Joh Piers aldermen
Joh Coventre [illegible] Civitat

Ordeinance
pur remover les estues

Pur ce qe devant ces heures plusours grevaunces damages abhominables disturbes murdres
homicides larcines & autres coes nusaunces ount sovent venuz & eschieuez deins la cite de
Londres & les suburbes dicell pour lencheson & cause del coe recourse receptment
& demoer qe les foles homes & femes de male & noisant [illegible] esteauntz ount & eyent en les
estues des homes & femes deins la cite & suburbes avauntditz Entant qest a doleir
plusours homes & femes ont este [illegible] tuez spoillez & robbez parmy lacause & enche-
son avantditz Et qe peiur est de iour en autre les femes filz files apprentices & servantz
des prodes homes de la cite sont subtilement per faux ymaginacion colour & covine
[illegible] diceux qe teignent les ditz estues come des autres pour un poy de moneye
retraitz & enticez & illoeqs [illegible] ils come autres psones reguliers & seculers sont
suffertz desire & executer les illeibles [illegible] de lour fole charne al grand abhomina-
cion & displesaunce al dieu & grand dishonour & damage de tout la cite As queux
cesser & ouster pour toutz jours le honurable home Robert Chichele Alderman de
mesme la cite promist de pure & charitable volunte pur doner al oeps & pffyt
de mesme la cite pour toutz iours en fee simple certeins terres & tentz oue les
appurtenantz en le countee de [illegible] amountantz a quarante marcz p an [illegible]
marcz esterlinges par la cite de mesme la cite annuelment appaiers al dit Robert
& sa feme durant lour ambedeux vies Et sur ce Henry Barton
Mair & Aldermans de la cite de Londres oue lassent des coes al plesaunce de Dieu
salvacion de lour almes remoever des males avantditz netteure & honestete de
la dite cite dun part & le grand pffyt & ese ausi dautre ordeinerent & stabilierent
pour toutz iours en apres a tenir qe desormes null home ne feme deins la cite
de Londres ne les suburbes dicell teigne nulles estues pour herberger
deins icelles par iour ne par noct nulles homes ne femes sur peine de cent
livres de paiers a la chambre a chescun foitz qe ascuny serra convict a lencontre
et oultre ce destre pris & de faire fyn al discrecion des Mair & Aldermans
Purveux toutz foitz qe chescun psone de la cite pur son honeste de mesme puisse
& lise avoir & faire deins son meason un estue ou autre chose honest al oeps
de luy & sa meigne.

Ordinance for the banning of stews in the City of London.

(*vide* Stow), but otherwise no records exist of further interest in the problem. Henry of Lancaster was a popular fighting monarch and a practical and energetic business man, but his reign was bedevilled with the unruliness of the powerful nobles. Constant wars with the Welsh took up a great deal of his time and in the later part of his reign he suffered the disaffection of his son, soon to become Henry V.

This lawless and disreputable prince turned into a self-righteous bigot and disciplinarian, and before he died in 1422 he found time to sponsor an Ordinance from the Mayor and Aldermen for the *ABOLITION OF STEWS WITHIN THE CITY OF LONDON*[10] and another one forbidding Landlords to harbour persons of an evil and vicious life.

The first Ordinance dated 20 April, 1417 was proclaimed by the Mayor and Aldermen and '. . . an immense multitude of Commoners . . .' and shows, at last, rising mass indignation on the part of the decent and respectable citizenry against a state of affairs doubtless aggravated by the civil and military unrest of the past 40 years, where law and order seemed to have broken down. The most convenient scapegoats at hand were the troublesome stews; consequently they thought that if they could rid themselves of this evil all would be well. The preamble sounds familiar:

> *'Whereas heretofore many grievances abominations damages disturbances murders homicides larcenies and other common nuisances have oftentimes ensued . . . by reason of common resort harbouring and sojourning which lewd men and women of bad and evil life have in the stews belonging to men and women in the City and suburbs . . . and what is worse . . . the wives sons daughters apprentices and servants of the reputable men of the City . . . are oftentimes . . . drawn and enticed thereto (the stews) . . . to the great dishonour of the City . . .'*

The upshot was that no man or woman within London or its suburbs should be allowed to keep stews (except the real hot baths in their own private houses).

[10] Letter Book I. fol. 193.

The next Ordinance then openly confirms that many of these houses belong 'as well to Aldermen and substantial Commoners . . . for the trifling gains that (they) have in letting these houses . . . ' and ordained ' . . . that henceforward no Alderman nor substantial citizen shall keep places for harbouring people of evil and vicious life, upon pain of very heavy fines . . . ' mainly because of the 'horrible damage and scandal' caused to the reputation of the City.

Early in the King's reign, about the same time that he was preparing his famous ordinance, Sir John Prynce, a chaplain, was taken in adultery with Petronella Albright, by the Constables of the Bridge Without. The curious part of this announcement is the mention of the area 'without', that is on the south side of London Bridge which, however, was not to become known as Bridge Ward Without for another 100 years, so it would seem that the City by virtue of its Charter of 1327 already anticipated its future complete ownership. There is no record as to what punishment was meted out to the reverend gentleman, but presumably he managed to have the matter dealt with by the ecclesiastical authorities. There is no record as to Petronella's[11] punishment. She was one of hundreds of Petronellas, since this fancy name had been a favourite with prostitutes for centuries.

Other lawlessness was also rife. Gangs of hooligans interfered with the poor laundresses and washerwomen by making 'imposts' on them demanding 'protection money' just as they do today:

> ' . . . *agaynst the pore comon people who tyme oute of mynde have fetched and taken their water and washed their clothes and done other thynges for their owne needs* . . . '[12]

To turn for a brief moment to the political situation, there is the important occasion when on 27 July, 1414 the king addresses the chief magistrate of London for the first time with the saluation 'To oure Worshipfull the Lord Maire' in

[11] Guildhall Letter Book I, p. 279.

[12] ORDINANCE AGAINST HARBOURING VICIOUS PERSONS. Letter Book I, p. 649. 1417.

English.[13] Curiously enough it is a title which, like Topsy, 'just growed' with the job: since for centuries the Mayor had been addressed as *Dominus*, certainly from October 1283.[14] It is thought that the title of 'Lord' stemmed from the great honour given to the City by Edward III, in his Fourth Charter dated 10 June, 1354,[15] of granting the Mayor a Serjeant-atte-mace, who was to walk before him always with his gold and silver staff of office. Hitherto only royalty had had the privilege of a mace-bearer, so it was a signal honour, and doubtless the king was well-paid for it in the end.

In 1420 the Paris Gardens come into the news again, when the gallant Duke John of Bedford became the Firmarius – a sort of Head Constable and Lord of the Manor combined. Long before the Abbot of Bermondsey had passed the property to the Knights Templar, who claimed the privileges of a Liberty by virtue of a Papal instruction:[16] 'That no-one shall lay violent hands on anyone seeking asylum in the House of the Templars under pain of excommunication'. Meanwhile the Templars had passed the property over to the Knights of St. John of Jerusalem, from whom the Duke now held a lease to farm out the property.

The Dukely regulations were not onerous, but conscious of his next-door neighbours and their daily and nightly goings-on, he had one clause which laid down that:

> '. . . *anyone who harboured by day or night any whore or allowed any fornication or adultery to be committed or supported any wrongdoer . . . would be fined 6s 8d and lose the benefit of asylum . . .* '

Doubtless the Duke's resident Bailiff would square up matters to everyone's satisfaction without troubling the Duke over much. The Liberty was very profitable to the former, who had a good run before he died in 1435.

[13] Cal. of Plea and Memo. Rolls. A. 43. 1413-1437 mem.9.
[14] Letter Book A. Guildhall. fol. 30 b.1283.
[15] Charter, 28th Edward III. 1354.
[16] W.Dugdale. *Monasticon Anglicorum* Vol.III. p. 189. 1686. *Ne quis injiciat manus violentes in confugientes ad domos Templariorum sub poena excommunicationis.* Pope Innocent IV. ca. 1250 A.D.

One of the first records in Henry V's reign had dealt with the adultery of a priest, and the last incident recorded in the City's Letter Book I for 1420, concerned yet another, Sir Roger Wattes, the Chaplain to the Guild of Fishmongers '. . . who was taken in adultery (*in luxeria*) with Alice Soureby of Bridge Ward near St. Magnus' Churche . . .'. Letter Book I shows that in the same year a very large number of reverend gentlemen were taken in adultery in the stews in Queenhithe and Billingsgate: they were at least patriotic, for judging by the names of the harlots cited, all were English women.

Then in the midst of his triumphs, King Henry V died in August 1422 and his infant son came to the throne as Henry VI, with his uncle, Humphrey 'The Good Duke' of Gloucester as Protector of the Realm. The course of lechery was slightly altered, but not impeded.

Chapter Seven

For to Eschewe the Orrible Stynkynge Synne

Duke Humphrey of Gloucester was popular with the Londoners. He built a palace at Baynard's Castle Liberty, infamous because of the existence for two centuries afterwards of a street of whorehouses called 'Duke Humphrey's Rents'.

His popularity helped him a great deal during his otherwise quite inept rule. The young King Henry VI was crowned in November 1429 but he already showed signs of the nervous instability which dogged him all his life. He was a pious, good-natured, disinterested weakling, remote in morals and manners from his coarse age. He was sent to Paris when he was ten years old and with typical *éclat* his hosts welcomed him at the Porte St. Denis with the pleasant sight of three naked *filles de joie* swimming round a fountain for his special delectation; but it seems to have had little effect upon his appetites.

One bright spot was the record in March 1427 when a number of people in Queenhithe successfully protested that they were carrying on honest stews – real clean hot baths, morally and physically for women, and were all mainprised (released on assurances) from responsible citizens. Washer-women, however, were still excluded from entering these stews.

That the other kind of stewhouse was still flourishing appears from a mention of '. . . le Stuehous in Love Lane . . . ' in 1428.[1] The first mention of this well-known street of whorehouses was in 1393 when it is referred to in a will as 'Love lane formerly called Roppeland . . . '. Its old name was never completely lost, because in 1455 there is yet

[1] Cal. Wills. ii 311, 464, 536

another reference in a will to '... Roperslane now Love Lane ...' – such is the tenacity of tradition and the persistence of whoredom.

The King's government was feeble and corrupt and bankrupt from the unceasing wars. But amidst all his troubles and preoccupations the pious King still had time to issue an Ordinance in Parliament in 1433 to try to restore some semblance of order in the Borough of Southwark and its stews and taverns, and also to settle another problem which was worrying the worthy Mayor and Aldermen of the City of London. In its quaint English, it is worthwhile setting it out:

> *'PLEASE HIT TO THE WYSDOME and high discretion of the worshipful Communes in this present Parliament assemblid, to consider a grete myschief in late dayes begonne amonge untrew lyvers and people without conscience and yet duellyng in a suspect and wycked place called the Stews in the Burgh of Southewerke in the Shire of Surr'. That ys to wete, how that ... diverse persones of right grete poverte and right disolute governance withinne a fewe yeres duellyng in the said suspect place ... have sodenly comyn to grett rychesse, and therwith purchasyd grett lyvelod of Londes & Tenementes to right grete value yerly: ... and been ofte retourned by the Shereve of the Shire and oyere Baillifs and sworen in Enquestes, as wel for felonies and trespasses betwene the Kyng and (other) partie ... and howe the said suspect people enhabyte hem in comune Hostries & Tavernes in the high strete ... these recettyng Theves, comune women & other mysdoers in like wyse as they deden at the ... stewys ... and that the Justices of the Pees ... punysche hem ... by fyne and raunson & imprisonyng of here bodies ... for the love of God and in the way of charites. LE ROY LE VOET.'*

Now this really was a pretty kettle of fish. Not only had several rogues made great fortunes after a few years as brothelkeepers but they had become respectable landlords in the Borough, had bought freeholds and lands bringing in at least 40 shillings a year and so become eligible to sit on juries, where they were able to obstruct and pervert the course of justice, and get their pals let off punishments even for murder and other heinous offences. Parliament reacted with unusual speed to decree that men who had once lived in the stews must be debarred from holding taverns or hostelries elsewhere in Southwark or from participation in any official bodies such as juries and inquests outside the stews.

This in fact links up with the City Ordinance of 1417 whereby men and women, who had once been indicted for bawdry inside one of the City's wards, had found other places of residence elsewhere, not only in the suburbs but in the houses of wealthy and respectable burghers. The problem was to come up again in 1453 when Robert Poynings, a substantial citizen of Southwark who had supported Jack Cade, and whose wealth had been amassed in such a manner, was indicted.

Even more curious is the moral obliquity which denied Southwark whoremongers from enjoying the privileges secured by their wealth and from reaching – so to speak – respectable bourgeois status, while the respectable burgesses of London who did exactly the same thing, had enjoyed all civic rights for centuries without anyone preventing them from serving on juries or at inquests. The mitigating excuse may well have been that if the profits from whoredom were spent on founding churches and chapels in the City to the Glory of God, the tainted source would be overlooked on high; in contrast with the wicked whoremongers in Southwark who used their money and the consequent legal freedoms just to defend other felons, here below. It is a nice point, still the subject of argument.

Even this comprehensive ordinance proved ineffective, for in 1436 the Lord Mayor addressed an appeal to Parliament with much the same content, but adding for good measure that there were in the main '. . . Frensshemen Piccardes and Flemmynges . . .'. A little xenophobia was always useful. They demanded that all these elements should be '. . . confined . . . to the Banke . . .'.

The City was troubled with adulterous priests in the paid service of various organizations, especially Guilds; so much so that they found it necessary to adopt a form of Charge Sheet for use in bulk (like today's Rate Summonses). An example is extant dated October 1437:

> '*The mayr commaundith on the kinges bihalf that no man from this daye forward w'in the fraunchise of this Cite of London holde in servyse ne give no maner salary to N.B. that here is, in peyn of payinge the doble sume to the Chambre of the said salaries to the Chambre of London for he is founden in suspect place in wey of synne for he is founde in doynge fornicacion (avowtri) w't J.N. that here is present . . .* '[2]

This was an attempt to hold the employing Guild or other organization responsible for the misdoing of its clergy, since the office of Chaplain in those days was well paid and also well esteemed. It says much for the laxity of priestly morals that it was necessary to go in for mass production of charge sheets.

The Harley MS 565 under the year 1438 says:

> ' . . . *also in the same yere in hervest tyme weren too baudes sett vppon the pillorye and iij strumpettes weren led to Neugate . . . how they shulde be putt owte of the franchise of London citie and no moo comyn withinne the walls* . . . '

Just to show that not all stews were for the purpose of bathing in the hot waters of lust there appears at this time a reference in Court to an honest stew[3] when Magdalen Johnson swore:

> ' . . . *thatte shee would kepe a respectable stewhouse* (balneum) *and not allow any prostitution adultery or fornication to take place there* . . . '

and to make sure she kept her word, Master William Wolnore, Citizen and Skinner stood bond for her in the sum of 10 pounds. The fact that such a large bond was demanded infers that in fact the *balneum* had not always been quite so respectable as Magdalen (surely a most apposite name) had averred.

[2] Letter Book I. fol.289. Guildhall.
[3] Cal. Plea and Memoranda Rolls. March 8th. Roll 66. 1439.

Before the same court a month later, a woman named Margaret was charged with:

> '. . . *procuring a young girl named Isabel Lane for certayn Lombards and men unknown; which Isabel was deflowered against her will in Margaret's house and elsewhere, for certayne sums of money which Margaret collected, and then afterwards took the girl over to the common stewes on the banks of the Thames in Surrey against her will for immoral purposes with a certain gentleman on four occasions against her will* . . . . '

This Margaret was a hard case, because in the same indictment she took a girl named Joan Wakelyn to a house in the parish of St. Katherine Coleman by prior arrangements with a 'certain important Lombard' who paid Joan 12d. for 'her wicked and unlawful behaviour'. Joan had to pay Margaret 4d. from that money; and so in turn Joan procured Margaret taking her at dark to the home of 'a very prodigal Venetian' and:

> '. . . *both women for a long time taking no thought for the safety of their souls had carried on this base and detestable manner of life* . . . '

The report shows that the Bordhawe was still functioning in the Coleman Street area, and also that the district was still frequented by Italian merchants and visitors, who were good, regular and appreciative clients.

To demonstrate that no part of London was now free from synne, the Court heard a case in January 1440[4] when Robert Large was Mayor, in examining '. . . immorality, common procurers and protestitutes . . . ' plying their trade in Tower Ward hard by the Tower of London . . . '. Their informers gave them the names of Katherine Frenssh, Sibil Eddon, Katherine Clerk and Alice Moysant as engaged in prostitution over a long period, who all admitted many acts of immorality with Ralph Hislam, Simon Strengere and many others in the preceding month. The first three women confessed their guilt, but Alice Moysant '. . . confessed that she could not

[4] Cal. Plea and Memoranda Rolls. Roll 67, fol.10. 1439-1440.

deny the indictment . . . ' which seems to be a curious plea of 'Not quite Guilty but . . . '.

In February 1445 George Fynse Esquier was taken and detained in prison on the complaint of Richard Crips (or Grips) a Cittizen and Wheelwright that Fynse had:

> '. . . *four yeres and mor had encouraged open fornication and adultery there (in Fynse' house) and had been an assiduous friend of many persons seeking and leading a detestable lyfe.*'

Mr. Fynse however had 'refused to find mainprise for obeying the law and appearing for judgement . . .' and so was remanded in the Sheriff's custody. Mr. Fynse was a Gentleman and thus entitled to be treated in a different manner. Since he certainly could have raised any necessary sureties, but for some private reason had refused to avail himself of his legal rights, the case was held open in case he wished to change his mind and secure someone to stand responsible for him. The presumption here is that he carried on a house of assignation to which repaired many a respectable lady and gentleman who would be well known to the jurors and the court, and it was preferable for him to stay mum so as not to give evidence which might incriminate any clients. Very probably Mr. Crips, a member of the Guild of Wheelwrights, made the complaint because his wife or daughter was one of the visitors to the establishment.

Things had gone so badly in Southwark over the years, that one of the last Ordinances which Henry VI issued during his last lucid period in 1460 when at Coventry, was to appoint a Commission of twenty reputable citizens to enquire into events:

> '. . . *owing to the number of prostitutes in Southwerk and other places adjacent many homicides, plunderings and improprieties have occurred, and although the ministers and officers of the church have cited such and others supporting their sins to the correction of their souls according to canonical sanctions, yet they continue in sin because the church cannot compel them to appear for their crimes by ecclesiastical censure only* . . . '

The Commissioners were therefore '... to remove all such prostitutes and others dwelling within the said Borough and places, if necessary by imprisonment ... ' and also to remove '... all persons who refuse submission to ecclesiastical correction as certified by the Bishop of Winchester or his ministers ... '.[5]

In 1460 Townley was constrained in his *Mysteries* to sum up the current scene in the words '... ye Ianettys of the stewys and lychouris on lofte!' (The Janets of the brothels and the lechers on high!)

The Commissioners' reform obviously did not work because long before the end of the century women were being recruited again into the stews.

In 1449 came Jack Cade's rebellion. This was no mob of disorganized miscreants, but an army composed of disgruntled peasantry and ex-soldiers, with a political programme so socialistic that Cade was known both as 'The Capteyn' and 'Jak Amende-All'. He roused the commons of Kent and marched them in good order to Southwark, where Hall's 'Chronicle' records:

> *'The Capteyn beynge advertised of the kynges absence came first to Southewerke and there lodged at the Whyt Harte, prohibiting to all men, murder rape or robbing, by whiche colour he allured hymselfe to the hartes of the common people ... '*

He had support from a great many powerful citizens of Southwark, and they included the rich inn-cum-brothel keeper Robert Poynings, who acted as Cade's sword-bearer and server. However for some unknown reason, discipline broke down and '... hys menne began to riful and to robbe ... '. Next day the commons of London welcomed him together with the men of Essex who had marched in to swell the rebellion: but they began to loot widely in the rich metropolis, and alienated thereby not only the sympathy of the progressive shopkeepers, but caused their whilom allies the London commons to turn against them. In the subsequent *mêlée* two very popular 'liberal' Aldermen were killed, the Capteyne fled into Sussex, where he was caught

[5] Cal. Patent Rolls. p. 610. 1452-61.

and slain, and his head, with many others of his companions', adorned London Bridge for years. While the king's revenge was murderous against the peasantry, it had to be mitigated in the case of the wealthier supporters, and Robert Poynings, being a man of consequence was amongst a number of other Southwarkians who had to be pardoned. He appears in later records as the owner of the 'Crossed Keys' which was a known brothel. (Centuries later this inn came into the possession of the father of John Harvard, the founder of Harvard University.)

In 1453 the King fell into a state of imbecility which lasted until the end of the next year. The Duke of York took up arms and the War of the Roses began. No questions of national interest were involved: it was a faction fight between two great families for the possession of the Crown and because no principles were involved there were frequent changes in allegiance purely on the grounds of expediency. It was a bleeding operation performed by the baronage upon its own body, and the mass of people were not involved, nor did the Londoners take sides. Some months later Henry VI was murdered and by 1461 Edward IV was secure on his throne.

King Edward IV was a cruel and treacherous man, but his pleasant manner made him popular and he was clever enough to ingratiate himself with the great citizens of London and particularly with their women, whom he greatly fancied, for like all his forebears he was a great voluptuary.

He was also a bit of a sybarite for his time, as may be seen from the glimpse of his toilet habits in his 'Householde Boke' for the period 1461-83:

> '*. . . thys barbour shal haue everie Satyrday nyghte if it please the Kinge to cleanse hys head legges or feet and for his shaving . . . (he shall get) . . . 2 loves, 1 picher of wine . . . .*'

At one time he had no less than three concurrent mistresses, Lady Eleanor Butler, Lady Elizabeth Lucy and the lovely Jane Shore, after whom the London Borough of Shoreditch is alleged to be named – although old John Stow says sourly that it was a 'sewerditch' running down to the Thames.

This beautiful girl, daugher of respectable parents, was married very young to a rich elderly Goldsmith and Mercer, Master Matthew Shore; but she was early seduced by the gallant Lord Hastings who was clearly her real love. Both her husband and Hastings however retired into the background when the king made her his official mistress. Fabyan gossiping:[6]

> '... *Jane Shor's husband who by the lyke glass (a mirror) saw the vnchaste embraces of hys wyf and king Edward the Fourth* ... '

The king is credited with the wisecrack according to the Chronicle of Edward Hall that he had three concubines '... whiche in diverse properties diversely excelled: one was the 'meriest', the other the wiliest, and the third the holiest harlot in the realme ...'. Jane Shore was certainly the meriest; she was a great favourite generally for her good nature and friendliness and '... when the kynge took displeasure with anyone she would mollify him and appease him to change his mind ...',[7] but on his death she was a victim of the reaction against all his mistresses and Fabyan remarks:

> '... *and shortly afftyr was a woman named Shore that beffore dayes afftyr the common fame ... alle her movablys weren attachyd by ye Shyrevs of london and she was lastly as a common harlot putt to opeyn penaunce ffor the llyffe that shee ledd w't ye lord hastynges and other grete astatys* ... '[8]

She died in 1527 at a very great age in dire poverty, but was remembered in many a ballad even a century later.

In the preceding hundred years many great changes had occurred. It was the age of Chaucer. It was the seed time of capitalism with the start of the new cloth manufacturing

[6] Ed. A.H. Thomas, London. 1938.
[7] Ed. A.H. Thomas, London 1938.
[8] Ed. A.H. Thomas, London 1938.

industry, which created a new species of rich wool cloth monopolists, army speculators, financial and commercial magnates. The general condition of the peasantry and artizan class had relatively improved, the Black Death having wrought great changes not only in earnings but also in social outlook; journeymen and field labourers had even struck and secured high wages. The growth of the new trade relieved the abysmal poverty of the cottagers and altered every aspect of life. Indeed in 1389 Parliament complained that:

> '. . . *artificers and labourers and grooms and servants kept greyhounds and other dogs and when good Christian people be at Church on Sundays and Holy Days these others disported themselves hunting in parks, warrens and coneyries of the Lords* . . . '

and Parliament was constrained to enact that ' . . . henceforth no laymen with less than 40/- a year in land . . . and no priest with less than £10 a year . . . be so bold as to keep sporting dogs or nets . . . '.

Chaucer's younger contemporaries now displayed their legs in ' . . . tight hosen' blazing in colours, wore jewels and costly materials with 'sleaves slod vpon the earth and harlottes (long pointed shoes with chains to the waist) . . . ' so luxurious that a contemporary exclaimed that they ' . . . carried their estates upon their backs . . . '.

The London merchants were making fortunes supplying these luxuries to the nobility and gentry and the rising middle class, thus incidentally spreading refinement and civilization by the very means being then denounced by puritans and moralists.

A change was occurring in the relationship between masters and men. Variety of function and greater inequality in monetary rewards altered the class structure. The Master became more an entrepreneur. Distinctions began to occur between small Masters manufacturing with a couple of journeymen and apprentices, and the great Masters who sold their products and waxed immensely rich in the process, thus further increasing the gulf. The City was governed by the rich merchants.

There were now 'gilds of Yeomen', embryo trade unions,

described by John Wyclif himself in *Select English Works*, Vol.II, page 333:

> '. . . *also men of sutel (subtle-that is, skilled) craft as fre masons and others (who . . .) conspiren togidere that no man of here (their) craft schal mak sade (the said) trewe werke to lette otheres mennus wynnynge at the craft and noon (none) of hem schal do ought but onlie hewe stone though he migght proffytt his maistere twenty pound bi o daies werk by leggyng on a wal without peyning to himself* . . . '

In other words, no craftsmen would do a steady day's work that might prejudice his mates' earnings: and only do what he had to do and no more, even though without exerting himself by laying a wall he could have earned his master another twenty pounds. It sounds depressingly familiar in 1973.

Meanwhile Londoners having become richer demanded amusements to take up their surplus energy and money. Bear-baiting, bull-baiting, and cock-fighting all became mass sports: football and cricket were still in embryo. All these diversions tended to congregate round Southwark and of course bring more and more business to the host of stews and independent prostitutes, bringing more business and prosperity to the shopkeepers and inn-keepers as well as landlords.

Occasional news creeps out about Bankside activities. For instance the ordinance of 1436 had made it clear that there was little to differentiate between inns and brothels. In 1470 a Conveyance mentions that the 'Cardinalls Hatte' later one of the best known brothels was '. . . rebuilt on a voyd place of ground by ye Steweside . . . ' and run by John Merston who leased it from William Hille. At about the same time the inn called the 'Castell uppon the Hoope' at the east end of the Bankside is flourishing, only to become a brothel before 1506 when the Whoremaster, John Sandes, a Cooper, was charged before the Bishop of Winchester's Court Leet '. . . with keeping it open on Feast Days and allowing women to board there against the Regulations of the Stewes . . . '.[9] It is extraordinary to discover that regulations contrived some

[9] P.R.O. Eccles.i. 85/i.

three hundred years earlier were still being observed and enforced. This brothel was still going strong in 1559 and is last mentioned in 1595 when the landlord, a jolly character named John Drew died and in his Will left 40 shillings to his Bankside tenants '. . . to make merry withal . . .'.[10]

Inns and hostelries were always full. There were public rooms for eating and drinking and a few private rooms for those wealthy enough to afford and demand privacy. In ordinary hostelries the beds were placed in recesses rather like bunks in ships – or rather like stables, since there were rushes on the floors and the bunks were in tiers, with straw bedding. Travellers of both sexes customarily slept in the nude (although they were always careful to wear a kerchief round their heads!) and wandered about in that state with little regard for the proprieties as we know them today. Small wonder they became brothels eventually. In most cases the barmaids and chambermaids were accustomed, for a fee, to attend to the sexual requirements of the guests. Indeed in some inns there was a room in which certain 'maidens' awaited calls from downstairs.

Because the kingdom was involved in war in one way and another during his reign little is recorded of the king's official attitudes towards his subjects' social and sexual problems, although Fabyan's *Chronica Major* for 1472 says that the Lord Mayor issued a prescription *De Correccio Meretricium* (Concerning the Punishment of Whores):

> '. . . *thys yere alsoo the mayer dyd dyligent and sharp Correccion vpon Venus servauntys and cawsid theym to be Garnysshid and attyrid wyth Raye hodys and to be shewid abowth the Cyte wyth theyr mynstrelsy beffore theym by many and sundry market dayis and sparid noone ffor mede nor ffor ffavour albe It that ffor some were offryd large Summys of money of have them prysed ffrom that opyn schame* . . .'

This Lord Mayor was Sir William Hampton whose severity in dealing with strumpets is noted in John Stow's *Surveigh* because he '. . . caused stocks to be set up in every ward to punish them and vagabonds . . .'. The times were admittedly

[10] Scott, Prerogative Court of Wills, Canterbury, 9.

troublous. Just two years previously there had been the uprising led by the 'Bastard Fauconbridge' and with much bloodshed in the streets of Southwark and London before he was beaten. It is not surprising therefore that in 1475 the Lord Mayor ordained '. . . that the keepers of stewes shall not harbour men or women at night . . . under penalty . . .' because there were still hundreds of refugees in hiding.

Another prime cause of unrest was due to the invention of printing, for it enabled the common tongue to be brought to the nation in a more or less uniform state and gave a tremendous stimulus to thinking as well as organizing. By the time Caxton died in 1491 new ideas were commanding change.

Then suddenly in April 1483 Edward IV died, and his son, a boy of twelve, became King Edward V under the Regency of his uncle, Richard, Duke of Gloucester. In the next month the Lord Mayor issued on behalf of the young king, the famous ordinance headed:

> *'For to Eschewe the Stynkynge and Orrible Synne of Lechery'.*

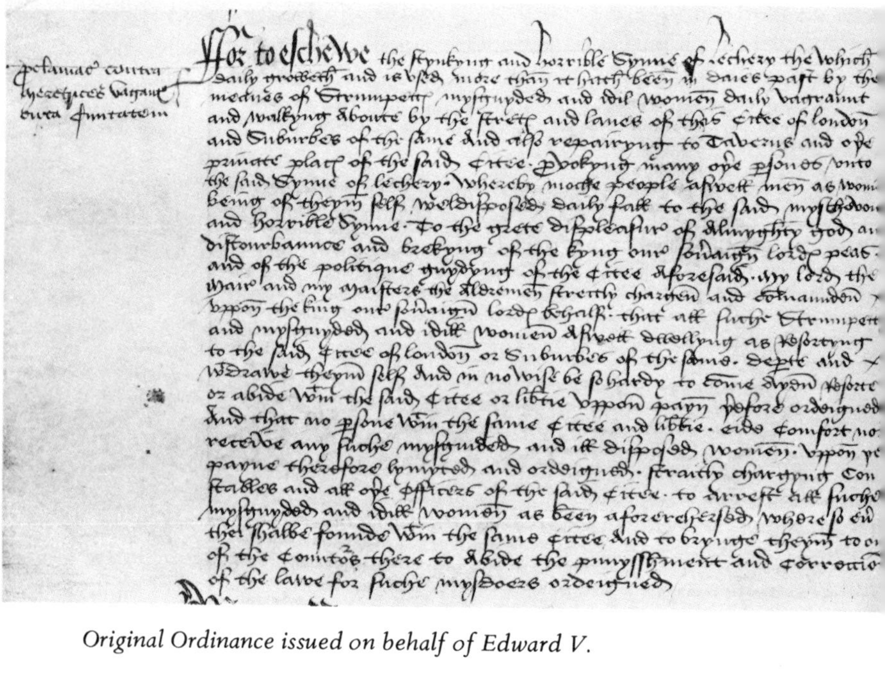
pclamac contra meretrices vagant circa Civitatem

For to eschewe the stynkyng and horrible Synne of lechery the which
daily groweth and is used more than it hath been in daies past by the
meanes of Strumpettes mysguyded and idil women daily vagraunt
and walkyng aboute by the stretes and lanes of this Citee of london
and Suburbes of the same and also repairyng to Tavernes and other
private places of the said Citee provokyng many other persones unto
the said Synne of lechery whereby moche people aswell men as wom[illegible]
being of theym self well disposed daily fall to the said myschevo[illegible]
and horrible Synne to the grete displeasure of Almyghty god an[illegible]
distourbaunce and brekyng of the kyng our sovereign lordes peas
and of the politique guydyng of the Citee aforesaid my lord the
Mair and my maisters the Aldremen streitly charchen and comaunden
upon the kyng our sovereign lordes behalf that all suche Strumpettes
and mysguyded and idill women aswell dwellyng as resortyng
to the said Citee of london or Suburbes of the same departe and
withdrawe theym self and in nowise be so hardy to come dwell resorte
or abide within the said Citee or libertie upon payn before ordeigned
And that no persone within the same Citee and libertie eide comfort no[illegible]
receive any suche mysguyded and ill disposed women upon pe[illegible]
payne therefore lymyted and ordeigned. streitly chargyng Constables and all other officers of the said Citee to arrest all suche
mysguyded and idill women as been aforerehersed whereso ev[illegible]
they shalbe founde within the same Citee and to bringe theym to o[illegible]
of the Comptours there to abide the punysshment and correctio[illegible]
of the lawe for suche mysdoers ordeigned

Original Ordinance issued on behalf of Edward V.

'. . . *the whiche daily groweth and is used more than it hath been in daies past by the Meanes of Strumpettes mysguyded and idil women daily vagraunt and walkynge aboute by the stretes and lanes of this Citee of London and Suburbes . . . also repairynge to Taverns and othere private places . . . provokynge many othere persones unto the said Synne of Lechery Whereby moche people . . . daily fall to the said myschevous and horrible Synne To the grete displeasur of Almighty God and distourbance and brekyng of the Kyng our soveraign lordes peas . . .*'

The boy king of course had never drafted any such ordinance, so it must have been prepared by his father who had died before he could proclaim it himself. However the two ordinances, although some years apart, show firstly, that despite the reforming zeal of a dedicated puritanical Lord Mayor in a drive against prostitution and corruption, there were many important people who perverted the course of justice by offering large bribes to be kept out of the public eye, or to get their particular paramour let off without scandal or punishment. The non-success of the Lord Mayor's sweep is evidenced by the second ordinance which demands now that all strumpets be forbidden the City and its liberties. Neither Lord Mayor, nor even the King could make their writ run in the liberties of the Clink where the Bankside stews still remained protected *hors de la loi* by their ancient safeguards.

This ordinance therefore was intended to clean up areas like Farringdon and Cripplegate, Holborn, West Smithfield and Finsbury, and certainly from this time onwards the reports about these 'red lamp' areas seem to be fewer, until they resurge in tremendous strength a hundred years later.

In the same month as the ordinance the boy king was to be murdered at the instigation of his uncle who, on 22 June, 1483 ascended the throne as Richard III.

Chapter Eight

Old 'Penny Pincher' Closes the Stews

Richard III's short reign ended ignominiously on Bosworth Field in 1485 with the triumph of the Welsh gentleman, Henry Tudor, aided by a few French adventurers. They defeated a king for whom the mass of Englishmen were ashamed to fight. The accession of Henry VII marked the end of the Wars of the Roses and also the end of the Middle Ages. The ensuing twenty-five years of peace contributed towards changing the entire fabric of English social life.

Many a feudal stronghold now lay in ruins, never to rise again. The day of powerful barons with large retinues was finished. Henry had disarmed them. But the disbanding of the many thousands of baronial retainers, as well as the increasing unemployment among the lower order of priests and 'clerks' caused a great increase in beggary and vagabondage. The emancipation of the serfs and the break-up of the Manors was already far advanced, with consequent increase in mobility of the very poorest sections of the people, who began to flock to the towns for work. The women amongst them swelled the ranks of the prostitutes and furnished fresh supplies for the stews. Indeed in 1494, Robert Fabyan, who had been Sheriff the previous year, says in his *Chronica Major*:

> '. . . *and vppon the xv day of August weren covyct ffor bawdry ij men John Northffolke and John Whyte whyche weren afftir punnysshid uppon the pyllory* . . . '

and in his notes for July 1495 he records:

> '. . . *uppon the secund day of Julii was sett uppon the pyllory a Bawd of the Stewys namyd Thomas Toogood*

the whyche beffore the mayer was provid gylty that he entysid ij women dwellynge at the Quene Hythe to become his servauntys and to have men comon whthyn hys howse . . . '

Moreover a significant change had taken place in the economic and political life of the country. Parliamentary members now rose from the lesser gentry or were lawyers and officials or even tradesmen and merchants. A strong and varied middle class had emerged, resistant to and impatient of the barons. They were not interested in chivalry. They were money seekers first and foremost, with the ambition and the means to advance their families in wealth and status. This was easier for them because they did not need a host of retainers and hangers-on like the nobles. They were prepared to accept an autocratic king just so long as he could maintain peace and order and control the new economic situation.

Then a more sinister event struck England. In January 1496 syphilis was first recorded in Naples. By March 1496 the City of Paris promulgated the very first public measures known to control this new and dangerous eruption. It reached England before the end of the century and by 1504 was reaching frightening proportions. It became necessary to curb the spreading of this disease.

In 1504, Fabyan reports:

' . . . *the stewis or comon bordell beyond the watyr ffor what happ or concyderacion the certaynte I knowe nott was ffor a seson inhybyt and closed upp. But it was not long or they were sett opyn agayn alle itt the ssame went that were beffore were occupyed xviij howsys ffrom hens fforth should be occupyed by xij . . .* '[1]

This is incidentally the first indication that there were in fact only eighteen of such licensed houses.

The information does not appear elsewhere, so neither the reasons for the closure nor the reopening are known, but it may assuredly be ascribed to the raging infection by the new strain of syphilis, which had aroused the apprehensions of the forces of morality, which the king was inclined to favour. He

[1] *Chronica Major* fol.57 v. Ed. A.H. Thomas, London 1938.

An 'honest' stew.

seems not to have inherited the family tradition of wholesale lechery, and his only known mistress was Mary Boleyn, elder sister of Anne who was later to be the second wife of Henry VIII.

Of course the ordinance was not designed to help the whores. It was designed to protect the clients. All the licensed whorehouses were therefore summarily closed, and after an examination of the girls and a general check-up, only enough of the women were sufficiently uncontaminated to enable the rapid re-opening of twelve brothels. There is no indication that any steps were taken to clean up the hundreds of unlicensed establishments in London and its suburbs; although shortly afterwards there was a regulation affecting 'honest' stews, which presumably were also thought to be sources of syphilitic infection:[2]

> '... *also if there is any House wherein is kept and holden any Hot House or Sweating House for Ease and Health of Men, to which be resorting or conversant any Strumpets or women of Evil Fame: or if there be any Hot House or Sweating House ordained for Women to the which is any comon recourse of young men or other Persons of Evil Fame and Suspect Condition* ... '

The penalty for infraction of the licence was £20. This ordinance clearly demonstrates apprehension about health rather than morals. 'Suspicious persons' would include the politically suspect as well as the religiously unreliable, for Henry VII was zealous in roasting heretics too.

The short prohibition had, as is to be expected, very little effect, for only three years later Fabyan again reports (*Chronica Major*. 1509, fol.79) the following very curious episode arising from Lord Dudley's treason, wherein one of his henchmen, Captain Canby, was indicted in the following pregnant words:

> '... *this Canby (who had been an officer in the Sheriff's own house)* ... *contynuyd hys weyward lyffe Not wythouth contyneull complayntis of brybory fforcyble Injuryes* ... *and pety Bawdry or covert by Reason of a Stewes that he kepyd by the watyrs syde insoomuche* ... *he Goderid soo money that by his Gyfftes he wan alle wayes* ... '

This is evidence of the wealth that could be amassed by people of high rank by brothel-keeping, in this case under the protection of the mighty – and greatly feared – Dudley, and the Sheriff too. Bribery, corruption and blackmail, as well as threats and beatings, were only uncovered because this

[2] Laurence Wright. *Clean and Decent*, pp. 60-61. Routledge, London 1960.

was a treason trial, otherwise it would still have been hushed up.

Within ten years the brothels had multiplied enormously, and had spread all along the High Street in Southwark, and on to the eastern side on the road to Bermondsey. There was great sport to be had there, as shown in one of Wynkyn de Woorde's plays when a character named 'Imagination' says:

'. . . *Hark! fellows! a good sport I can tell you.*
At the stewes we shall lye tonight
and, by my troth, if all go right
I will beguile some pretty wench
to get me mony, at a pinch . . .'

and this seems also to imply that he could procure a girl to earn some money for him by prostitution, so that he and his companions could enjoy themselves on the proceeds. It also shows that ca. 1509 the Southwark bawdy houses were going strong, and that the syphilis scare had not dampened down the demand. However the great influx of beggars to the City had led to an increase in all types of crimes, so that about this time the Lord Mayor, Sir William Capell, issued an instruction that 'smal howses' (cages) had to be up in every ward, and stocks fixed inside them '. . . for to punnysshe sterk beggars and vagabaundys . . .' with the Beadle keeping the keys. Two of these cages were put on London Bridge as well as two pillories, which are shown on an old map of that time; and they were still there in Bloody Mary's time. The unrest was so great that there was even a revolt in the Marshalsea prison, and many prisoners succeeded in breaking out and rioting. The ringleaders were caught and hanged upon a nearby tree.

Chapter Nine

Of the Clink and the Cucking-Stool for the Correccion of Loose Women

King Henry VII performed on his death bed a notable act of charity, and thereby also gives us the earliest reference to the Clink prison, by name. In his Will he left a list of monies to be distributed at his funeral, which took place on 28 April, 1509, '. . . to the poore at the Clinke . . .'.

When the Bishop of Winchester's Palace was built in 1107 there was undoubtedly built beneath it a place of detention. This is made clear by the references in the Ordinances for the Regulation of the Stews which existed in 1130, to the prison of the Lord of the Manor, who was the Bishop of Winchester. This can only have been the Clink, although at that time it had no official name, although in common parlance it must already have been known as the Clink. The next reference to the Bishop's prison is in the Will of Cardinal Henry Beaufort (also Bishop of Winchester) in 1447, when he left £400 to be distributed to the poor prisoners in various prisons, including '. . . those confined within my Mansion of Southwark . . .'. A reference, about a hundred years later, mentions that the prison was '. . . lying under the Manor House of the Bishop (of Winchester) . . . being waterlogged at high tide . . .'

Neither the origin of the Clink as the name for the ancient Liberty, nor of the prison, is known. As regards the prison there are a number of suggestions, the most favoured being the onomatopoeic from the clanking of the prisoners' fetters, and is cognate with the Old Dutch word *klinken* meaning to make a clinking sound, and also meaning to confine, in the sense of 'clinch' or 'clench'. This would give the word an origin going back to King Edgar's time and perhaps provide a link with St. Swithin's original stone monastery built nearby in ca. 850.

If it is to be credited with a Norman-French ancestry,

there is the Old French word *clinquer*, meaning to clank or make a clinking noise as of fetters; this word was in use about 1500.

If it be connected with the old waterlogged prison built in 1107 it would undoubtedly be a place where many fatalities would occur. The Old Latin name for a sexton or gravedigger is *Clincus*, and his job would have been, so to speak, to bury the evidence, the inference being that once you were unlucky enough to be put in, your chances of getting out alive were poor.

It might have developed through dog-Latin and the painful efforts of untutored English-speakers trying to master the hated Norman-French tongue of their new masters, and refer to the whorehouses themselves. In Roman times the profession of Bawdry was known as *lenacinium*, and would-be clients coming up to the Bridge Head sentries would ask their way to *haec lenacinium* and over the years this difficult mouthful would elide into 'hic linc', and thence to Clink.[1]

It was certainly known as a prison in 1514, for Alexander Barclay, in his *First Eclogue* states baldly and with feeling '. . . tho' thou be guiltless thou shall be convict: thou art clapped in Flete or Clinke . . . ' giving us in passing a glimpse into contemporary justice. In 1524 it is called 'The Clynk' and in 1553 the Bishop's own Palace is referred to as 'The Clyncke'; thereafter the word passes into the vernacular with the meaning of prison, much as 'in the jug' or 'in stir', and it is so used to this day. At that time too it is described by John Stow as a prison:

> '. . . *in olde tyme for suche as shoulde brabble or frey or break the peas on the said bank or in the brothell houses* . . . '

It was also used for incarcerating scolds and petty criminals. From time immemorial there stood at the junction of Clink Street and the 'waye to the Banke' a pillory and a cage and a ducking stool; originally known as a much more fearsome instrument, the cucking-stool. This latter punishment seems to have originated in the Teutonic lands, *vide* Tacitus (*Germania*, 12):

[1] The author's own pet theory.

'... in Germany. cowards sluggards debauchees and prostitutes were suffocated in mires and bogs ... useless members ... and pests of society ...'

'Cucking' derives from Old Icelandic 'kuka' originally, Latin 'caca'-shit, which meaning it also has in Old English. It was much used in Anglo-Saxon times. Although in modern times generally regarded with some amusement, it was a much more sinister instrument when first devised, for the victim was dipped deep into muck and excrement so as to choke ignominiously to death. It is no accident that the Saxon word is 'sceathing-stole' i.e. 'choking stool'.

It was carried over into Norman times as a punishment for delinquent bakers and brewers given to adulterating their bread and ale, and the ale-wives of mediaeval times were frequently before the courts for this offence, as well as brawling and screaming and soliciting and disturbing the peace. In Scotland 'ail-wyves' were set in the 'cock-stule', from 'cukkyn' (to shit).

There are two references contained in the Domesday Book. In the account for the City of Chester is stated: '... the culprit should be placed *in cathedra stercoris*: ('in a shitting chair') ...'; and elsewhere it is described as ... *cathedra in qua rixosae mulieres sedentes aquis demergebantur* ... ('a chair in which scolds are seated and submerged in water').

Originally in fact the offender was bound on to her shitting-stool, in front of her house, and then carried to the nearest water, a pond or a river, and then ducked two or three times until she gasped for breath, when the lesson was supposed to be learnt. Indeed ca. 1150 it is called a '... goging stole ...', 'goging or gonging' meaning a dung-stool or close stool. Gong-farmers were scavengers who carried away excrement each night, 'gong' meaning dung.[2] There are two references in the Stews Ordinance 1161 to the stool as a punishment.

As the distinction between ale-wives and female 'huksteres', and whores was sometimes very fine, and at all times prostitutes congregated for soliciting in the streets and

[2] MS. *De Legibus*. Burgi Villas de Montgomerie. fol. 12b.

habitually called after men, sometimes creating disturbances, small wonder all were lumped together as 'scolds' liable for this punishment. It was a comparatively simple device, being a chair or stool attached to a long pole on a fulcrum: the chair being suspended over the water. Sometimes it had wheels to enable it to be wheeled to its destination. In the Register for the City of Southampton for 1540 is an account for a total of '... x shillings and viiij pence ...' paid to Robert Orchard for making a 'scooldyngestoole', which included tenpence for the timber, threepence to carry it up the hill, eightpence for sawing 'iij peces' of wood; sixpence for 'iij boltes and lj pinnes ...' and no less than three shillings and threepence for '... ye wheeles to convey the seid stole by commandement of the mayre ...'.

On the other hand, in 1572 the Corporation only paid twenty three shillings and fourpence, and that included '... three brasses and three wheeles ...' which cost four shilling and tenpence alone. By this time it was called a 'ducking-stool for scolds'. It is shown in a contemporary print referring to the ducking of 'light sisters of the banke' or 'light housewives of the banke': and the last recorded use in England was in 1801 at Chelmsford when an old woman was ducked thrice '... by the proper officers ...'.

No accurate description of the 'thew' is known, but it must have been a special type of pillory devised to hold women down, and in the earliest period used almost exclusively to punish harlots, although later there are a couple of references to men being condemned to the thew.

The pillory was an upright cross, into which the victim's head and wrists were locked. It was effective as a punishment by ridicule for short periods. But in the course of our civilization it developed into another means of torture by being extended from hours to days. There are cases on record of up to eleven days. Friends and relations would feed him, but others would delight in pelting him with bricks, pebbles, rotten vegetables and of course, dung, as the fancy would take them, and the target was nicely fixed so that they could not miss. Defecation and urination then had to be done *in situ*, and as the victim was usually fully clothed the mess remained and the stench increased, so that what started as a comparatively harmless way of taking the mickey out of a local misdemeanour, became something the victim would seldom be able to live down, apart from any physical damage incurred by the straightened position. A later refinement locked the legs into the pillory as well, so that in addition to the foregoing tortures the victim was locked into a position of great distortion, leading to permanent injury.

By contrast, the stocks, wherein the malefactor's legs were locked, was comparatively comfortable, although the pictures which show merry victims happily smoking their pipes philosophically can be taken as contemporary Establishment P.R.O.'s nonsense.

Sometimes pillories were made for two or more offenders. Often they were built on a raised platform to make them more conspicuous. It goes without saying that they were exposed to the vagaries of the weather and in no way protected by day or night.

There was for centuries a pillory and stocks on Old London Bridge, but about A.D. 1503 it was ordained that 'small houses'

Woman in the Cage on London Bridge in the time of Queen Mary

of punishment should be set up in every ward, so one was erected on London Bridge. Most of the women thus exposed were prostitutes, as part of their punishment; afterwards they were shaven and paraded about the City in a cart with red and white striped hood, and then put outside the gates of the city.

In Queen Mary's time there was an additional refinement, in that the pillories were erected inside a cage. The cage is of very ancient Near Eastern lineage. Originally it was a cage wherein the victim was locked up like an animal, and put on show, sometimes hung on a city wall for all to see. In the west it reached refinements not dreamt of by the savages in the east. Men as well as women were encaged in hatches too small for them to stand or sit or lie down, and they wallowed for years in their own ordure. Cases are on record where some were so encaged for the whole of their lives. The contemporary mob would add to their torture by flinging muck and slops as well as screaming insults. Most went insane after a while, while the lucky ones met an early death. King Edward I hung the Duchess of Buchan in a wooden cage on the walls of the City of Berwick 'so that all who pass by may see her'.

Although the Clink prison was by no means a first-class hotel,[3] the unfortunate women who were condemned to the 'Houses of Correccion' like Bridewell went literally to a hell-on-earth, granted that they were not exactly shrinking violets in the first case. Their sojourn had been preceded by public humiliation; they had been stripped naked or at least bare to the waist; their heads had been shaven bald: they had been covered with a red and white striped hood, on which was stuck a paper recording their offence and the cart was followed by a jeering mob of *hoi polloi* throwing refuse as well as screaming insults. If they were very unlucky, they were tied to the cart-arse and whipped, while being paraded through the main thoroughfares of the City, before finally ending in Bridewell, where their real troubles then began.[4]

[3] John Taylor (1580-1653) called 'The Water Poet' listed 'five jayles' and 'Then there's the Clink where handsome lodging be . . . '.

[4] A suitable epitaph comes from the old ballad 'Honest Posture Moll'.
'Oh! Bridewell, what a shame thy Walls reproaches?
Poor Whores are whip'd, whilst rich ones ride in coaches!'

Bridewell stood on a spot where once stood a royal palace even before the Conquest. It was rebuilt by Henry VIII for the reception of the Emperor Charles V, who called it Bridewell because of the miracle well attached to the nearby Church of St. Bride's. Edward VI gave it to the City as 'a house of correccion' and of it Ned Ward the 'London Spy' said 'T'was once the palace of a prince . . . ' and continues:

'No prince or peers to make a feast
no kettle drums or trumpets,
but are become a shameful Nest
of vagabonds and strumpets.'

Once in the prison, they were subject to 'correccion' to make them repent. This took the form of repeated whippings, repeated beatings, repeated rapings, frequently being locked up in cells, starved and otherwise ill-treated; and all this usually for an unspecified period. Unless someone came to buy them out, or to bribe the venal keepers handsomely, the unfortunate victim could stay there indefinitely. Small wonder, then, that the threat of Bridewell made every harlot shiver. Nonetheless, it was a risk inherent in the trade, and they had no option but to take this risk, for no other livelihood was readily open to them.

This was the reverse side of the harlots' medal. Such punishments were to be continued almost until the reign of Queen Anne; and even then it is recorded that the vicious 'Society for the Reform of Manners' in 1720 caused prostitutes to be whipped by the police, and that despite the fact that as far back as 1640 prostitution was no longer a crime but a misdemeanour.

One of the last official references to the Clink Liberty and its inhabitants is found in the *Reminiscences* of the venerable Archdeacon Louth of Nottingham in the form of a *cri du coeur*:

' . . . gentle reader, yow muste remember that Stephen Wynton (the Archbishop Stephen Gardiner also Bishop of Winchester) preferred this Henry Francis to the Baylywyk of the Clynke, that ys he mad hym capteyn of the stews and all the whoores thereto belongyng. And in dede he

> *proved an excellent cutter and Ruffyne. Lerne, lerne, reader . . . by this unchristian prelate . . .* '[5]

Archbishop Gardiner was himself a notorious lecher and a pander to Henry VIII. Henry Frances was one of his most servile henchmen, and as the old Archdeacon complains, he managed to get excellent cuts out of the revenues, besides being a ruffian. One of the Church's perks in earlier times had been the selling of indulgences, and this was a very profitable sideline. For a scoundrel like Frances who was also the Bailiff and thus in control of the prison as well as the Bankside stews, the appointment was a real goldmine. This revenue from indulgences is referred to in Shakespeare's *Henry VI* Act I scene 3, where Richard Plantagenet, Duke of Gloucester, accuses Cardinal Beaufort, then also Bishop of Winchester of being ' . . . an arrogant prelate . . . thou that giv'st whores indulgences to sin . . . ' and as a final insult calls him a 'Winchester Goose', meaning a frequenter of the stews, which incidentally gives us the information that this sobriquet goes back as far as 1460. Hence, to be bitten by a Winchester Goose meant to have a venereal disease.

[5] Camden Society. Vol.77 p. 48.

The Clink Prison.

Strangely enough there are no extant illustrations of the early Clink Prison, except that in the Manuscript of the Bodleian Library at Oxford to be dated about 1580 in which there is a satirical verse referring to ' . . . fydlinge knaves . . . ' who had been confined ' . . . in their auncient howse . . . called ye Clynke . . . '. There is a little sketch of a prison with barred windows behind which can be seen some prisoners, and this must certainly be the first pictorial representation of it. More interesting perhaps is the fact that there is a Swing-sign outside with a device of a fiddle: and this is the earliest note of the expression 'fiddling' in the sense of something illegal. It also demonstrates that it was a 'clink' in which people were confined for petty offences.

In 1624 when one Robert Davison was ' . . . the Keeper of the Clincke . . . ' he also leased the adjoining property, thereby presumably adding some revenue from whoredom from the very houses whose inmates he cheerfully incarcerated from time to time, in itself a classic fiddle.

The Clink prison probably began to decline in use about 1649 when the Bishop of Winchester's House and property described as:

> ' . . . *the Mansion in Southwark . . . called Winchester Libertie* . . . alias *Clink Libertie . . . three and a half acres . . . nine messuages and nine tenements . . . and the Clink Gardens (stretching) to the Cage on the west of the cawsey (causeway) leading from the stewes bank towards the Clink Gate . . . (were sold . . .) . . . to Thomas Walker . . . . for £4380.8.3 d . . .* '

but still in 1661 the Surrey Quarter Sessions discloses that a number of vagabonds were ' . . . . inmates of the jail *infra libertatem de le Clinke . . .* '.

By the end of the century it does not appear to have been used any more as a prison.

Chapter Ten

Henry VIII Closes the Stews

When Henry VIII succeeded to the throne in 1509, he was to utilize the Tudor strongmindedness and aggressiveness to transform the kingdom into a modern power. He had the great advantage of succeeding to a kingdom at peace and with money in the treasury, and with no powerful nobles able to oppose him successfully. Nevertheless, with all his power and prestige he could not alter the human frailties in his people.

Within a year of Henry's accession that good old gossip, Fabyan, records a carting:

> '. . . *and vpon the vij daye of Junii yood abowth the cyte certayn comon harlottys weryng Raye (striped) hodys (hoods) w'th shame. Inowth and afftyr they hadd been soo punyshid by thre market dayes they were banyshed the toun at Sundry Gatys of the Cyte* . . . '[1]

Although the country was at peace, the land was infested with 'vacabunds' and 'mysdemeanourid persons'. Henry, concerned with the effects of immorality amongst his troops, was led in 1513 to issue Proclamation No. 73 ordering severe punishments for ' . . . bordel keeping in the host . . . and the branding of whores . . . ', this last a new and savage penalty hitherto not known in England.

By 1519 the unrest was becoming so serious that his most powerful henchman, Cardinal Wolsey, ordered a thorough search throughout London and suburbs for 'suspected persons', which included all men without occupation or masters and, for good measure, loose women. Although the measure was designed to catch disgruntled elements and dissenters, some otherwise quite harmless people fell into the Cardinal's net.

[1] *Chronica Major*, 1510.

For example, in 'Padyngtone' four men were committed to the care of the Constable because they '. . . had played all night until 4 o'clock at tables . . . '.

As may be expected, in Southwark the catch was much greater and more interesting. Twenty-two such persons were apprehended within the Liberty of the Archbishop of Canterbury on 17 July '. . . including seven Frenchmen taken in the Spittle of a Frenchman's house called John Drokes . . . ' (probably Jean des Roches). Others were taken in the houses of Kechyns, the King's servant, and of John Howell in Blewemeadaly (Blue Maid Alley – a most notorious street of whorehouses).

> *'. . . Persons taken in the stewehouses within the Liberty of the bishop of Winchester, the same day: 54 men and women including Jo. Willyams, footman to the king, at the signs of the 'Castle', the 'Bull', the 'Hart', the 'Olyfant', the 'Unicorn', the 'Bear's Head', and other houses designated by their owners' names . . . '*

The bordel known as 'The Castle' is mentioned by Stow.

In the nearby Gilde Alley (Golden Alley) several others were arrested, among them Will Borage, yeoman of the guard, who was commanded to appear the following Tuesday before the King's Council, doubtless to be punished by a military court.

Six people were arrested in the Liberty of 'my lord of Barmsey' (The Abbot of Bermondsey), including one 'David Glynne, scholar, the King's servant . . . ' and the others at designated houses with the names of the Madams thereof, Joan Reynolds and Katharine Thomas.

The Cardinal's minions swept extremely wide. In Clerkenwell they raided houses in 'Tirmyl Street' (still functioning two hundred years later as Turnmill Street), and as far as Islington, Hackney and 'Stoke Newenton'. Five were picked up in the stewhouses in Queenhithe.

The Cardinal's sweep was partly due to the demands of the respectable citizens of Southwark that something be done to clean up the area which brought much trouble and shame on them. Indeed ten years later the Bishop of Winchester, Richard Fox, in a report to Cardinal Wolsey stated that there was little known crime in his diocese except in Southwark.

It was not seriously to be expected that this arrogant prelate would concern himself overmuch with such matters, for his own morals left nothing to be desired. He had already procured for his natural son four Archdeaconries, a Deanery, five Prebends and two Rectories. He was at this time reported to be richer than the King and had already built his magnificent Palace at Hampton Court, wherein it was reported:

> '. . . *the celebrated Cardinal Wolsey over a door of a particular part of his palace had these words in Latin: "the House of the Whores of my Lord the Cardinal* . . . . " '[2]

Nor was it seriously to be expected that the King, himself one of the greatest of royal lechers ever known, could be interested in the ethics of the 'synne', although from the context of his various Ordinances his Court ought to have been unbelievably virtuous. But the King was already visiting Winchester House for the purpose of consorting with unvirtuous ladies. Indeed, towards the end of his reign, Henry Brincklow attacked both the King and the Archbishop Gardiner for the immoral goings-on in 'Wynchester's Gardyn' – a very witty play on the Primate's name and address. In 1542 he was again to attack the arrogant Archbishop, saying:

> '. . . *Steuyn Gardner (Stephen Gardiner)* . . . *is it not manifest and openly known that he kepyth other mennys wyves which I could name* . . . '[3]

Moreover, the King himself was enjoying the same felicitous arrangement as his late Cardinal for, says Rabutaux:

> '. . . *notons enfin que les rois d'Angleterre et les seigneurs du Royaume avaient aussi leurs gyneces sous le règne d'Henri VIII, un écriteau etait placé sur la porte "Chambre des filles de joie du Roi* . . . " '[4]

[2] Rabutaux. *Histoire de la Prostitution*. Paris 1851.
[3] *Complaynt of Roderick More* E.E.T.S. extra 22. London.
[4] *De la Prostitution en Europe* 1851, fol. xxxiv apud Saboteux 1821.

The City authorities then revived a very ancient institution, the Ward Mote Quest, one of whose terms of reference was '... ye shall truly enquire if any person keep any bawdy house gaming house or house of ill-fame ...'. Henry Brincklow, an early Puritan complained:

'... *There is a custom in the cyte ones a yeare to haue a quest called the warnmall (Ward Mote) to redress vices, but alasse to what purpose cometh it, as it is used. If a pore man kepe a whore besyde his wyfe and a pore wyfe play the harlot they are punysshed as well worthye. But let an Alderman, a ientleman or a riche man kepe whore or whores what punishment is there?.* ..'[5]

The City's authority over the 'Guildable Manor' was never accurately defined, and its control had been circumscribed somewhat in 1327 by the powers of the King's Bailiff; so in 1539 the Mayor and Corporation made an Ordinance prohibiting spinsters from *le estewes* visiting the Guildable Manor except for market, and providing punishment for those who practised bawdry within the Guildable Manor, of 26/8d for a first offence and carting for a second offence.[6]

Buggery, although frequently observed as a vice amongst the highest and the lowest in the land, had been regarded as an ecclesiastical offence from the time of Henry I, and there is little evidence that the temporal courts had ever been called in to do anything about it. It certainly flourished amongst the clergy, on whom the rule of enforced celibacy lay hard.

Under the reforming zeal of Henry VIII, it was time to make an end of this lax state of affairs, so in 1533 Parliament passed Act No.21 *FOR THE PUNISHMENT OF THE VICE OF BUGGERY*, the preamble reading:

'... *Forasmuch as there is not yet sufficient and condign punishment appointed and limited by the due course of the laws of this Realm for the detestable and abominable vice of buggery committed with mankind or beast* ... '

Henceforward, sodomy was to be a felony, punishable by death and burial without benefit of clergy, as well as

[5] *Complaynt of Roderick More* E.E.T.S. extra 22. pp.91 ff. London.
[6] Southwark Court Leet Book, 1539.

forfeiture of all property. The Justices of the Peace were empowered to try and to sentence.

From 1542 there dates a unique and valuable piece of evidence about Southwark in the form of a rough map (now in the Public Record Office in London). It shows for the first time the two stone staples at the foot of old London Bridge which marked the end of the City's jurisdiction, and a few yards further south is the important phrase '. . . here endeth the Mayor and here beginneth the king . . .'. It shows also '. . . the waye to the Banke . . .' and the positions of the pillories at the Clink nearby the Bankside. It also depicts a large pillory and cage in the north east of the borough near the riverside, which must approximate to the area of the ancient Bordich owned in 1270-1290 by Isaac, the Jew of Southwark. The presence of the pillory, which is drawn extraordinarily prominently on the map at this point, lends substance to the view that this was not a timberyard but a brothel area, since pillories, stocks and cages were customary adjuncts to the whorehouses but had no purpose near a timberyard.

Of even greater interest is the depiction of 'Blue Maid End' (or lane) and 'The Sink', known streets of whorehouses, and also a mention of the 'Half Moon' which was rebuilt in 1690 and was still functioning as a brothel in 1740 or thereabouts.[7]

Internal unrest was growing and so the King began to devise ways and means to channel his subjects' energies into more useful or less dangerous ways.

Accordingly in 1545 he issued an Ordinance *ORDERING VAGABONS TO THE GALLEYS*, the preamble to which is a remarkable giveaway:

> '. . . *notwithstanding the sundry good and wholesome laws and statutes . . . for the good and virtuous occupations of his people . . . the persuasion of the same from idleness, the mother and root of all mischiefs, and the punishment of vagabond ruffians and idle persons . . . there do remain in this realm and specially about the City of London . . . vagabonds and ruffians to*

[7] W. Rendle. *Old Southwark and its People.* London 1878.

A Proclamation to avoyd the abominable place called the Stewes

Rex Maiori et vicecomitibus Civitatis London. Salutem. Vobis mandamus &c.

The kings most excellent Matie, considering, howe by toleracion of such dissolute and miserable persons as putting awaie the feare of almightie God and shame of the worlde, haue bene suffered to dwell beside London and elswhere in common open places, called the Stewes, and there without punishment or correction, exercise their abhominable and detestable synne, there hath of late encreased and growen such enormities, as not only provoke, iustly the anger and wrath of almightie God, but also engender such corruption among the people, as tendeth to the intollerable annoyance of the Common wealth, and where not only the youth is provoked, enticed and allured to execute the fleshly lusts, but also by such assemblies of euill disposed persons, haunted and accustomed, is daily devised and conspired, howe to spoyle and robb the true labouring and well disposed men. For these consideracions, hath by the advise of his Counsell, thought requisite, utterly to exterminate such abhominable licence, and clerely to take awaye all occasion of the same; Wherefore his Matie straightlie chargeth and commaundeth, that all such persons as haue accustomed most abhominably to abuse their bodies, contrary to Gods lawe, and honestie in any such common places called the Stewes, in or about the Cittie of London, doe before the feaste of Easter next comyng, depart from those common places, and resort incontinently to their naturall Countries, with their bagges and baggages, upon paine of imprisonment, and further to be punished, at the Kings Maties will and pleasure. Furthermore his Matie straightlye chargeth and commaundeth, that all such householders as under the name of Bawdes, haue kept the notable and marked houses, and knowne hosteries, for the said euill disposed persons, That is to saie such householders as doe inhabite the houses whited and painted, with signes on the front, for a token of the said houses, shall avoid with bagge and baggage, before the feast of Easter next comyng, upon paine of like punishment at the Kings Maties will and pleasure. Furthermore the Kings Matie straightlye chargeth and commaundeth that such as be dwellers upon the Banke, called the Stewes nere London and haue at any tyme before this proclamacion, sold any manner victualls to such as haue resorted to their houses, doe before the said feast of Easter, cease and leave of their victualling and forbeare to retayne any

Henry VIII's Proclamation closing the Bankside stews.

> *whom God hath given strength apt and able for labour . . . yet . . . they give themselves to no labour or honest kind of living but entertain themselves with theft & falsehood in play whereby many* simple young men be polled *(beguiled) and* some utterly undone *and with other* detestable vices *and fashions* commonly used at the banke *suchlike naughty places where they much haunt and . . . lie nightly for the accomplishment and satisfying of their vile wretched & filthy purposes . . .'*

To reform them, the King ordered '. . . that all such be apprehended and impressed to serve him in these his wars in certain galleys and other vessels . . .'[8]

By this time, also, the syphilis from which His Majesty suffered was already in an advanced stage, and what with his marital and other preoccupations and his naturally irascible temperament, he was led to enact one of his most famous edicts *ORDERING LONDON BROTHELS CLOSED* in April 1546:[9]

> *'. . . This Yeare at Easter the stewes was putte downe by the King's proclamation made there with a trumpett and an harold atte armes . . . (and all) those householders as do inhabit those houses white and painted with signes on the front for a token of the said houses shall avoid with bag and baggage before the feast of Easter . . . and that all such as dwell on the banks called the stewes near London . . . (who have) sold victuals to those who frequent these houses, should cease from doing so or harbour any guests . . .'*

For good measure, the King then commanded that from Easter there should no longer be any bear-baiting '. . . on that side of the bridge called London bridge . . .' and that the places where bears and dogs were being baited be abolished.

That the arch-lecher should seek to make others eschewe lechery was hypocrisy of a high order; but to deprive the

[8] Steele MS 273. Royal Soc. Antiq.
[9] C. Wriothesley . *Chronicle of England* 1875-79, Camden Soc. Vol.I, p. 163.

populace of such traditional pastimes as bull- and bear-baiting was unheard of, and can only be due to the King's spleen or the mental deterioration due to his syphilis,[10] coupled with his fears of subversion. That it could not have been meant seriously is shown by the fact that shortly afterwards he assented to a request preferred by Mr. Secretary Pagett to grant 'A Licence for John Allen yeoman of my lord Prince's bears to bait his bears in Southwark or thereabouts or elsewhere from time to time for his most commodity . . . '.

The Liberty of Paris Garden first appears as a hide of land called Widflete which William the Conqueror had assigned to Robert Marmion, who gave it in 1113 to Bermondsey Priory. Later on it formed part of the dowry of the unlucky Jane Seymour. It had come to the King with the dissolution of the monasteries. He granted his henchman a Royal Licence for Baseley's sumptuous public gaming house with its outdoor bowling alleys and indoor facilities for ' . . . cardes dyze and tables . . . '. In 1546 it may not have actually been a brothel but it was certainly an open place of assignation and certainly became a brothel afterwards because it was widely known for its brazen licentiousness for generations thereafter, reaching its pinnacle of infamy in Charles I's reign, when it became known as Hollands Leaguer.

Moreover, to demonstrate that the banning of the brothels was an irritable quirk, is shown by the fact that although the edict forbade bear-baiting, in September 1546 Thomas Fludde, Yeoman of the King's bears, was also granted a licence ' . . . to make pastime with the kinges beares at the accustomed place called the Stewes . . . '.

It had taken the King 37 years to get around to his banning of the people's most favourite relaxation and for all the good it did it might just as well never have been done, for he was dead and buried next year. His son and successor, Edward VI, instructed the stewhouses to be re-opened in the second year of his reign, stressing that they must again be shown by their whited signs as of yore. Perhaps his wise mentor, Lord Somerset, sensed the degree of resentment

[10] He may have caught syphilis during the junketings on the Field of the Cloth of Gold in 1520. McL. Yearsley. *Le Roy est Morte* p.73. London 1935.

at Henry VIII's interference with popular pastimes and swiftly reversed the situation. A further degree of tolerance was also shown when the Laws against Buggery were re-enacted in the first Parliament of 1548 when the punishment was softened by exempting the felon's property and the rights of inheritance, which were still held more sacred than the felon's own life.

The King was, perhaps, too young to have been corrupted by the dreadful atmosphere of his father's Court, or by the very synnes he had restored to daylight. Nor does he seem to have interfered any more with national pastimes, for that sturdy fearless old preacher, Bishop Latimer, in his 'Third Sermon before the King', thundered:

> '. . . *I say that there is now more Whoredome in London than ever there was on the Bancke . . . you have put down the stewes, but I pray you, how is the matter amended? What avayleth it that you have but changed the place and not taken the whoredom away . . . ?*'

That the young King was only listening with half an ear is shown by his renewal of a lease to one of his father's old and faithful servants, the details of which recall the old synne, way back from the time of Henry VII. It will be recalled that William Baseley had bought the lease of the Manor House in Paris Gardens in 1542, and had been shown exceptional favour by Henry VIII in 1544 to run bear-baiting and other sports in spite of that king's own Ordinances. Edward VI's document reads:

> '. . . *(the king) allows 39 acres now or late in the possession of William Baseley in divers parishes in St. Georges Fields and all our other Park in Southwark and all messuages . . . called the Antilope therein . . . all our lordship lately pertaining to the late monastery of Bermondsey . . . (a) house or tenement called the Swanne, messuages or tenements called (respectively) Mermaid, Rose, the Lock, White Hart, Crown, Blue Mead . . . at 10½d rent . . .* '

All these were the fruit of the diligent Baseley's profitable usage of his privileges as King's Bailiff of Southwark, a remarkable collection of taverns and brothels and sites, whereon later the Rose and the Swan theatres were to be erected, as well as the hospital to tend the sufferers from the diseases they had acquired from the inhabitants of the Bailiff's other 'houses'. Baseley must have paid well for the renewal of his leases, although by 1552 the King had leased at least the Rose messuage to Henry Polsted, who in turn disposed of it to Edward Alleyn's father-in-law Philip Henslowe who built the Rose Theatre.

In a lighter vein comes a small paragraph from the records of Southwark Court Leet of 1549 which:

> *'presentid that certaine persons doe not onlie their easements in fowle lane but cast chamber pottes whiche is a grete anyaunce to the people that way passynge . . . '*

The miscreant in this case was fined twenty pence. Foul Lane was aptly named for it led to the Bankside, and also to the pillory and stocks. There were such pleasant resorts as 'Lowsie Mead', 'Sluts Well', 'Whores' Nest', 'The Sinke' (which referred to a brothel or a privy), 'Durty Lane', 'Deadman's Place', 'Naked Boy Alley', and 'Theeves Lane' are but a few; others were so frankly named as to be too obscene for the historians to put down in writing. 'Durty Lane' led right up to the stocks.

'The Merry Man's Resolution', a Roxburghe Ballad of the time, informs us that the orrible synne was rampant in Southwark:

> *'Farewel to the Banckside*
> *Farewel to Blackman's Strete*
> *where with my bouncing lasses*
> *I oftentimes did meet . . .*
> *and all the smirking wenches*
> *that dwell in Redriff town . . . '*

Blackman Street was the continuation of the High Road, and the mention of Rotherhithe (Redriff) indicates that the brothels on the south-east bank of the river were now spreading further east. At the end of the Bankside still stood the inn-cum-brothel, the 'Castell on the Hoope',[11] established

[11] See p. 118 for the history of this place.

as early as ca. 1400.

Small wonder, therefore, that a contemporary versemaker wrote of St. Saviour's church and parish:

> '. . . *Blessed St. Saviour*
> *from his naughty behaviour*
> *that dwelt not far from the stewes;*
> *for causynge infidelitie*
> *hath lost his diginitie* . . . '[12]

[12] *A Booke entitled the Fantaisie of Idolatrie* ca. 1540. Foxe V., p. 406.

Chapter Eleven

How the City Controls Southwark

At last in 1550 the City of London realized its cherished objective. Edward VI granted it the farm of the borough of Southwark for an enormous sum of one thousand Marks. The City immediately began to enforce jurisdiction:

> '. . . *This moneth of Aprill the Lord Mayor of London caused all the Aldermen to cause their Wardmotes . . . to sitt and inquire of all misrule done in their wardes since Candlemasse last past . . . caused persones to be arraigned . . . for bawdry whoredomes and scouldings . . . execution to be made immedyately by rydinge in cartes with ray hoodes (striped headscarves) . . . after the lawes of the Citie so that he spared none . . .* '

The Ward Mote was the last trace of the public ward meeting of citizens where everything would be discussed openly. So, for obvious reasons, it was rarely convoked, for it was not often advisable to wash public linen in public. What makes this particular entry very curious indeed is the next paragraph – and even the more curious for the fact that it is almost a non sequitur:

> '. . . *for wher there was one Ferdinando Lopus a phisitian which was a straunger dwellinge within St. Helenes, which was cast for whoredome and condempned for the same . . . and within vi daies . . . he shoulde be banished the realm for ever . . . this straunger was a Jewe borne . . . and shoulde have been once burnt in Portingale . . .* '[1]

This may very well have been Dr. Francisco Ruy Lopez, a Portuguese Marrano (crypto-Jew) who had fled to England

[1] C. Wriothesly. *The Chronicle of England.* 1875-79.

and arrived in London at the beginning of Queen Elizabeth's reign, and although a practising Christian, was well known to be a Jew. He was held in very high esteem, becoming House Physician at St. Bartholomew's Hospital and attending to many of the nobility. Eventually in October 1593 he was appointed as Physician-in-Chief to the Queen. He may have been sowing a few youthful wild oats in 1550, for he certainly was not banished, seemingly because his powerful protectors and patients at Court would not allow it.

At Whitsuntide, Sir John Aliffe (Ayliffe), was sworn the first Alderman of Bridge Ward Withoute, as Southwark was afterwards to be known, although by some curious quirk this new ward never had a properly elected council, nor Alderman, during all its subsequent existence.

The City's authorities were still on the warpath against synne, and in August of that year arraigned one Middleton, a member of the powerful Guild of Haberdashers, and his wife, for bawdry. This was a curious case because the lady was charged:

> '. . . *shee for a common adoulterix with one Nicholas Ballard, gentleman, booth with her owne bodie and also bawde to hym for her owne daughter also and a mayde of tenne or eleven yeares of age her servaunt which the said Ballard occupied all three carnallie . . . (and were) . . . sentenced to be carted immedyately with ray hodes and whyte rood (rods or sticks) in their handes according to the oulde laws of the cittie* . . . '

Nicholas Ballard, being a Gentleman had to be treated rather differently, but they had to make an example of him, albeit it was a delicate situation when a worthy Guildsman's wife was found to be whoring with him and prostituting her daughter and her maid to boot. Eventually he pleaded guilty to rape and was punished by a short term in prison and had his hand burnt. Honour was seemingly thus satisfied all round.

Another adjacent haunt of prostitutes was the Savoy, since it lay on the main highway from London to Westminster, from the Bankers of the City to the King's Court, and was always thronged with the wealthy or the curious, and therefore always good for lecherous pickings. It had little changed its character from 1381 when Wat Tyler's London allies had burnt it down.

Although Richard II had in 1385 levied a toll for paving the road from the Temple Bar to the Savoy, the Strand road was not completed until 1553.

King Edward VI's reign was brief, for he died early of a combination of congenital syphilis and tuberculosis, a part legacy from his father's lecheries.[2] In the same year 1553 his sister, Mary, came to the throne and inaugurated eight bloody years of savage reprisals against Protestants in her passionate determination to restore the power of Rome.

She immediately repealed most of her father's legislation which likewise meant that the stews were given another lease of life; and one side-effect, too, was that sodomy was not punishable during her reign. She ordered, however, that stocks, cages, pillories, should be set up in various places and although they undoubtedly confined their usual quotas of strumpettes and scoldes, they also contained even larger numbers of men and women who dissented from Mary's fanatical religious persecution.

Amidst what would otherwise be an unrelieved tale of gloom, one small gleam of humour appears in Wriothesley's *Chronicle for 1553:*

> '. . . *In the first year of Queen Marie . . . Friday Nov. 24 one Sir Thomas Sothwood priest alias parson Chekin of St. Nicholas old Abbaye in Ole Fysshe Strete rode about the citie in a carte with a raye hode for sellynge hys wyfe whiche he said he had marid . . .*'

This is one of the comparatively rare occasions when a man is reported to have been carted for a sexual offence. A carting was accompanied by a howling mob of people running in front banging metal bowls – often hired from barbers who made a few extra pence on these occasions by hiring out their 'shavynge bowles' – and shouting obscenities. Sometimes the malefactor was flogged at the cart-tail and this spectacle was so revolting to some foreign observers that they commented adversely, not only on the deed but the mob's

[2] Dr. J. Rae. *Deaths of the Kings of England,* p. 78. London 1913.

obvious enjoyment of these dreadful scenes. Of course it was a coarse and cruel time and there was plenty of encouragement from the highest in the land for various bestialities, such as burning at the stake and decapitation and racking and other tortures.

Mary Tudor's insensate religious and persecution mania may well have had its roots in the congenital syphilis she inherited from her father, for Haggard asserts that:

> '. . . *Queen Mary shows in her facial expressions a typical congenital syphilis . . .*'[3]

The same source opines that Henry VIII suffered from cerebral syphilis in addition to a syphilitic lesion on one hip.

[3] H.W. Haggard. *Devils, Drugs and Doctors*, Harvard 1929. McL. Yearsley says 'that it was syphilitic rhinitis and quotes a Lady in Waiting "there was a disgusting smell from her nose." '

Chapter Twelve

Of Sex and Sewers: of Schetyng-pannes and Syphilis

Hitherto we have been investigating the morally murky background of our forefathers. With Henry VII's solution to the problems regarding syphilis discussed earlier, it is apposite to have a look at the equally murky background which played its part in bringing about the disease scourging the kingdom.

Not to put too fine a point on the subject, the English people were for centuries coarse in manners and coarse in their physical habits and consequently coarse in their speech. They were both dirty and smelly, and the circumstances in which they lived did little to alleviate their situation.

When London was comparatively rural, sanitation was a simpler matter. The people defecated or urinated in their gardens and thought nothing of it:[1] but after the Norman Conquest when the township began to develop mightily, problems of sanitation arose that never existed before. Naturally old habits were hard to break, and when gardens were fewer, easements were done in the lanes and alleys. The consequent stench and obstructions were casually referred to as Pissing Lane, Stynkyng Alley, Shiteburnlane or Foul Lane. If the lane were additionally used for fornication it might also bear a suitable title such as Gropecuntlane – assuredly a hark-back to Saxon times – or Codpieće Alley, or even Whores Lie Down. These places, as may be expected,

[1] Disposal was easy in 1387 still, *vide* Ranulph Higden. *Polychronicon (Trevisa)*. Rolls Service. iv.329. London 1865.

'. . . they wolde . . . make hem a pitte . . . whanne they wolde schite . . . and when they hadde-i-scete they woulde fill in the pit ayen . . . '

eventually were deodorized into Grape Lane, Coppice Alley and Horsleydown. Where there were whorehouses, the streets would bear names like Whores Nest or Sluts' Hole or Mayden lane (in which were no maidens at all) or Rose Alley (to pluck the roses of maidenheads) or Golden Lane, whence gold could be so earned.

Although the Romans left one legacy of indoor latrines at this time, seated and trenched lavatories were usually just cesspits. The first recorded English latrine (from Latin 'Latrina' – a cave) naturally was a royal one, installed by Stephen in 1141 in his palace at Woodstock: and the next one dates to 1152 at the royal palace at Clipstone, when it was to be glazed.

Bathing and washing were perfunctory or non-existent pursuits, although wooden tubs were utilized occasionally as baths. Bathing in the Thames was of course frequent in the summer time when the water was warm. Some idea of standards of cleanliness amongst the highest in the land may be gauged by the report after Thomas à Becket was murdered in Canterbury Cathedral in December 1170. When the king's four murdering knights had departed, the acolytes plucked up enough courage to approach the body. They peeled off garment after garment and at the end clouds of fleas jumped off the holy man's stinking carcase, thus demonstrating that cleanliness was not close to godliness in the 12th century – although this did not prevent the canonization of this turbulent priest. The fact that he had farmed out the brothels in his diocese in Southwark was also no bar to sainthood. Brothel-keeping was not especially frowned upon by the Church. Fornication was another matter, especially priestly fornication.

Incidentally this butcher's son, the first Englishman to reach such eminence, was baptized in the crypt of St. Mary Colechurche, of which the famous Bridge-Master, Peter de Colechurch was later the Prior. The builder of Old London Bridge dedicated the lovely little chapel in its midst to St. Thomas à Becket and it remained a shrine until it was converted some centuries later into a grocers' warehouse.

Dirt and squalor were the norm in all walks of life. However after a number of fires had ravaged London, King

Richard I in 1189[2] ordered that all new buildings in London must consist of stone or brick up to the first floor and some of these presumably had cubicles for lavatories, since in that year the City of London laid down standards of size and distance one from the other:[3] at least 2½ feet apart if the pit were lined with stone (5½ feet if unlined).

Since most houses however were still constructed of wood and thatch, although they had at least one upper storey, they had no space nor means to build a privy. The inhabitants took to throwing the full chamberpots out of the casement into the street, hoping to reach the 'channel' of running water which was the only means of sanitation.

Another domestic utensil (less well known than the ubliquitous chamber-pot whose history is likewise a legacy from Roman times) was that used by Master Huberd of London, who in his Will of 1386[4] bequeathed '... *melioram patellam meam, vocatum* schetyng panne ...' (My easement bowl, called a shitting-pan). This may mean the metal pan used in his close stool which would normally be situated at the top of the first storey stairs on the landing and would be for family use. The contents likewise might have been thrown from the upper storey into the street. In any case, even in 1386, only the more wealthy citizens could possess such a useful internal refinement: a wooden board over the cesspit usually sufficed.

The job of clearing up all the ordure was that of the Guild of Scavengers (also known as Gong-farmers – 'gong' meaning dung) who had to convey it at night into laystalls or dunghills, of which there was one to each Ward: and the contents were then eventually emptied into the Thames. Farming this dirty job out was a lucrative business and the tendering was fierce, with price-cutting rampant, as the City records show. Then as now, jobs went to the lowest tenderer.

Bathing, that fine old Roman habit, neglected for about five hundred years, came back into fashion during the Crusades when the returning soldiers had savoured the

[2] *LIBER ALBUS* III/II fol.211.b. *De Cameris Necessariis in Domibus.*

[3] Interesting details may be found in Laurence Wright's *Clean and Decent*, London 1960.

[4] Register of Wills: Somerset House. 1386. London.

The Stews as an amorous rendezvous in the Middle Ages.

delights of the oriental 'hammams', and it became a great vogue. Public baths flourished: 'hot stews' abounded. Such stews were set up in England, notably in Queenhithe, at first separately for men and women. By about 1100 such 'estuwes' were known on the Bankside, and gave their name to the official whorehouses when recognized in 1130 by the Church and in 1161 by the Law.

In royal circles bathing seems not to have been so popular. It is related that King John took a bath about every three weeks.

The first stone bridge of London, when built in 1209, had

recesses for use as public latrines and it was the duty of the Bridge Wardens to keep them clean. These niches however also became shelters in which harlots lurked: presumably taking their clients to the Bankside houses conveniently near or doing the job on the spot. Certainly moral and street dirt were closely linked in the authorities' minds, for in 1273 Edward I issued his decree 'Of Cleaning the Streets and Lanes and the Punishment of Thieves and Whores'.

Public latrines appear at a very early date, and they were usually built over a running stream. Queen Maud (ca. 1140) built a 'necessary house' at Queenhithe 'for the common use of citizens' and it was enlarged in 1237 'to have access to the Thames'.[5]

The introduction of a privy began to spread, although by 1250 it was still rare enough to excite comment. It was of course still the prerogative of the wealthier citizens. Nevertheless, the ordure was still thrown out into the streets and collected by the scavengers. That the streets were still used as latrines is evidenced by the existence in 1263 of Pyssinge Lane (between St. Pauls and Paternoster Row) (Ekwall, *Early London Street Names*) which Ekwall says stems from the much earlier Saxon name (and habit) 'mihindelane'; from 'micgan', to piss: there was a Mihindelane in Gloucester about that time too. It was still there as Pyssinge Alley in 1425.

As to the habits of kings, we have the note that in 1256 Henry III would repair to 'the Wardrobe at Westminster . . . where the king was wont to wash his head . . . '. It does not say how often his Majesty indulged in this dangerous pastime: and doubtless he remembered the foppishness of the Danes in mediaeval times, when they were criticized:

> '. . . *following the usage in their country (they) used to comb their hair every day, bathed every Saturday, and often changed their clothes . . .* '

While there is no record of the sanitary conveniences in brothels at that time we do know about one prison, Newgate; for there is a note that in 1283 it required no less than

[5] Close Rolls. 564.

thirteen workmen to clear away the accumulated ordure. It took them five days to clean the '*cloacum*' and their pay of 6d. a day was about three times more than unskilled workers then earned.

Some years before that King Henry III (in 1245) had written to his Master of Works, Edward Fitz Otho:

> '*. . . since the prevy chamber of our wardrobe at London is situate in an unsuitable place wherefore it smells badly, we command you . . . that you in no wise omit to cause another privy chamber to be made in the same wardrobe in such more fitting place . . . even though it should cost an hundred pounds . . .*'[6]

This would be about £4000 in today's money, a very expensive seat for a royal backside in any generation.

The houses situated on London Bridge very early seized on the idea of putting their privies in little cubicles overhanging the river-side of the Bridge, which solved their problems very neatly, and also rendered their houses sweeter smelling and much more healthy. It is related that during the Plague the mortality amongst dwellers on London Bridge was much less because of the clean air and cleaner physical state.

Although by that time a very large number of houses had cesspits, there were still those who continued the old custom of throwing the muck into the street, so much so that in 1306 the inspectors reported that Ebbgate Street was choked up (*quarum putredo cadit super capitas hominum transeuntium*) from the shit falling on the heads of passers-by.[7] (It was still stopped with filth in 1420!)

In this period however, the King's 'Ingeniators' were gaining more experience and building was going on apace: and there are thus many mentions of the installations of privies: but very few hot baths.[8] In 1370 eighteen shops were built in Paternoster Row, and ten privies and a cesspit were provided.[9] The City of London was insisting that something

[6] Cal. Close Rolls. 1245.
[7] H.T. Riley. *Liber Custumarium*, p.449. 1859.
[8] L.F. Salzman. *Building in England to 1540*, p.276 lists only six 'stews' in the period 1351-91, all royal properties. OUP 1967.
[9] *Ibid.* p.478-79.

be done on London Bridge in 1377 because '. . . the necessary houses there were in a dangerous state of repair . . . '; and again in 1382 these same latrines were said to be '. . . filthy and stynkynge . . . '.[10]

However in 1388 a spark of civilization appears in the statement that King Richard II installed the first Ladies' Lavatory – a *Latrina Dominarum* – in one of his residences.

As regards hot baths, there was a running battle for hundreds of years between the City authorities and those, particularly in Queenhithe, who insisted they were running honest stews, especially for women. Presumably the sight of nude women excited concupiscence in passing males and they quickly became, despite the efforts of the proprietors, brothels. For some reason washerwomen were forbidden access to the women's baths, possibly because the dividing line between them and prostitutes was very finely drawn: or because they were easily enticed. It may however have been a more mundane matter. The heating of these baths became ever more costly as the number of stewhouses increased with rising prosperity and growth of population, and the washerwomen wasted water and the precious wood fuel, which was running short, before the advent of sea-coal brought in barges from Durham in later years. There were hot baths and whorehouses side by side in Queenhithe almost until Queenhithe ceased to exist as a thoroughfare.

It is clear that such lack of facilities would affect the brothels' hygiene. Lack of water meant lack of washing. Lack of washing meant the encouragement of disease. For centuries the only prophylactic generally known both for men and women was hard pissing in the chamberpot. The clients came dirty or unwashed and brought diseases with them or acquired them from girls unlucky to have received them from the last client. As for public hygiene, almost nothing was known, except the use of water and vinegar, or white wine by the more sophisticated. By the 16th century the position had somewhat improved, perhaps because of the expertise of the Dutch and Venetian Courtesans, who had developed their profession efficiently – there was even a

[10] Cal. Plea & Memo Rolls. A.22. Feb.1377: and Letter Book 'H'. 1382. 6.Ric II p.212.

Guild of Courtesans in Venice, the first (and only) whores' trade union! They certainly had acquired some prophylactic techniques, but to what degree these had been adopted in England is quite unknown.

When in 1417, therefore, Henry V had ordained the first closing of the Southwark stews, it was followed up by an attack on the physical misdemeanours of the citizens: and about 1420 a city-wide series of raids was made.[11] A selection of the details is set out here, to give an idea of the actual life and habits of ordinary Londoners of that time: and very instructive it is too! The Inspectors reported *inter alia*:

> *Item: Filth is thron out of Welles' house in the Vinesterie (Vintry) and pushed under the walls of the house of Mildenhalle the Skinner.*
>
> *Item: Adam Semy and Richard Kere . . . are comon usurers. Also Guyse Pawnsner and Willyman his wife are common Bawds and keepe a stew in their house in St. Bartholomew.*
>
> *Item: Behind the Pye in Quenehythe is a privy place which is a good shadowing for thieves and many evil bargains have been made there: and many strumpettes and pimps have their covert there . . .*
>
> *Item: (in the Tower Ward) . . . also the Porter of the Tower does grete extorcion and wrong to the City by taking barges and other vessels and ferryboats into the Tower so that the owners must buy them back '. . . as it were in Fraunce . . .'*
>
> *Item: that in Dowgate Ward the common lane called Ebbegate is stopped with filth . . . and that Ermenterslane is common (a public highway) and stopped with filth and the stair is broken so that none can get water from the Thames: that Wolsilane is common but is stopped up with filth from privies on either side: that Turnylane is common and full of filth and the pavement is*

[11] Cal.Plea & Memo. Rolls. A.50. 1413-1437. Cal.Plea & Memo. Rolls. A.51. 1423.

broken . . . that Hayswharflane is obstructed by fullers who wash their cloths there so that no one can draw water or make their easements there, to the great nuisance of the commonalty . . .

Item: *In Bradstrete Ward . . . two dunghills on both side of the common privy dore are defective owing to default of the Chamber . . .*

Item: *Farndon (Farringdon) Ward, the Common prevy at Ludgate is defective and perilous and the ordure thereof rotteth the stone wall and makyth an orrible stenche and a foul sight to the great discomfort and nuisance of al folk dwellynge thereabout and passing thereby: and it is a disgrace to the City that so foul a nuisance . . . though often presented (complained about) hath no remedy yet bene ordayned. The mud wall in the Great Bayli (Old Bailey) . . . is falling bit by bit into the street: the timberwork of Flete Brigge is perilous . . . and a dunghill within the Temple Gate encumbers the high way . . . Moreover they indite and present White the Carpenter and his wife for being as Common Bawds as any in London and for being recyvers of strumpettes and although they have been twice indicted . . . yet no execution hath been done therein . . .*

Item: *William Emery for laying dung in the highway all through the yeare and for casting out horse piss that had stood under his horse a month so that no man can pass there for styngle (a pungent stinging stink) . . .*

Item: *In Crepulgate (Cripplegate) they indite Gerard Clayson and his wyfe of the Estewehous in Grub Street as evildoers and receivers and maintainers of harlotry and bawdry . . . of horrible life, and of strumpettes and other malefactors . . . They present John Sherman, Cooper also of Grubb Strete for keeping ducks to the nuisance of his neighbours: . . . They indict the Stew House in the Ward as a nuisance . . . because it is a comon*

> *house of harlotry and bawdry and a grete resort of theves and also of priests and their concubines to the great disgrace of the City: . . . and likewise they indict the privy of the Stew House as a nuisance because of the great corruption: and further indict four privies in West Yard because they stop up the common watercourse running into the ditch of the Moor: and also the privies of Robert Brynkele the Goldsmith and Thomas Lucas, Grocer, which stand about the common watercourse and stop the flow of water: also they present that three ancient watercourses . . . are stopped up whiche is a nuisance whenever there is . . . a flood of rainwater: and they indict the cart of John Riche of Wood Street, Brewer because the wheels have iron strakes which destroy the pavement and make a great noise when the cart is loaded with barrels and draskes (malt refuse) as often happens . . . .*

It can be seen that the Inspectors certainly had a field day! These remarks give us a refreshingly clear insight into the daily life, and rather coarse, not to say free and easy habits of the citizens and their off-hand disregard of laws and ordinances. They disclose the presence of individual unlawful brothels in the Moorgate area, and castigate their own superiors for their lack of attention to matters often brought to their notice. They try to take care of the 'pavement', that is the cobbled roadway (for in those days there were no pavements for pedestrians: the cambered surface ran down to 'kennels' (channels) on either side into which the household refuse of every kind was thrown, and the old and the weak would be jostled off the crown of the highway and literally 'went to the wall'); refer to the ancient streams of clear fresh water that had been fouled up by over-hanging 'houses of easement' (privies) or used as urinals; they uncover the fact that clergymen frequented these low-class whorehouses 'with their concubines' and they use the word 'pimp' almost for the first time on record: they disclose there were public latrines in Ludgate and in Broad Street in 'orrible' condition; they inform us that Ebbegate (which was stopped up with filth way back in 1306) is still in the same condition; and they uncover the Tower Porter's little racket of blackmailing ships just as if they were foreign vessels (he was entitled to hold those up by ancient law). They also disclose a sleazy side of life usually ignored by historians.

Of great interest is the mention that in the late fifteenth century, excreting into running streams – the old shite-bournes – was still going on. Likewise the existence of the Pyssing Lanes. Both Shitteburne Street and Pissing Alley still bore these names, although the first was soon to be transmogrified into Shirebourne and then Sherbourne, while the second was to change its name to Chick Lane and later to Blowbladder Street.[12] A certain prurience was beginning to manifest itself to cover up down-to-earth descriptions with euphemisms: but these words have irreproachably respectable lineage from earliest times in standard inoffensive use.

The word 'shite' or 'shit' stems from the Old Teutonic 'Skit', which in Old Frisian became 'Skitj' (sk' – 'sh') and in Old English 'scitan' thence to 'shite', meaning to evacuate or shoot out. In German today it is 'scheissen', in Dutch 'schijten' and a similar sounding word exists in all Northern languages.

The earliest written record in English dates to about 1300 concerning the superstition that snakes excreted jewels:[13]

> '*. . . the addres (adders) shiteth precious stones . . .*' followed in 1367 by the phrase '*. . . and he sched out hys bowels . . .*'[14]

Chaucer writes (about 1386) '. . . and schame it is if a Prest take keep, A shiten shepherd . . .'[15]: and he is followed by William Langland in 1393 translating a Latin phrase '. . . the wolf shiteth woolle . . .'[16]

[12] This was a street leading to the Cokkes Lane stews off Newgate: Blowbladerer street may very well mean it was another pissing lane.
[13] K. Alis. 5670. from O.E.D.
[14] Ranulph Higden. *Polychronicon (Trevisa).* Rolls Service v.152. London. 1865.
[15] *Prolegomena* 504.
[16] *Piers Plowman* X.264 from Latin '. . . *lupus lanam cacat* . . .' Macro Plays, *Castle Perseverance* 136. 1969 ed.

To shit from fear is a favourite expression in the next century one example being '. . . thei schul schytyn for fere . . .', and this is echoed at least twice by Caxton about 1484.

Thus far still everyday usage, only in 1500 comes the hint that the word can be used as a term of abuse:

> '. . . *a vyllany it were . . . to slaye a shitten-arsed shrew . . .*'[17]

which may equally mean a condemnation of slaying a poor woman, or a description of her abject poverty.

A little later it appears in the medical sense, in the phrases '. . . an ounce for them that spetteth blode, pysseth blode or shytteth blode'[18] and in 1583 an instruction '. . . stampe hym downe tyll he shyte . . .'[19]

By this time euphemisms are becoming common, one of which was the word 'jakes' or 'jaques' for the privy, and one of Elizabeth's favourites, Sir John Harington, announcing his invention of the Water Closet[20] states that 'the jakes' was '. . . in plaine Englishe called a Shytinge place . . .'. This was not yet considered vulgar since in 1659 it appears in a translation of French proverbs into English for the use of children '. . . it is not alle butter that a cow shiteth . . .'.[21] From this time onwards the term becomes one of abuse, and 'not decent' or 'vulgar', although still used habitually amongst many sections of the people to this day.

The other excretory function has an even longer lineage in respectability; this is the noun and verb 'piss'. It comes from the Old French 'pisser', to make water or urinate and the first written record in English is in 1290 in the statement '. . . ywane he wolde pisse . . .'[22]. There are a number of examples extant until it is used by William Langland at least twice in *Piers Plowman*. For instance the character Gloton

[17] Chester Plays. *Innocents* 157.

[18] Andrew. *Brunswycke Distill. Waters* C.iv.b from O.E.D.

[19] Bale. *Three Laws* IV.E.5.b. from O.E.D.

[20] Sir John Harington. *Metamorphosis of Ajax*, p.56. Ed. Elizabeth Donne, Routledge. London 1962.

[21] N.R. Proverbs 'English-French'. No.68 1659. O.E.D.

[22] S.E. Leg. I. 45. 381.

' . . . pissed a potel in a Paternoster-while . . . '[23]

About the same time in 1494 John Isell bequeathed in his Will: ' . . . a grete cawdren and iij pyssing basons . . . '[24] which must be the original name of the chamber-pot. In 1591 Shakespeare[25] uses the expression ' . . . an pissing while . . . ' in the acceptable sense of a few minutes delay. Thereafter there are a number of references to ' . . . pyssinge vessels . . .' which are again chamber-pots: in 1602 there is the expression '. . . and pisse vinegar . . .'[26], as a description of a disagreeable person, and in 1623 ' . . . rods in pisse . . . '[27] are a form of punishment.

Shakespeare uses it in a description in *Henry VI* Part I, Act IV. Sc. vi:

> *'. . . I charge and command you . . . (that) . . . the Pissing Conduit run nothing but clarret wine the first year of our reigne . . .'*

referring to the Water Conduit in Cheapside which was thus known owing to its propensity to spurting in gushes.

The word was frequently in ordinary use in the 18th century, as was the expression ' . . . pissing pins and needles . . . ' to describe gonorrhoea. Then suddenly in about 1800 it is deemed vulgar, although used in serious literature and medicine until 1870. It has returned to daily speech, still in a pejorative sense, but its accolade was surely during the Versailles Peace Conference in 1920 when Clemenceau, then Prime Minister of France, admiring Lloyd George's eloquence exclaimed 'Ah! si je pouvais pisser comme il parle!' (Ah! If I could only piss as fluently as he speaks!').

Today's expression 'to take the micky out of someone' or 'take the mike' out of someone can be traced back even earlier, for in the form of 'taking the piss out of someone' it goes back to about 1000 A.D., probably from Old English 'migan', from Old Norse 'migan' from the Latin 'mingere' – to piss, to make water.

[23] A.5.92.
[24] Register of Wills. Vox.1.f.21/4 B. Somerset House.
[25] *Two Gentlemen of Verona* and other plays.
[26] *Return from Parnassus* II.iii II.ARB.40 O.E.D.
[27] Mabbe. MS. Cotton-Virgil Travesta. Brit. Mus.

In the year 1000 an expression '. . . and his micga byth hwit . . .'[28] in its context may well be a reference to gonorrhoea, while the expression 'mig of lecherie',[29] is very early known. At the same time there is a medical prescription ordering a patient '. . . drince eft buccan micgan . . .'[30]

The religious work 'Ancren Riwle' (Rules for Anchorites) written by the monk Layamon (The Law-Man) in 1200 refers to lechery as 'Grickische fur' (Greek Fire) and may even be referring to a venereal disease:

> *'. . . and tet (that-the Greek Fire) ne mei no-thyng bute migge and sond & eisil ase me seith a cwenchan . . .' ('as far as I can see only piss and sand and vinegar can quench the Greek fire')*[31]

and to make quite sure his meaning is not lost the old zealot goes on:

> *'. . . micge as ich er seide that acwentheth grickische fur is stynkynde ulesshes luue thet acwenteth gostlich luue . . .' ('as I said, the piss that quenches Greek fire is like the stinking lues (syphilitic discharge) of Ulysses which quenches carnal love . . .')*[32]

and in 1400 occurs the reference to the stinking piss of lechery, to show what the old monks thought of it.

It is strange how men make taboos of ordinary words; for words *per se* bear only the meaning men put on them and can have no innate vulgarity or obscenity.

From this brief excursion into ancient philology emerges the closeness of the relationship between excretory functions and carnal love and venereal disease: and these were intimately tied up with the insanitary ignorance of the times. The theology doubtless satisfied the unslaked latent lechery of the religious: but unluckily the practical result of the

[28] *Saxon Leechdoms* III/132. 'His piss is white'.
[29] Apollonius Loll. 58. O.E.D.
[30] T.O. Cockayne. *Saxon Leechdoms* I/354. 'Drink frequently buck's piss': the anti-septic quality of fresh urine was known from very early times.
[31] Cotton MS.Nero. B.M.402/22.
[32] Cotton MS.Nero. B.M.406/13.

physical carnal love had now thrust itself into King Henry VII's ambit and had compelled him to make a decision. Syphilis was now a 'named' disease: no longer the *morbis indecens aie cunnientis* but something specific; affecting all sections of lecherous mankind, from kings and popes down to the commonest commoner.

A number of clever 'physitians' and '*chirugeons*' had been examining the effects while trying to establish the cause. In the reign of Henry VIII the Ingeniators were tackling the questions of sanitation. Both in their way played (then as yet unrecognized) great parts in the way of eliminating the scourge: but as their effects fall effectively into the next reign, we shall deal with them in a later chapter.

Chapter Thirteen

Of Buggery, Bear-baiting and Bawdy-houses

Elizabeth I is known as Good Queen Bess or as the Virgin Queen and rightly famed for her intelligence, literacy, statesmanship and wit. While her virginity is a matter of conjecture – Henry IV of France wisecracked that there were three things that nobody believed: that Archduke Albert was a good general, that he (Henry) was a good Catholic, and that the Queen of England was a virgin – there can be no doubt that in other ways she could gain no encomiums.

Her ill-manners and exasperating behaviour were those of a selfish and ruthless and foul-mouthed vulgarian, who in any other contemporary station of life would have been summarily dealt with and even carted by the civil power. Swearing and oaths were forbidden by ordinance to the people: the Queen indulged in it unchecked, to quote Alexander:[1]

> '. . . *Queen Elizabeth of England was not only much addicted to swearing but even the most vulgar and familiar oaths were uttered in a vulgar and indelicate manner . . .*'

She was without feeling for those less fortunate than she, and this despite her harrowing childhood experiences and her apprehension for her own safety during Queen Mary's reign, which should have made her more tolerant and understanding of others. Even when she was old, with:

> '. . . *her vast violence of temper . . . the greatest vanity . . . here in her 66th year with wrinkled face, red perriwig, little eyes, hooked nose, skinny lips and black teeth . . .*'[2]

[1] Dr. W. Alexander. *Women*, vol.II. p.264.
[2] T. Pennant. *Some Account of London*. p.134. 1813.

she was still demanding unceasing flattery about her beauty from her courtiers. To quote one of her most recent admirers:[3]

> '. . . *there can be no doubt that she encouraged, indeed exacted adulation . . .* '

It is not therefore to be expected that she would have shown much tolerance towards or interest in the horrible lot of 'fallen women' in whorehouses. Thus when she re-enacted her father's various laws in her second Parliament of 1563, including that of closing the stews, she also renewed the Law Against Buggery on the grounds that:

> ' . . . *divers ill-disposed Persone have been the more bold to commit this most horrible detestable vice to the High Displeasure of Almightie God . . .* '

Detestable or not, this vice flourished in the Virgin Queen's Court which included such famous homosexuals as Sir Francis Bacon, Henry Wriothesley, Earl of Southampton (whose name was later linked with King James) and Lord Henry Howard. Outside the court the most famous is perhaps Christopher Marlowe, most of whose works refer in one way or another to his predilection for boys – indeed 'Come live with me and be my love' is addressed not to a maiden but to a boy! The Queen's favourite cousin was thought also to be involved in this perversion. This was the Lord Hunsdon (who was supposed to be under mercury treatment for venereal disease) against whom the Satirist John Marston jibed ' . . . quicksilver was in his head but his wits were dull as lead . . . '. Marston's couplet:

> ' . . . *at Hoxton now his monstrous love he feasts*
> *for there he keeps a bawdy house of beasts . . .* '

is also supposed to refer to Hunsdon. There would be nothing surprising in that because he had already farmed out his demesne in Paris Gardens to Francis Langley and others for bawdy houses.

The cruel streak in Elizabeth's nature was clearly manifested in her deep enjoyment of those most horrible

[3] A.L. Rowse. *Elizabethan Renaissance.* p.33, London 1971.

sports of bear and bull-baiting. A contemporary account in *Letters from Killingworth Castle* (page 23) dated 1575 described a bear-baiting session very vividly:

> '. . . *if the dogge in pleadynge wool pluk the beare by the throte the bear with trauers (by traversing) woold claw him agayne by the skaip (scalp) thearfore thus with fendynge and proouynge (probing) with pluckynge and tuggynge by plain tooth and nayll a to side and toother (to one side or another) such erspes of blood and leather (skin) was thear betweene them az a moonths licking I ween wyl not recouer (recover) and yet remain as far oout az euer they wear. It waz a sport very pleazaunt of theez beasts; to see the bear with hys pink nyez (nose) leering after hiz enemiez approach, the nimblness and wayt of ye dogge too take his aduauntage (advantage) and the fors and experiens of the beare agyn to auoyd the assauts* . . . '

One attraction, also, was the price of admission, which was, to quote Lampard: '. . . 1 penny at the Gate; 1d at the scaffold; and a third for a quiet standing . . . '[4]

Another unbelievable piece of cruelty was the 'sport' of whipping a blind bear, the bear being tethered to a stake and whipped by five or six men standing in a circle!

All this was going on merrily in Good Queen Bess' golden reign.

That 'evill life' continued to flourish undiminished is attested by innumerable sources. One particularly revealing remark is in the broadsheet published in 1584 entitled *A Mirrour for Magistreates of Cytees*:

> '. . . *a man may find many of these neat Panders . . . hies to some blind Brothell House about the suburbs . . . where for a pottle or two of wine, the embracement of a painted Strumpet and the French Welcome (the pox) for a reckoning, the Young Man payeth 40 shillings or better* . . . '

This was an expensive and easy way to get gonorrhoea and doubtless with this sort of thing in mind the Common

[4] W. Taylor. *Annals of St. Mary Overie*, p. 142, London 1833.

Council of the City of London on 17 July, 1565 under a Minute headed '. . . Shaving the Heads of Harlots . . .' instructs its minions as to the:

> *'. . . cutting the hair off heads of harlots as have been sent to Bridewell, who will not be content to amend themselves, to be whipped and other punishments . . . (and) to be confined,. . .'*

In November 1555 they had ordered that '. . . an ill woman who kept the Grehonde in Westminster . . . be carted abowte the City . . .' and in the next year recorded that '. . . a woman who kept The Bell in Grassechurchestrete was carted as a Bawd . . .'. In November 1568 they ordered '. . . a special punishment for Bawds in Queenhithe . . .' although the details are not published.

From Henry Machyn's 'Diary' there are also a few gems, which we cannot forbear to narrate: he reports three cartings in such a way as to make it clear that these were important events which had to be diarized:

> *'1559 . . . the v daye of January ryd a-bout London iiij women for baudre . . .*
> *. . the xviij day of Desembre dyd a women ryd a-pone horsback with a paper on her hed for bawdere with a basen ryngynge . . .*
> *. . . the xx day of Desember dyd ryd a cart a-bowt Lundun the wyff of Hare (Harry) Glyn a gold-smyth for behyng bowd to her owne dowther . . .'*

And the *pièce de résistance*, which also shows what could really happen when gentlemen's girl-friends were incarcerated in Bridewell in 1559:

> *'. . . the xiij daye of aprell ther cam vnto Brydwell dyvers gentyllmen and ruffelars an servynge-menne an ther begane a tymult and or fray that the constabulles and Althermen deputte (Aldermen's deputies) cam to see the pesse (peace) kepte but they wold haue serten womene owt of the brydwelle and ther they druw ther swordes and be-gane myche besenes (business. i.e. trouble) . . .'*[5]

[5] *Machyns Diary*, ed. J.G. Nichols. 1848.

Despite the awful spelling, the respectable old Funeral Director throws a clear light on early Elizabethan goings-ons, and we are much indebted to him, also for the following vignettes which uncover the skeletons in the cupboards of some city worthies and their ladies, in the years between 1555 and 1562.

On 2 May, 1555 Master Manwarynge, a Gentilman, and two women dwelling in the 'Harry' in Cheapside, one of the ladies being a Goldsmith's wyff, were carted to Aldagate for baudry and hordom. A couple of years later John a Badoo (presumably of Bordeaux), himself a Bawd, and his wife, also a Bawd were arrested, but '. . . shee was wyppyd at the cart-arse . . . the odur woman being a nold harlot of iij (3) skore and more ledd the horse lyk a nold hore . . . '.

In 1560 Mastoress (mistress) Warner, wife of the sometime Sergeant of the Admiralty was arrested for bawdry, and both she and her daughter, whom she had prostituted as well as the mayde 'weren wyth childe and shee a hore . . . '. The next year a Waterman was whipped at a post in Quen-heyff '. . . for opprobyous wordes and sedyssyous wordes agaynste the magystrates . . . ' and several others were punished in various ways for ' . . . nostylevynge' (naughtiness) by bawdry. To make up for it all the worthy old gentleman informs us that a feast was given by the butchers and fishermen with 'grete cheere . . . (with) ij (2) fyrkyns of fresse sturgeon . . . and gret plente of wyne that itt came to viij (8) pence . . . '.

Volume I of the Middlesex Court Rolls lists no fewer than 25 cases under 'Disorderly Houses and Disorderly Women' around every part of the periphery of the City walls: a few of the more interesting are given here:

11 June, 1575	*John Holybring, Gent., of evil life, pimp, adulterer fornicator, kept a common brothel in St. Giles with (four women listed by name). Sentence* quod vehetur in carruce a Newgate vsque Giles *(to be taken in a cart to Newgate from St. Giles) . . . '*
31 March, 1578	*John Belman hath lodged lewd persons in his house also iij or iiij lewde wommen delyveryd of childe . . . '*

1 April, 1601 *Susan Newland in Nortonfollgate next Bishopsgate infernally and diabolically kept a brothel . . .*

Most of the others were sent to Bridewell after carting for such crimes as playing cards, or dicing or for other manifestations of 'lewde and euill lieffes'.

This was of course the viewpoint of 'Aucthorite' and as a change from their dreary recitals, we are indebted to John Marston's play *The Dutch Courtesan* for what can be termed the Bawdes-eye view of her excellent profession by Cocledemoy.

COCLE. *'List then: A Baud, first for her profession or vocation, it is most worshipfull of all the twelve companies;*[6] *for, as that trade is most honorable that sells the best commodyties – as the Draper is more worshippfull then the poyntmaker, the Silkeman more worshippfull then the Draper and the Goldsmith more honorable then both – so the Baud above all. Her shop has the best ware, for where these sell but cloath sattens and jewels, shee sels divine vertues, as virginitie, modestie and suche rare jemmes: and those not lyke a petty chapman, by retaile, but like a greate marchant, by wholesale. And who are her Customers? Not base corn-cutters or sow-gelders, but most rare wealthie knightes and most rare bountifull lordes, are her Customers.*

'Againe, where as no trade or vocation profiteth but by the losse and displeasure of another – as the Marchant thrives not but by the Licentiousnes of giddie and unsetled youth: the Lawyer but by the vexation of his client: the Phisition but by the maladies of his patient – onlie my smothe-gumbed Baud lives by others pleasure and onely grows rich by others rising. O! Mercifull gaine!: O! Righteous

[6] He refers to the 12 Great Livery Companies or Guilds who always dominated the governing of the City of London.

> *income! . . . 'tis most certayne they must needs both live well and dye well, since most commonly they live in Clearkenwell and dye in Bridewell . . .'*

Some continental brothels of the better sort had the pleasant conceit of hanging out a laurel wreath over the front door to announce the arrival of a virgin, although this term was a little elastic and could mean perhaps that she had not been in use for (say) four days or perhaps a week. By ancient custom, she was kept available for the wealthiest or the most important patron. Although some degree of luxury is evidenced from some English brothels, there is no record of the fantastic extravagances and elegance of the Italian houses of the same period. In Rome it was stated that Pietro Riario used to put gilded chamber pots under the bed of each of his favourite whores.

Another delightful whore's eye view comes in Robert Greene's *Theeves Fallinge Out*. Greene himself was one of the most debauched and bitter of all the contemporary dramatists and this vignette obviously is a first hand account of a dialogue between a women named Kate and her Thief Friend as to the respective merits of whoredom as opposed to thieving. Kate proves that it is more profitable and less dangerous to be a prostitute:

> '. . . *When a Farmer Gentleman or Citizen comes to the Tearme (finally makes up his mind) . . . perhaps he is wary of his Purse, and watch him never so warily yet hee will never bee broghte to the blow .is it not possible for us to pinch him ere hee passe? Hee that is most chary of his crownes abroad and will cry "Ware the Coney-catchers (Confidence tricksters)" will not bee afraid to drinke a pint of wine with a pretty Wench and perhaps go to a trugging house (brothel of the lower class) to ferry one for his purpose; then with what cunning wee can feede the simple Fopp, with what faire words, sweet kisses, fained sighs, as if at that instant wee fell in love with him that wee never saw before. If wee meet him in the Evening in the Streete . . . we straighte insinuate into his company and claim acquaintance of*

him by some meanes or other, and if his mind be set to lust . . : then let him look to his Purse, for if hee doe but kisse me in the Streete Ile have his Purse for a farewell although hee never commit any other act at all . . . But if he come into a house, then let our trade alone to verso upon him, for first wee faine ourselves hungry for the benefit of the house although our bellies were never so full, and no doubt the Pander or Bawde shee comes forth like a sober Matron and sets store of Eates on the Table and then I fall a boord on them and though I can eate little yet I make havock of all and let him bee sure every dish is well sauced, for hee shall pay for a Pippen pie that cost in the Market foure pence, at one of the Trugging houses eightpence. Tush! what is dainty if it bee not deare bought? . . . and ere we part the world goes hard if I foyst him not of all that hee hath . . .'

Elsewhere she makes the valid point '. . . fair Wenches cannot want of favours while the world is full of amorous fooles . . .'.

Kate says that if the Fop does not pay up he is then threatened by one of the house bullies with physical harm, by which time he is stripped of his money and even his underwear and turned out into the street, a sadder poorer and perhaps wiser man. The Trugging house was another name for a clip joint of the lower sort, the word 'trug' being a corruption of the German-Flemish 'troll', short for 'trollop' which was another form of 'strumpet'. 'Foysting' meant thieving or stealthy chicanery, and derived from the word 'fart', particularly a silent fart, which a synonym for silent trickery in those coarse times.

Kate herself remarks elsewhere that she had contempt for men '. . . as base knaves tearme us Strumpets . . . but we are more than cunningest Foyst or Nip (a 'nip' being a sneak thief who stole in the markets) . . . he that pickes the pocket is called a foist . . .', thus keeping the meaning of stealthy silent thieving.

Kate also lets on to another trick. There was a class of thief-cum-whore called a Bawdy Basket, being:

'. . . women thatte walke with baskets or Cap-cases on

theire armes, wherein they have laces pinnes needles white silke girdles and suchlike. These will buy Cony Skins (rabbit skins) and in the meane time steale Linnen or pewter. They are faire spoken and will seldome sweare whilst they are selling their wares, but lye with any man that hath a mind to their commodity . . .'

Kate clinches her argument with a telling phrase that explained very clearly why, despite prohibitions and maledictions, prostitution could never be stopped, by telling her Thieving friends:

'. . . and (in whoring) there is no danger therein but a little punishment, at the mooste the Pillorie and that is saved with a little "unguentum Auream" . . .'

to the constable or warden; although she looked back on her experiences in Bridewell with unfeigned horror, as well she might from many contemporary accounts of this hell-hole.

At this time, too, we have more information about the other areas of prostitution all over London through a Roxburghe Ballad, already quoted, which goes on:

'Now Farewell to St. Giles
that standeth in the Fields
and Farewel to Turnbal strete
for that no comfort yeeldes.
In Whitecross strete and Golden Lane
do strappinge lasses dwell
and so there do in every strete
twixt that and Clerkenwell.
At Cowcross and at Smithfield
I have much pleasure found
where wenches like to fayres (fairies)
did often trace the ground.'

The Clerkenwell area was just outside the boundaries of the City of London and was known from time immemorial for its roughness and lewdness. Turnbull Street was known in the time of Henry IV in the early 14th century as Trymil strete, which infers there were three mills at or before that time. As a resort of loose women, it was also known to

Shakespeare. In *Henry IV* Part I, Falstaff makes reference to Turnbull Street. Another Roxburghe Ballad mentions the 'Fleur de Lis' in Turnbaull street as a house where a whore makes an assignation with a client. (It is now known as Turnmill street, of impeccable ordinariness!)

In 1595 Nash, in his *Pierce Penniless His Supplicacion to the Deuil*, remarks ' . . . I commend oure uncleane sisters in Shoreditch and the Spittle (Spitalfields) Southewarke and Westminster . . . to the Deuil . . . ' thus introducing three more areas where his 'unclean sisters' operated.

Nothing can better give an indication of the down-to-earth speech of the Tudor period than the following excerpt from an English-Latin crib which was used in the schools about 1550. These are generally known as *Vulgaria*, in the sense they were translating from the Latin into the vulgar or vernacular tongue. The *Vulgaria Stanbrigiana* thus teaches 10 to 16-year olds to translate into Latin such wholesome and doubtlessly useful and certainly commonly accepted phrases as, page 17, line 14: I am almost beshitten; page 17, line 15: Thou Stynkest; page 23, line 17: He lay with a harlot at nyght.

In the period between 1650 and 1750 there is frequent use of phrases like Coney-catchers, Coney-hunters, Coney-hanters, generally thought to refer to tricksters catching innocent 'rabbits' or 'conies', but in fact the word derives from Cunny, a euphemism for the much older standard word 'cunt' which, however, owing to its strong sexual connotations and great popularity amongst soldiers (and similar rough people) became softened down. These watered-down phrases stand in fact for men who had successfully accosted a woman for sexual intercourse, or one who was seeking it, or those who haunted places and houses where sexual intercourse could be secured. A Cunny House or Cunny Warren was a well known pseudonym for a brothel, particularly in the middle of the 18th century.

Mediaeval people and the Elizabethans were not shy in expressing bodily and other functions. When Shakespeare writes of whores like Doll Tearsheet, Mistress Quickly and Mrs. Overdone, he is describing women he actually knew and probably slept with and thus pithily describes their individual quirks. The poet Herrick, better known for his delicate poetry about love and lovely girls and beautiful chaste heroines, just as easily writes about a couple of well-known whores whom he knew, informing us *inter alia* that many fresh young whores looked so wholesome and clean that people mistook them for respectable girls:

'. . .*Jone (Joane) is a wench that's painted*
Jone is a girle that's tainted:
yet Jone shee goes
like one of those
whom Purity has Sainted.

Jane is a girl that's prittie
Jane is a wench that's wittie
yet who'd thinke
her breath do stink:
and so it doth! that's pittie . . .'

But to revert to Kate and her praise of the benefits of her profession: there is another side to the story and not all houses were as pleasant as she made out. For instance Henrie Chettle in *Kind Harte's Dreame* 1592, writes:

'. . . *Landlords turn dye houses into tenements . . . and do a large stroke of business in this way. A little room with a smoky chimney lets for 40 shillings yearly . . .*'

and expresses his sympathy for the wretched women in the following passage:

'. . . *for in euerie house where the venereal virgins are resident, hospitalitie is quite exiled: suche fynes, suche taxes suche tribute suche customes as (poore soules) after seuen yeres service in that vnhallowed order they are fayne to leaue their sutes for the old Lenos*[7] *that are shrine keepers, and themselves . . . seeke harboure in an Hospitall . . .*'

Amongst the fines and tributes and customs duties

[7] A *leno* was a Bawd or Procuress. The word is Latin and it was in use without interruption for centuries. It appears in an Anglo-Saxon Glossary ca. 1300, as 'Lena/Leno' A Bawd.

mentioned above were the taxes extorted by the delinquent Constables and Watchmen, who are the subject of many references in contemporary plays; amongst the perks of their jobs was the offer of a fine fresh young wench when demanded. This was in addition to blackmail of the clients and protection money from the Madams. Shakespeare in *King Lear* Act.IV.Sc.vi describes these despicable practices:

> '. . . *thou rascal Beadle, hold thy bloody hand.*
> *Why doest thou lash that Whore?* . . .
> *Thou hotly lusts to use her* . . .
> *for which thou whip'st her* . . . '

Of course there were different grades of whorehouses, and Thomas Middleton in his *Black Book* written about 1595 describes a better-class brothel; albeit in irony it shows the immunity of such Houses. An Army Officer is surprised in a raid and at once reprimands the constables for interfering with his honest pleasure:

> '. . . *come you to search an honest bawdy house this seven and twenty years in fame and shame? Dare you balk us in our owne mansion?* . . . *our castle of come-down and lie-down* . . . ?'

From this we can now see that our perennial traveller in search of sin now had alternatives: 'prithee! Pard, which way to the Estuwes?' since, if he entered from the south he would be directed to Bankside and if he entered at Aldgate or Moorgate he would be directed to Cripplegate or Cock's Lane.

Chapter Fourteen

The Playhouse is Their Place of Traffic

When the Privy Council decreed in 1571 that all strolling players '. . . who were not the servauntes of noblemen . . .' should be dealt with as vagabonds it was because insofar as their artistry was devoted to the amusement of the lower classes, their lives and morals accorded with the type of company they performed to. The Lord Mayor of London had much earlier written to the Lord Chancellor that:

> '. . . *the players of plays used at the theatre and other such places and tumblers and suchlike are a very superfluous sort of men* . . .'

and he was referring to the clowns and 'jigs' or drolls singing and dancing as well as the lewd jokes. The entertainment included also feats of arms and sword-play and other diversions. These performances were usually in inn-yards or taverns: riotous places for riotous people. The nobility and gentry participated because it was a less expensive form of escapism for them, instead of maintaining their own hired companies. The plays were lewd when they were not actually obscene. Even as early as December 1559 the young Queen Elizabeth's stomach was turned, to quote Machyn's *Diary* (page 221):

> '. . . *the same day (December 29th) at nyght at the quen court ther was a play a-fore her grace the whyche the plaers plad schuche matter that they wher commondyd to leyff off* . . .'

and these were a troupe of Court Players. Forty years later they were not any better as witness the *cri de coeur* of a churchman in 1597:

'. . . will not a filthy play with a blast of the Trumpett call a thusand, than an hour's tolling of bells brings to the sermon an hundred . . . '

In the same year Nashe and Ben Jonson's play *Isle of Dogs* was so obscene that even the unsqueamish Privy Council sentenced Jonson (who was acting in it) to prison, and ordered the Swan Theatre to be closed down, thus causing great financial embarrassment to the unsavoury character, Francis Langley, who owned it.

Of course the quality of the plays was in accord with the quality of the audiences and from that time until this day, plays with bawdy or salacious content were the most popular, and hence the greatest money-spinners. This allowed the 'impresarios' to chance their arms and their money later on the drama which developed from this mumming.

The first actor/manager, James Burbage, and his troupe were originally on the payroll of the Queen's favourite, Sir Robert Dudley, but the Lord Mayor intervened because of the disturbances at their performances as well as the dissoluteness of the company and its hangers-on. When Burbage then asked the Earl of Leicester in May 1574 to obtain a Royal Patent, the mumming vagabonds became officially, 'Players'. Nevertheless, the Lord Mayor and Corporation would not heed the royal patent. They would grant permission to perform only with their own licence which carried a stipulation that half the profits must go to the poor. In the next year they banned players altogether from the taverns and inn-yards or open spaces within the City's Liberties.

The tavern owners naturally also had used their monopoly of venues to squeeze the players by increasing rentals.

Burbage circumvented both the City's prohibition and the rapacity of the tavern-owners by building his 'Theatre' in the Liberty of Holywell just outside the City's jurisdiction.

When, nevertheless, the City forced The Theatre and its neighbour, the Curtain, to move, The Theatre was moved lock stock and barrel to Southwark in 1598-99, gravitating naturally to the bankside area, which was the Soho of its day, subsequently becoming known as The Globe. On the

Bankside it competed successfully with all the existing amusements for the masses, incidentally helping to further the interests of the stews and the independent prostitutes who found, as their Roman forbears had found long before, that the theatre was a good place for picking up more business.

With the removal to Bankside the number of theatres also increased, some, like The Swan, The Rose and The Hope, being especially constructed for the purpose and '. . . chiefly employed in an inferior species of amusement . . . the bankside being frequented by libertines of the lowest sort . . .'[1].

They were open every day in the week including Sundays, until the puritans of Cromwell's Commonwealth decided otherwise.

The credit for the birth of the theatre is often given to the nobility for their help in circumventing the various prohibitions and taboos by forming their own companies of players, but their purpose was less noble than expedient, since they wanted crude amusement and diversion and there was no other way to get it. The glories of the drama came much later. Although the entertainment was suitable for the lower sort of man, the nobility frequented such places. 'Lord Strang's men, Lord Pembroke's men and the men of my Lord Admiral . . .' were to be found playing at The Rose theatre in 1593 to 1598.

At the back of The Rose theatre lay Rose Alley and Gilde Alley, both brothel streets. Rose Alley is yet another relic of the older tradition when a Rose was a euphemism for a harlot and to 'pluck a Rose' was to go a-whoring. Many a Rosengarten and Rosenstrasse remain in Continental cities, to remind the present of the past, and not a few Rose alleys and lanes in England have nothing to do with the flower. In fact, the association of the rose with illicit love goes back to remotest times, for it was the symbol of silence consecrated by Cupid to the god Harpocrates to conceal the lewd pranks of his mother, Venus, whose behaviour even for a goddess was to say the least extremely unconventional. Warburton quotes:

[1] Concanen and Morgan. *History and Antiquities of Southwark*, p. 194. London 1795.

'... *huic Harpocrato Cupido Veneris filius parentis suae rosam dedit in munus, ut scilicet, si quid licentius dictum vel actum sit in convivia* ... '[2]

Elizabeth I's favourite, Lord Hunsdon, sold Paris Garden to Francis Langley in 1589. In the very same year '... householders were ordered not to take lodgers into their houses without the permission of the Constable; and simultaneously Langley (who was the landlord of the messuages) was instructed to mend the Cage, the Cucking Stool, the Pound and the Stocks ...'. These instruments of punishment were still standing and in use in 1629 and shown in an old map of that year,[3] .

Langley built The Swan playhouse in 1594 and it quickly gained a very bawdy reputation. Francis Langley sold the property in 1601 to Hugh Browker. The Swan, however, carried on with ever-declining fortunes till it eventually closed down. The last mention of the theatre is in an anonymous tract entitled *Hollands Leaguer* dated 1632[4] when it was described as '... a famous foundation now fallen to decay and like a dyinge Swanne hanging down her heade and seemed to singe her ownne dierge ...'.

Many famous playwrights began to emerge. Shakespeare, of course, is the most famous and he lived in a house near the 'White Bear' and frequented the Bankside and its whorehouses using, indeed, in his dramas many phrases and situations arising from his experiences. Robert Greene, Thomas Middleton, Shakerley Marmion, Christopher Marlowe, Ben Jonson, the Burbages, all played their parts in the development of the theatre.

The writings of Dekker, Middleton and Greene clearly show they frequented the stews, and posterity owes them a great debt for these descriptions. The Bankside brothels gave them constant sources of inspiration.

The social and economic changes stemming from the confrontation with Spain, as well as the results of Henry VIII's tremendous overset of the church lands and

[2] Bishop William Warburton (1698-1779).
[3] L.C.C. SP/38-15. P.R.O.
[4] *An Historical Discourse.*

consequent financial troubles, had led to a trend for economy in certain noble quarters. A footnote to Thos. Dekker's tract *The Belman of London* mentions that in the period ca. 1580:

> '. . . *Great men had the fashion of keeping no house and reducing their households, especially in the country, which led to a decay in hospitality and was a common subject to complaint amongst the workers because of the unemployment* . . . '

The nobility took chambers in London and kept a servant or two, instead of large households. Because men now looked outside for their entertainment, the theatres and other Bankside amusements flourished and more girls and women began to seek a living by prostitution or as serving wenches in such houses and taverns. The Elizabethan brothels were also gambling joints where fortunes could be won and lost. The streets were the haunts of every kind of swindler and confidence trickster, of every kind of skullduggery and theft, of beatings, mayhem and murders.

Contemporary literature stresses again and again the close relationship between the theatre, the malefactors and the whorehouses. Plays especially give us a wealth of detail of the manners and language of players, thieves, confidence-men and courtesans.

Two men, later closely related to each other and both destined to become renowned in different spheres, now emerge. Edward Alleyn, son of a Grays Inn Road innkeeper, later actor, musician, usurer, property speculator, whore-master and later still the founder of Dulwich College: and his father-in-law, Philip Henslowe, property speculator, usurer and whoremaster, and famous for his theatrical activities.

Henslowe started life as a joiner '. . . having no education nor vocation . . . ' but he secured employment with a Mr. Woodward, and on his death married his widow, Agnes, who brought him a fortune which he began to expand rapidly by speculating and money-lending. He also bought up many of the Bankside brothels on the unfailing pragmatic principle that '. . . when playhouses were closed the stewes flourished . . . '. In his heyday he was undoubtedly the Grand Potentate of the Bankside: 'freeholder, leaseholder, Dyer, Maltster, Pawnbroker, Stew-holder, Banker, Playhouse owner and Bear Gardener . . . '.[5]

Lending money to actors often gave him a lien on them when eventually he managed (in partnership with Edward Alleyn) The Rose theatre, the site of which he had bought some years before.

The history of this site goes back probably to Edward II's messuage 'la Roserie' built in 1324,[6] sold in 1361 to John Trig, Cittizen and Fysshemongere, when it was described as ' . . . a Garden and Pond at the Stewes . . . '. Twenty years later the property turns up as the stews belonging to William Walworth, Mayor and Fysshemongere, which Wat Tyler destroyed. In 1474 in the reign of Edward IV it is described as ' . . . the Roose with the Bole . . . (and is) left by Robert Colyns, Cofferer of London to his wife . . . for Almesse dedes . . . '. The tenement called the 'Roose' is also mentioned in Edward VI's conveyance to William Baseley in 1550.

The Rose was ready at Michaelmas 1587, having cost £103 2s.7d.[7] and carried on as a theatre until 1603 when it was turned over to other *divertissements.* Alleyn was still paying tithes on the theatre in 1622.

Edward Alleyn was an actor and a musician and an astute business man, who by dint of property speculation and some judicious usury became very rich. He was early a partner with Henslowe in running a Bear Garden in Bankside, which Alleyn was still running in King James I's time. In 1592 Alleyn married Joan Woodward, Henslowe's stepdaughter, who was an actress. Shortly after the marriage Alleyn's connection with the stews came to light when Joan and some of her companions were 'carted' in her husband's absence during a squabble in the stews on Bankside. (In fairness to Joan Woodward, her 'carting' may have been due to a more technical matter in failing to carry out a Government order to close the brothels during a sudden eruption of the Plague.) At that time her stepfather owned

[5] W. Rendle and P. Norman. *Inns of Old Southwark*, London 1888.
[6] H.M. Colvin. *The King's Works*, Vol.I, footnote to p. 508.
[7] W. Taylor. *Annals of St. Mary Overie*, p. 142.

Elizabethan Ice Fair with Bankside stews overlooking. Amongst them are The Barge, The Bell, The Cock, The Rose and The Unicorn.

much brothel property on and near Bankside and she may have been just minding the shop in a perfectly innocent (sic) capacity since she was his heiress as well as Alleyn's wife. However, taking into consideration the loose morals of the time, it is more than likely that she was acting as a Madam and, perhaps, as an occasional whore. Alleyn would not have been the first husband to prostitute his wife or use her as a Bawd – it would not have occasioned much comment at that time or in that stage of his career. Alleyn's letters to her do not show anger nor shock at the carting, rather a mild surprise that it should have happened.[8] The founding fathers of the English theatre were nearly all men of loose morals, rough and ready and not too scrupulous in their business activities.

Alleyn's brothels were seemingly of a superior type, as evidenced by the many pictures and other *objets d'art* which were catalogued when being sent to embellish his new home in Dulwich.

Alleyn was already planning to become 'respectable' by taking the first steps to carry out the wise injunction of the anonymous author of *Ratseye's Ghost*:

> '... *when Thou feelest Thy Purse well lined, buy thee some Place or Lordship in the Countrey* ... '

Thus in 1603 he acquired the ancient Manor of Dulwich (first assigned by Henry I in 1127 to the Abbot of Bermondsey), from Sir Francis Calston whose family had received it from Henry VIII on the dissolution of the monasteries. Alleyn secured it in default of a debt of £5000 due to him by Sir Francis, thus becoming at one stroke not only a Gentleman of Property but also a Lord of the Manor, although not without some bitter expostulation from Sir Francis who stressed he had been gypped. The resultant lawsuit went on for years.

Alleyn's purchase of the Bear Gardens merits more study. In 1540 the Bishop of Winchester leased to William Payn the

[8] George Warner. *Catalogue of MSS & Muniments at Dulwich College*, 1891; p. 6. Alleyn's letter to his wife, 2 May of, 1593, mentions he was sorry '... that she had been by my lord maiors officer mad to rid in a cart ... ' with all her fellows.

tenements standing on this land, called 'The Barge', 'The Bell' and 'The Cock' ' . . . alle stewe houses on the Bankside . . . '. In 1532 King Henry VIII leased to Henry Polsted ' . . . the tenements known as 'The Unicorn' and 'The Rose', which before 1537 had belonged to the Priory and Nuns of Stratford-atte-Boghe, the deed of 1537 saying:

> *' . . . alle that hys tenement sometimes called the Rose set upon the Stewes Bancke . . . (as far south as) . . . unto Mayden Lane . . . '*

All this property fell to Alleyn on Joan's death in 1623 after many years of a very happy marriage. Alleyn's ultimate bid for respectability paid off when he married as his second wife Constance, daughter of that eminent poet and divine, John Donne, Dean of St. Paul's Cathedral.

This did not preclude the final irony that the three stews, The Bell, the Barge and The Cock, went into the marriage settlement of this doubtless virtuous and respectable Christian lady, who saw no reason to reject such a tainted source of income. It is only fair to state that on her death the revenues from the properties went to charities.

Before he died, Alleyn had become a Churchwarden of St. Saviour's in Southwark in 1610. The 'Bawds' rents were paid to Churchwardens to distribute, and some quite well-to-do persons were noted as recipients of 'Bawds of the Banke' monies.

In his will in 1626, Alleyn had bequeathed vacancies in Dulwich College for six men and six women who were to receive 6d. per week stipend and a new gown every two years. A sad footnote fifty years later says that: ' . . . these monies were not paid because there were not sufficient funds . . . '. Dulwich College stands as his monument and its dubious beginnings are rightly forgotten. His will also includes the brothel called 'The Unicorn', in addition to the above.

Eventually the theatres resembled convenient brothels, to which the play became incidental. Dryden's Prologue to Thomas Southern's *The Disappointment* sums it up succintly:

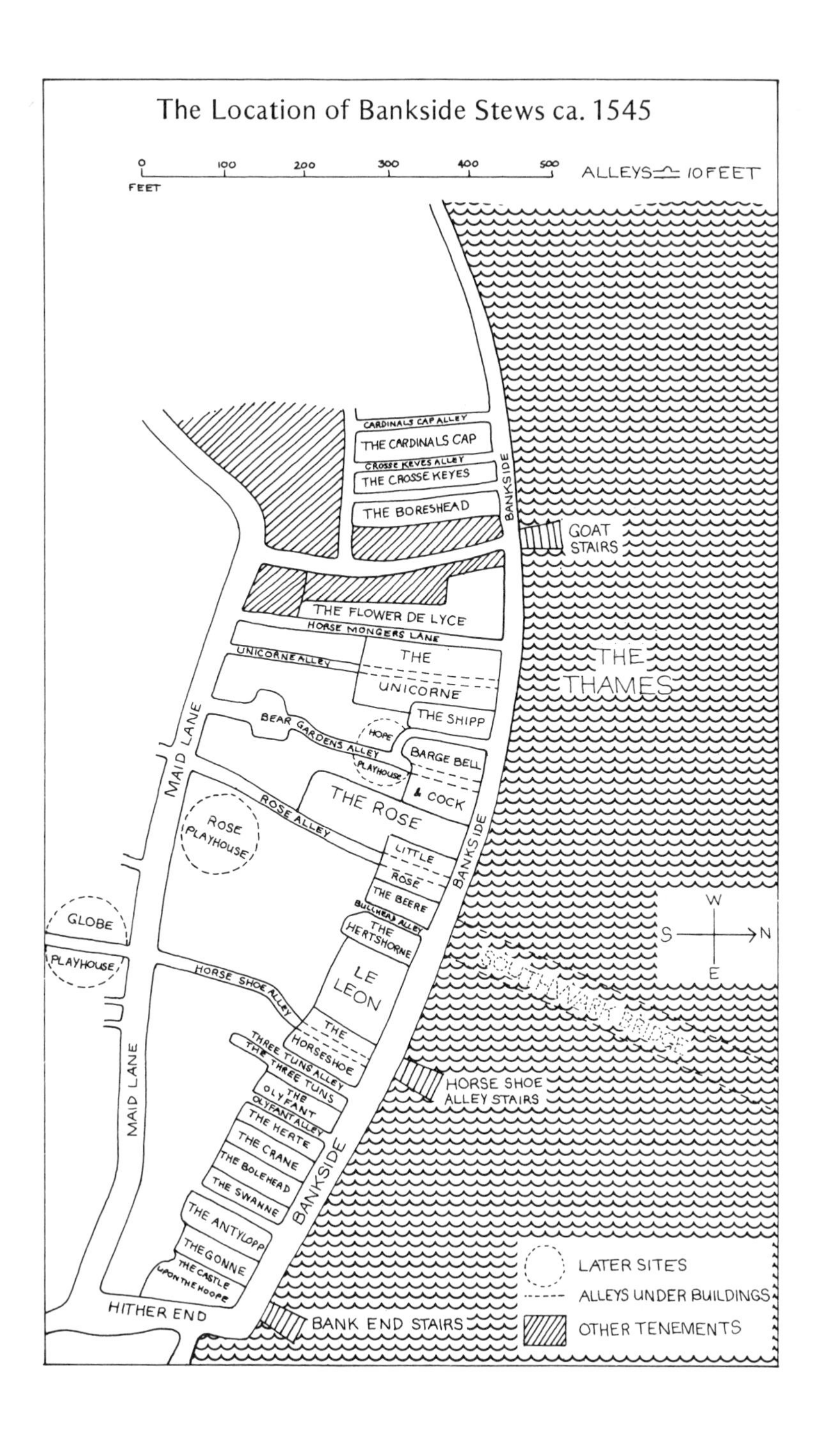
The Location of Bankside Stews ca. 1545
0
100
200
300
400
500
FEET
ALLEYS = 10 FEET
CARDINALS CAP ALLEY
THE CARDINALS CAP
CROSSE KEYES ALLEY
THE CROSSE KEYES
THE BORESHEAD
BANKSIDE
GOAT STAIRS
THE FLOWER DE LYCE
HORSE MONGERS LANE
UNICORNE ALLEY
THE UNICORNE
THE THAMES
THE SHIPP
BEAR GARDENS ALLEY
HOPE PLAYHOUSE
BARGE BELL
& COCK
MAID LANE
THE ROSE
ROSE PLAYHOUSE
ROSE ALLEY
LITTLE ROSE
BANKSIDE
THE BEERE
BULLHEAD ALLEY
THE HERTSHORNE
GLOBE PLAYHOUSE
W
S
N
E
SOUTHWARK BRIDGE
HORSE SHOE ALLEY
LE LEON
THE HORSESHOE
THREE TUNS ALLEY
THE THREE TUNS
HORSE SHOE ALLEY STAIRS
THE OLYFANT
OLYFANT ALLEY
MAID LANE
THE HERTE
THE CRANE
THE BOLEHEAD
BANKSIDE
THE SWANNE
THE ANTYLOPP
THE GONNE
THE CASTLE UPON THE HOOPE
LATER SITES
ALLEYS UNDER BUILDINGS
OTHER TENEMENTS
HITHER END
BANK END STAIRS

> *'The Playhouse is their place of Traffic, where*
> *nightly they sit to sell their rotten Ware.*
> *Tho' done in silence and Withoute a Cryer*
> *yet hee that bids the most is still the Buyer:*
> *for while he nibbles at her am'rous Trap*
> *she gets the Mony: he gets the Clap . . .'*

Elsewhere he calls the 'commoditie' the 'tawdry Cracke' – the *trousse puteyne* of old, put into English!

Chapter Fifteen

'Eschewe Vile Venus' Toys...'

By the end of Elizabeth's reign, the political and economic changes in England had been profound. Its mariners, privateers and merchantmen sailed all over the world, bringing back rich loot and fantastic stories to fire the imagination. The country began to be outward looking. London had grown enormously in size as the result of the population explosion generally, and now had more than 100,000 inhabitants. Its boundaries had spread westward and northwestwards and northwards. In the Borough the spread was south-eastwards and attracted principally the working and artisan classes. It now also included thousands of Dutch and European Protestant refugees who had settled with their crafts and skills, and they brought with them a stern and fervent puritanism, thrift and order, and a desperate attachment to the ideals of religious freedom and freedom of speech.

Although they doubtless brought with them other Flemish elements of a less sterling character, nonetheless despite the generally dissolute character of Southwark a much stronger body of decent citizens was growing and making its weight felt.

Although the poor were still very poor a noticeable rise in living standards had been reached by quite a number. In the home, bolsters had replaced straw pallets, pillows had replaced log headrests, pewter had replaced platters and wooden utensils. In 1601 even a rather strange utensil called a fork was coming into fashion in aristocratic circles. Streets had been widened and main roads 'paved' with cobbles. A Dutchman's[1] engines piped water into thousands of the

[1] Pieter Mauritz (Morice) arranged with the City Corporation in 1574 to instal his 'water engines' and by 1580 was piping water into the houses in the upper part of the City: in gratitude they granted him in 1582 a lease for 500 years!

City's households from an arch under Old London Bridge. Coaches were beginning to be known. For some it was a golden era.

Yet by a curious paradox, the position of women at that time was in the main worse than it had been a hundred years earlier despite the glowing accounts of foreigners who exclaimed with wonder on the beauty and lovely dress of English women as well as their engagingly free and easy ways. Izaak Walton found the common people singing 'Come live with me and be my love!'. Travellers enthused over the habit of greeting guests with kisses on all occasions, although this pleasant quirk had already been noted by Erasmus during his stay in England half a century earlier. Others commented on the splendid dress of English women, especially that the unmarried girls wore tightly fitting dresses which hugged their figures with deep cleavages exposing their breasts and even their nipples.

This enticing habit aroused rather different emotions in some English male breasts:

'Youre faces tricked and paynted bee;
Youre breastes al open bare
so far, that a man may almoste see
vntoe youre lady ware . . . '

Harlots had started the style of naked breasts, even 'paynted': and there are references to 'laying oute their naked breastes' and again doing this ' . . . affter a whoorishe manner to be seene and touched . . . ' and such was the obsession that writers alternate with praise and condemnation in phrases such as 'paps embossed layed forth to mens view' and 'nipples lyke yong-blossomed jessamines'. Nipples were often rouged to make them more prominent. And since many a fashion originated in a brothel, it is not surprising to learn that the fulminations extended to the same décolleté in Dames and Damsels, who were warned that walking about with bared breasts 'is daungerous . . . '.

Others appeared to be worried because they could not tell the ladies from the whores. Thus 'Merrie Englande' as seen by wealthy travellers and as enjoyed by the middle-classes, the gentry and the nobility. At the other end of the scale were the working people, the peasants and even a remnant of bondsmen. For them life had effectively changed very little, for their womenfolk mostly for the worse.

The nascent manufacturing industries were still too small to engage even the numbers of men fleeing the land and the smaller centres into the metropolis: there were even fewer jobs for the women. The children of the landless peasants had no economic value to their parents and their females were regarded as inferiors, whereas in the previous centuries they had been welcome and essential helpmeets on the farm or domain.

They were lucky if they found jobs as servants in comfortable households, although they would often be the legitimate prey of the master of the house or his sons. They were natural prey to the nobility and gentry. But even those women who had hitherto practised a profession, such as midwifery, or had been in business with their husbands, were also affected by their men's drift to work or a business outside the home. They began to be housewives and household 'slaves'. Often they looked for other outlets in less reputable fashion.

It is no accident that the main source of supply for the ranks of prostitution, as well as for brothels, were the unmarried children of the peasantry and working classes: the stupid and dull ones being the easiest prey. But most of these maidens were aimless and innocent and certainly not born degenerate. For none of them, however, was sex a mystery. When man, wife and children all share one small room, there is nothing the children do not know by the time they can understand speech. Their 'innocence' is lost long before puberty. So is their sensitivity to coarse words, since they would hear little else. Down-to-earth expressions would be more common than elegant euphemisms. For example they would hear their parents use the common word 'fucking' for what they were doing, and the children would possibly know no other to describe the function. Nevertheless the girls from this background frequently resisted losing their 'virginity' until the pressure of circumstances compelled them to. Their demoralization was a gradual process. Most likely they would begin by giving away that which they would later be instructed to sell.

If a girl became a harlot she had a modicum of choice of partners, but she was a prey to everyone around her – the butcher, the baker, the candlestick maker, for her meat, her bread and the candle to light up the room in which she plied her trade. All would savagely overcharge her, while treating her like dirt for the same services supplied to others with civility. However much a girl earned, she seldom had much left after a lifetime of prostitution, after the ponce and the pimp and the procurer had had their share, not to mention the protection money to be paid to the Beadle or Constable.

There were also excessive fees paid to 'doctors' for treatment of venereal diseases: or even to help girls hide the fact that they had it. In this connection it appears that many of these Quacks were Dutchmen; *vide* a rather sinister reference in 'The Poor Whores' Complaint to the Apprentices of London':

> '*. . . too manie of us scab'd and mangy be;*
> *our Leeches who would us to health advance,*
> *hasten away to France . . . confounded Dutch-men*
> *only you we curse with all our heart . . .*'[2]

and in 'The 'prentices Answer to the Whores' Petition' they too criticize the doctors:

> '*. . . so long as Rogues and Whores are trading,*
> *the Surgeons will have work . . . who . . . gain more*
> *by Venus then they do by Mars . . .* '[3]

The certain harvest of promiscuous relations was venereal disease and in those days the girl who escaped it was very lucky indeed. But it may also be seen that the quacks often took their money and decamped.

The girl in the bordell was not much better off. The greatest advantage was a roof over her head and some guarantee of food and raiment. The work was harder because they were on tap day and night. They had no power to refuse any customer however vile or diseased he might be. They risked being bashed by drunks or sadists. They had to pander

[2] *Bagford Ballads.* Ed. J.W. Ebsworth. London 1876.

[3] *Ibid.* pp. 509.

to the most despicable requirements of the most horrible lechers. They had to cope with the ragingly lustful young gallant, and the desperate impotency of the aged *roués*. They had to be particularly careful not to vex unwittingly these rich aging lechers who could take offence at anything which sounded remotely like disparaging their failing powers. Worst of all, they had to submit to every posture and offer the use of every part and orifice in their bodies to the most exigent and lubricious client.

It must have been appalling for a fresh young country lass to adapt herself to the profession. They had to learn to be hard and to avoid anything more than the strict commercial relationship. There were 'Manuals of Instruction' on every aspect of their new profession. Above all, says one sage Madam ' . . . When Fortune deserts a Man, let the Whore do so too . . . the destruction of credulous whores attests to disregard of this Rule . . . '.

A girl had to learn to be well-mannered, learn how to talk to men of all stations, even to learn a foreign language: to dress tastefully and keep herself ' . . . free from alle vitious diseases . . . and . . . alle ill-smells from breath or under the arms or elsewhere . . . '. Her bed must be clean and so must her 'Hollands Smocke' – her nightgown of fine linen, which seems in those days to have been a *sine qua non*, so much is it stressed.

There were many other tricks of the trade – alas! literally, tricks which they had to use to cozen ever more money into the whoremasters' pockets. For now they were cogs in the big business of pleasure-giving to men.

Of course brothel-keeping is a business like any other enterprise, with the added attraction that except for unforeseen disaster, it is very highly profitable, even after all the legitimate and illegitimate expenses have been met, and the more so if the owners are well-connected or well-protected. The original ordinance must have proved a gold-mine for the 'gret howseholders' on Bankside, as it gave them a monopoly. However monopolies also lead to black-marketing and price-cutting, and so history records faithfully the steady increase in 'illicit' whorehouses decade after decade. This profitability was quite realized by the astute Bishops seeking the best returns of their investments: and by generation after generation of inn-keepers using their premises for the purpose, eventually launching out into property-developing in which brothels, and later theatres, became an integral part of the project. Running a brothel was little more complicated than running an inn.[4] Fresh stock was always and immediately available even though the turnover was great, and it had the supreme merit of being cheap to buy and dear to sell, and in constant unflagging demand. Efficient 'Dutch' Madams could wring the maximum profit for themselves or for the hidden owners. Not for nothing appeared the saying 'In matters of Commerce, the fault of the Dutch, was giving too little and asking too much'. Indeed one could parody this by saying 'In matters of whoring the art of the Flemish, is producing good whores without any blemish . . . '.

Thomas Middleton put his finger on it when he says:

> *'. . . one acre of suche Wenches will bring in more at a yeare's end than an hundred acres of the best harrowed land between Deptford and Dover . . . '*

Originally the bawdy houses did not differ in appearances from ordinary dwellings, but before long they developed into places more suitable for the purpose, and were designed more like inns. An illustration of one of the Tudor brothels shows a gateway leading into a stable yard, in which horses could be stabled, watered and fed. The entrance would be on the ground floor from the yard, and lead into a reception room, attached to which would be a dining room, with the kitchens somewhere at the rear. Other ground-floor rooms would be reserved for gambling or card games or drinking in company with the harlot of their choice. The bedrooms were generally on the first floor, with casements overlooking either the gallery running round the yard or the street outside. Up till Tudor times, most brothels would be standing in their own grounds, like most other houses.

[4] Aaron Holland, builder of the Red Bull theatre was an inn-keeper and the son of an inn-keeper. Edward Alleyn was the son of an inn-keeper. Francis Langley was involved with the Boar's Head inn-cum-theatre in Whitechapel.

Terraced houses came somewhat later. At the back of the yard there was probably an exit because wagons and coaches could not easily turn and had thus to go straight through, and also at the rear would be the privies and a dunghill. The latter would perhaps be cleaned out weekly or less often depending on the arrangements with the gong-farmer. The floors would be covered with rushes which were replaced from time to time, but nevertheless were always full of fleas, lice and other vermin.

In the better class brothels life might be superficially easier in so far that the girl would have a well-furnished room with pictures perhaps of famous harlots on the walls, a bed with a vallance and a quilt (sometimes 'on or off the bed for dayly vaulting for the vse thy trade').[5] On a bedside table 'vialls filled with rare waters to make thee faire' and a cabinet for powders and perfumes, and another with plasters and medicaments to sweeten the breath, and some 'devotional books' as well as 'Amorous pamphlets and merie commedies . . .' to rouse the senses of the jaded client. One essential piece of furniture was 'the groaning chair' (a close stool) and '. . . of chambre pottes, a paire . . .', since it was the custom for the man to piss into one, while the whore held it (a refinement of the very best brothels and doubtless included in the enhanced price) and the other for her use in 'pissing . . . till I made it whurra and roar like the Tyde at London Bridge to the endangering the breaking of my very Twatling – strings with straining backwards for I know no better way or remedy more safe than pissing presently to prevent the French Pox, Gonnorhea, the perilous infirmity of Burning or getting with Childe which is the approved Maxim amongst Venetian Curtizans . . .'.

The over-work, the psychological strain, the need for constant drinking, the irregular hours, the need to be constantly 'obliging', the large numbers of clients, as well as the submission to their beastly vagaries, all too soon ravaged even the youngest and strongest woman. It also coarsened them into vicious, ruthless females to whom trickery and theft were everyday parts of normal life. The *Belman of London* in a chapter entitled *The Sacking Law* says:

[5] *The Wandring Whore*. Anon, p. 13. 1660. Issue No.1.

> '. . . *the Companion of a Theefe is commonly a Whore: it is not amise to pinneon them together for what the theefe gets the Strumpet spends* . . . '

but it was more likely to have been the other way round.

Dekker then goes on to say of the hierarchy in the Brothel:

> '. . . *The Baud, who if she be a woman, is called a Pandarelle:*
> *The Apple Squire who is to fetch in wine.*
> *The Whore, who is called the commoditie.*
> *The Whore House which is called a Trugging Place* . . . '

Amongst the whores themselves, the name for their *vulva* was the Commodity, appositely, because it was this they were selling: on the well-known maxim that '. . . a Man will pay for a Dutchesse . . . yet he embraces in reality a Common Strumpet . . . '.

In the end the girls might leave literally with nothing but their smock, since what the other extortioners did not get, the whoremaster robbed them of their earnings by every possible pretext. Whether it was a base or high class brothel, the only basis was cash, and 'How much?' in every language. No one knows how long these women endured such lives. Many would have married, since immoral relations amongst the working classes were quite usual – all knew the stresses which led to such lives. A few might get wealthy 'protectors' and put something aside for a rainy day. Most would have sunk to menial work when worn out or ravaged with disease, or might become procuresses for younger girls. A very few would live to become old hags scrabbling in the Gropecunt-lanes. Perhaps most would die prematurely, or be murdered, or commit suicide, or be beaten to death in Bridewell.

Nevertheless throughout the ages there was never any lack of Kates thronging up to the metropolis in search of work, or life, love, adventure and romance. And there was never any lack of consumers for the goods they offered. For to the Elizabethan men 'women were more hotte thanne goates . . . '[6] and it was genuinely believed that '. . . wymmen be

[6] L. Wright. *Display of Dutie*, 1616. Carroll Camden. *Elizabethan Women.* Cleaver-Hume, London 1952.

more desirous of carnall luste thanne man . . . '. Charles Bansley in 'Schole-House for Women' 1572 goes even further; he has a doggerel verse reading:

> *' . . . That the woman is far more lecherous (and goes on in Latin) . . . while fifteen hens will satisfy one Cock fifteen men are not enough for one woman . . .'*[7]

In contrast to this is the moan by an English bride:[8]

> *' . . . of alle this nyghte til the cock crew*
> *he would not once turne for me to kisse.*
> *Everie nyghte he risith for to pisse*
> *and when he commeth againe vnwarme*
> *dooth turn his arse vnto my barme . . . (my lap)'*

Nonetheless, says Fynes Morison in his *Itineraries 1617*:

> *'England in generall is said to be the Hell of Horses*
> *the Purgatory of servauntes and the Paradice of Women.*
> *The Londiners pronounce woe to hym that buyes a horse in Smyth-feilde, takes a servaunt in Pauls Churche, that marries a wife out of Westminster . . . '*

the reference being to the crowds of whores who infested Westminster Hall: which Shakespeare also echoes in *Henry IV* when the page tells Falstaff that Bardolph has gone to Smithfield to buy a horse, the old man replies:

> *'I bought him (Bardolph) in St. Pauls and he'll buy me a horse in Smithfield: an I could get me but a wife in the Stewes, I were manned horsed and wived . . . '*

All this makes Old Stow's remark ' . . . that English women disdayned to be baudes: Froes of Flaunders were women for that purpose . . . ' appear to be rank hypocrisy, since as a contemporary he must have been well aware of all the above happenings.

[7] Hazlitt. *English Popular Poetry*, Vol.IV. p. 119. London 1864. *'Gallus gallinis ter quinque sufficit unus sed ter quinque viri non sufficiunt mulieri . . . '*

[8] Charles Bansley. *Scholehouse for Women – English Popular Poetry* Ed. W.C. Hazlitt, London 1864.

Then as now there were also the part-timers such as:

> '. . . *a housewife that, by selling her desires, buys herself bread and clothes . . . as tis the strumpet's plague to beguile many . . .*'

and the extremely revealing incident of the '. . . poore but honest servant . . .' Elizabeth Boteler, who complained bitterly to the Bishop of Durham that she:

> '. . . *had been decoyed by one Thomas Boyd, Inn Holder at the Stewesside . . .*'

who asked her whether she wanted good service when he met her at a friend's house in London, and then took her by wherry to the other side of the river:

> '. . . *then he would have compelled me to do suche service as othere hys servauntes done there, which (the petitioner) fully denyed and yet doth: and would rather die than be of that disposition . . .*'

Boyd had then arraigned her before the Bishop of Winchester's Court in Southwark and secured judgement against her '. . . in soche a sum of mony as Yr.sd.Oratresse shall never be able to content it (never be able to pay it) . . .' and also that 'he kept her in prison for three weeks . . .'. Somehow she had managed to get someone to write an appeal to another Bishop asking him to intervene and issue an order *corpus cum causa*. The outcome is not known.

So much for the 'living furniture' and its means of supply. We have seen too, the primitive ideas about avoidance of disease and contraception. The Elizabethan-Stuart period was to show considerable advances in both spheres of knowledge, if not in actual practical success.

One of the first discoveries was the contraceptive sheath which is attributed to the famous Italian gynaecologist Dr. Gabriel Fallopio (1525-1560) who gave his name to the Fallopian tubes. The first sheath was supposed to have been made of fine linen, although there is no record. Nor is there any report of its success or non-success, although by its interruptive function in copulation it must have been better than nothing at all, albeit it would have been uncomfortable.

for both partners. Whether it was designed as a contraceptive or a prophylactic is also not known.

Contraception is as old as civilization. As early as 1850 B.C. the Egyptian *Papyrus Petri* and 1550 B.C. the *Papyrus Ebers* have recipes for contraception, a mixture of herbs and magic. These may seem laughable or grotesque today, but they were based on the abortive properties of certain plants and must have been effective to a degree. In 1000 B.C. another recipe mentions the vaginal use of honey and crocodile dung. The early Hebrews used moistened sponges inserted into the vagina, the early Greeks used wads of wool soaked in alum.

According to Ovid intercourse *per anum* was resorted to by Roman women to avoid pregnancy. Martial cites Cornelia, mother of the Gracchi, Julia the wife of Pompey, and Portia the wife of Brutus who accepted anal intercourse against this contingency. Timid brides on the bridal night were taught by their mothers to substitute their anus for their vagina as the simplest and safest form of contraception. Whether it was the most pleasurable was another thing, although throughout history women seem to have accepted penetration in either orifice as a matter of course, perhaps as one of their husband's marital rights. Suetonius relates that the Emperor Tiberius kept a picture in his bedroom, showing Atalanta bending to allow penetration *per anum*, and the same theme may be seen often in Etruscan tombs.[9]

The Cundum or Condom, better known in the English-speaking world as a 'french letter' is reputed to have been the brain-child of a military doctor Colonel Conton who invented it in 1665. However there is some vague evidence that in much earlier times sheaths made from animal membranes (such as used for sausages) were tried. Dr. Conton's was probably of thin leather and the sheaths intended rather as a soldier's protection against venereal disease than for contraception. They at once caught on in Court circles and were hailed by the irrepressible Earl of Rochester who published a pamphlet in 1667 entitled *A panegyrick vpon cundum*

[9] Suetonius. *Historie of 12 Caesars – Tiberius Nero*, p. 204. para. 43. Philemon Holland, 1606.

extolling at some length the advantages both as a prophylactic . . .

> '. . . *happy is the man who in his pocket keeps a well-made cundum . . . nor dreads the Ills of Shankers or Cordes or Buboes dire . . .* '[10]

and as a contraceptive '. . . unknown big Belly and the sqawling Brat . . .'. According to this expert lecher the cundum was to rule '. . . not only the chaste Marriage Bed but Filthiest Stewes and Houses of Kept Dames . . .': it was the 'open sesame' to unlimited sexual intercourse. Indeed the poem contains the sad warning of the Young Blood who contemptuously rejected '. . . his old Grannum's advice . . .' – a bit of anachronism surely? – to use one and in consequence caught a dose of the clap.

The 'french letter' therefore appears too late to have been of use in the pre-Elizabethan and Elizabethan bordels and as late as 1668 there is still no mention of it in any of the relevant literature of the day. Apart from Rochester, Boswell is the next biographer to mention it. This experienced but adventurous lecher, who got gonorrhoea at least three times, complained that his sheath '. . . gave him dull satisfaction . . .' and he was writing about 100 years after its invention. Lechers and others had to wait until the 19th century when the discovery of the useful properties of the rubber plant were suitably exploited.

As for the recognition and treatment of venereal disease, not all the doctors were the Dutch quacks, so detested by whores. Despite the avalanche of lewdness spilled out by Elizabethan playwrights, noble lechers, debauchees royal and ignoble, and the like, the Tudor and Stuart periods witnessed the birth of modern science. Despite the constant wars and upsets, there was exchange between English and European savants in every sphere. It is said that in the Elizabethan age, Apothecaries became Doctors and Leeches became Surgeons. Certainly from the time of Henry VIII deeper enquiry was made into the scourge of venereal disease. Indeed, perhaps because such diseases were rife in royal bodies, royalty tended to encourage such research in self-interest.

[10] Poems of the Earl of Rochester. 1667.

The Surgeon Dr. William Becket (1684-1738) published an article in 1717 'On the Antiquity of Venereal Diseases long before the Discovery of the West Indies',[11] and remarked that Henry I's Ordinance of 1161 had referred to the '. . . perilous disease of Brenning . . .'. He had also noted with great perspicuity that the original MS of 1130 of the Bishop of Winchester's regulations, which had Latin Rubrics, contained one which read:

> '. . . *de hiis qui custodiunt Mulieres habentes Nephandam Infirmitatem* . . .'[12]

followed by a paragraph in English:

> '. . . *thatte noo stewholder keep noo woman wythyn his house that hath any Sycknesse of Brennynge but thatt shee be putt out vpon the peyne of makeit a fyne vnto the Lord (of the Manor) of a hundred Shylynges* . . .'

and he had noted too that the preamble referred to the custom of the regulations as '. . . tyme oute of mynde . . .'.

Because the fine was so heavy, it was clear that the disease was known even then to be very dangerous and widespread although its nature and cause was unknown.

Gonorrhoea was known from the time of Galen (about 200 A.D.) who had named it from 'gonos'-seed or semen: and 'rhoia' – a flowing. Venereal disease was known in China more than 5000 years ago, according to modern archaeological research: the ancient Hebrews legislated against it as unclean 'genital discharges' ('zab' for the male: 'zabah' for females) which was 'unclean' when they were thick enough to block the penis. (In their view all semen discharged in intercourse was 'unclean' and both partners had to bathe in running water or a spring thereafter.) Even, very much earlier the Akkadians had a word for an unpleasant female illness 'Shiktu' – something rotten or foul smelling – which may very well have been V.D. None of them however differentiated between the diseases, and all of them came under the general heading of Leprosy, which embraced all sorts of purulent and contagious diseases, giving rise to the earliest

[11] *Journal of the Philosophical Society*, London 1717-18.

[12] 'Of those in charge of women having the filthy disease'.

form of *apartheid* known to mankind.

Both the Bishops and the Royal Ordinances called for weekly examination for the *morbis indecens aie cunnientis.* This Roman description infers that they too had realized that the *vulva* played a part in the transmission of the disease, but were not advanced enough to connect it also with men as disseminators.

In any case, according to male codes from time immemorial, the female was the receptacle for all sorts of 'uncleanness' including menstruation, even though that was recognized as being not a disease.

The English surgeon John Arderne (ca. 1320-1370) physician to both King Richard II and Henry IV had, before he died, defined the disease as '. . . a certayne Heat and Excoriation of the Urethra . . .' which was caused by '. . . the virulency of the matter injected into the urethra from the infected woman, which also attacked other parts of the Urethra . . .'. Arderne indeed invented a palliative labelled *Contra Incendium. Virgae Virilis Interius ex Calore & Excoratione . . .*, to be injected by syringe to relieve the burning sensation and the ulceration of the urethra. For him, the removal of the symptom would be the cure, for the nature of the disease was unknown.

Becket also discovered an ancient MS dated 1390 which was a prescription for *Brennynge of the Pyntyl yat men clepe ye Apegalle* (Burning of the Penis which is called Apegalle.) In Old English a 'galle' was a running sore. The word 'Ape' was short for Apron which had the bawdy meaning of something covering a woman's genitals. Hence Apegalle meant sores received through a lady lifting her apron for sexual intercourse. Later the word 'Apron' became a euphemism for the *vulva* itself, for three hundred years later Lord Rochester refers to the Fleet Street cheap whores:

> '. . . *known by their white aprons, bartering low with Cit(izens) or Lawyer's Clerk, at cheaper rates . . .*'

One of the Bankside brothels was known as 'The Ape and Urinal' perhaps referring to the habit of urinating after fornication there, or perhaps the 'Apes' was a general nickname for the whore. In fact Dr. Becket found yet another MS, this time dated 1430 referring to '. . . the BURNING in that Part (the Apron) by a Woman . . .'.[13]

Syphilis is supposed to have been brought by Columbus' sailors from America in 1493. In March that year Pope Alexander's physician Dr. Pinto had observed the first appearance of the *morbus gallicus* (the French disease) in Rome, alleging that the French Army had brought it into Italy. During the next two years it spread like wildfire in Europe, and when the French army occupied Naples in February 1495 the malady infected many French soldiers, who, naturally, called it *mal de Naples.* In August 1495 the Emperor Maximilian issued an edict calling it *malum francisum*, and when the French returned to France in October 1495 they spread it through France. Voltaire's savage epigram however clarifies the French point of view:

> *'. . . when the French went hotfoot into Italy they easily won Naples, Genoa and the Pox. When they were driven out they lost Genoa and Naples, but they did not lose everything for the Pox stayed with them (. . . car le vérole leur resta!)*

The disease was officially recorded first in Naples in January 1496: eight weeks later Paris promulgated the first measures of public control.

Due to the great promiscuity occasioned by the many military operations in Europe, it spread with malignant rapidity. Caesar Borgia is supposed to have caught it when in France, but Pope Julius II and many Cardinals were also infected. It reached England about 1500; and in 1504 Henry VII ordered the Bankside stews to be closed, and after the medical examinations, only twelve were reopened a few weeks later.

Up to this point the disease was being treated without being named. But in 1521 the Veronese poet Girolamo Fracastoro wrote a 'Georgic' type of poem 'Syphilis or the French Disease' (*Syphilis sive de morbo gallico*) about the suffering of a Greek peasant Syphilus who had angered the

[13] The expression 'tied to her apron strings' certainly meant originally that a man was more tied to what was under the apron and so far too amenable to a woman's demands.

god Apollo, who punished him by infecting him with poisonous vapours in the air and causing horrible ulcers all over the peasant's body, which were later cured by the god Mercury. Fracastoro expressed doubt that it came from America and had observed that '. . . it did not manifest itself and remained latent for a certain time, a month . . . even up to four months . . . before the ulcers appeared . . . to eat away the skin . . . '.

Skin diseases and pustules had long before been treated with mercurial unguents: from 1496 onwards mercury became as popular a cure-all as today's penicillin.

The means of contagion was still unsure, but in 1530 a Protestant Divine Dr. Simon Fish, fulminating to Henry VIII against 'Romish priests' says:

> *'. . . (These who) . . . catch the Pockes of one woman and bear them to an other; that be BURNT with one woman and bare it vnto an other; that catch the Lepry of one woman and bare it to another . . . . '*

thus showing that the connection was now known.

Henry VIII closed the Bankside stews again in 1546 allegedly for the highest moral reasons but undoubtedly the real reason was the continuing spread of syphilis, from which the King himself now suffered and which by then was affecting his brain. The King was unlikely to have been responding to any public pressure because he never paid any attention to the wishes nor welfare of the mass of the people, but he knew of the researches being made and like every other sufferer, wanted a cure.

No one was safe from its ravages. In 1556 Dr. Hugh Weston, Dean of Windsor, was deprived of his office for adultery, and in the MS (found also by Dr. Becket) it was disclosed:

> *'. . . at this day is lecherous Weston, who is more practised in the arch of Brench (breech) Burning than all the Whores of the Stewes . . . had been bitten with a Winchester Goose and was not yet healed thereof . . . '*

This is not quite the first reference to getting infected by a Winchester goose, who would be any whore in the Bishop of

Winchester's stews. In 1553 there is a reference to this Burning concerning Archbishop Stephen Gardiner, pander to Henry VIII, which may have given both those lecherous men reason to think (although by this time Henry was long dead), but both were known to have sampled the wenches of the nearby stews in their time.

In the year that Henry VIII died, Dr. Andrew Boord, Doctor in Physick, published his *Breviary of Health* the 19th chapter of which begins:

> ' . . . . *if a Man be BURNT with an Harlotte and doe meddle with an other Woman within a Day he shal BURN the Woman that he shal meddle withal* . . . '

and he recommended immediate washing of the genitals two or three times a day ' . . . with white wine or ale or else with Sack and Water . . . ' but if the disease had got a hold, he was to go to an ' . . . expert Chirurgeon to helpe . . . '

To make clear his meaning he states in paragraph 34 of his 82nd Chapter that ' . . . burning is . . . by a Woman through carnall Copulation . . . ' and in a later chapter he advises what to do ' . . . iff hee get a Dosser or two . . . ' a dosser being a syphilitic bubo.

Both Dr. Boord and the earlier Dr. Arderne had certainly studied the venereal diseases in the regular inspection of whores in the stews, Dr. Boord probably more intensively than usual because of the raging epidemic. Otherwise such examinations were normally very perfunctory and inexpert. Dr. Boord indeed gave a remedy against 'Erection of the Yerde to synne' which is of classic simplicity:

> *'that is, to leap into a grete vessel of cold water or putte nettles in the Codpeece about the yerde and the stones* . . . '

The last (Elizabethan) word comes from Dr. William Bullein in 1562 who in a 'dialogue' in a book writes: ' . . . rather eschewe the Cause of thys Infyrmitie and filthie Rotten BURNING of Harlottes . . . '. So the women, as usual were saddled with the blame. Prostitutes were undoubtedly the main vehicle in spreading the disease. In the course of business they might copulate with any number of men between ten and thirty in a twenty-four hour stretch – perhaps even more in a low-class brothel. If the disease were a virulent new strain, as is now supposed, and there was no resistance built up, the results could be devastating. Experienced whores could easily hide any manifestations of the disease when examinations were perfunctory and unskilful, even ignorant. Most examinations lasted a couple of minutes. They were carried out with unwashed hands or dirty instruments thus merely passing the disease on from sick to healthy whores. The quacks who clustered round the hopeful whores were hardly likely to be better.

Let us give Dr. Becket another hearing. He had pointed out that in 1130 syphilis would have been common '. . . amongst the lewd women who had a licence for entertaining their paramours . . . ' and that:

> '. . . *Persons myghte be secure from anie Contagious Malady after their Entertainment at these Houses . . . for the same Powers that granted a Liberty to keep open suche lewd houses must find it to their Interest to secure all Persons from receiving Injurie there lest the . . . Misfortunes shoulde deter Others from frequenting them and so the original Design (of grouping the brothels and harlots together to limit the disease) . . . cease from the entire sinking of the Revenue . . .*'

The worthy doctor may have been right about the Church's motives, but although thousands of whores and clients caught both the French Pox and the Great Pox the revenues never decreased. Indeed this history has shown that the brothel business mushroomed over the centuries to reach uncontrollable proportions. Despite the wise words of Mempricious, 'Eschewe Vile Venus' toys She cuts off age . . . by Pox; Death sudden; begging harlots' end . . .', the pitchers will always go to the well even when they know it is polluted and however defiled. Not for nothing did Sir John Harington, almost a hundred years before Dr. Becket, observe:[14]

> '. . . *the cheefeste of alle oure sensual pleasures . . . whiche some calle the sweet synne of letcherie, tho'*

[14] *Metamorphoses of Ajax. Op. cit.*

> *God knowes it hath muche sowre sawce to it . . . for it . . . grieves oure hartes to keepe this Law . . . '*

Pleasure was of the Devil, but the revenues went to extol the Glory of God. In the end penicillin was more effective than prayer or the pillory: streptomycin better than stocks, cortisone better than the cucking-stool, although none of them yet has ended prostitution or indeed venereal disease.

Chapter Sixteen

Hollands Leaguer

Some reference has been made in previous chapters to the Hollands Leaguer as an example of the top quality brothels on the south bank, so it merits a little further explanation.

The gardens in Southwark were quite numerous, and are mentioned in the Domesday Book as 'Widflete', but their first mention as Paris Gardens is from 1380 when the plot of land was held by Robert de Paris in Richard II's time. It was then described as a place into which butchers' offal and entrails were thrown as into a laystall or dunghill, and part of the land was occupied by the kennels for 'the Lorde Mayors' dogges'. That it was still stinking in Mrs. Holland's time is attested by a complaint of a prisoner in the nearby Marshalsea Prison in 1618 '... that the gayle stank more than the Lorde Mayor's Dogge House or Paris Garden in August ...'[1]; although old maps still show it laid out as fair gardens with river water sluicing through many ditches.

In 1542 the King's Bailiff of Southwark, the ubiquitous William Baseley, bought the lease of the Manor House of Paris Gardens and secured a licence from Henry VIII to turn it into a gambling joint '... with cardes and dyze and tabells ...' (although it is recorded that there were 'outside' bowling alleys there as early as 1505 built by William Udall) and various other activities. From this time it acquired its later widespread reputation of ill-fame.

After Edward VI's all-too-short reign, his sister Queen Mary purposed to have brothels generally re-established, one of her supporters preaching that brothels '... were as necessary as the jakes (latrines) in a man's home ...' a curious reflection of the opposing attitudes of Christians

[1] W. Rendle. *Old Southwark and its People*, London 1878.

professing Roman Catholicism with the intolerance displayed by those professing Protestantism.

Good Queen Bess granted the Manor and its lands to her favourite cousin Henry Carey, Lord Hunsdon, who in turn granted licences to stew-holders. Some of these newer brothels in Paris Gardens were from the start of much higher class, catering for the nobility and gentry and the rising upper-middle class, interlarding bawdry with dicing and gambling, wine and refreshments, like the superior type of club they in fact were. About this time, just before 1600, the Manor House was supposed to have been run as a brothel by the legendary Amazon 'Long Megg' of Westminster. But it changed hands several times for the worse until it was acquired in 1603 by the lady known as Donna Britannica Hollandia. The *nom de plume* – or rather *nom de guerre* – was intended to show that she was a Flemish Madam skilled in management and offering efficient whoredom.

She was already a noted procuress, having operated in the 'Italian' quarter near Cripplegate as a whore, then as a Madam in the City Libertie of St. Andrews-by-the-Wardrobe with great success and *réclame*. She was arrested and thrown into Newgate Jail, whence she escaped by a stratagem artfully carried out by friends, undoubtedly because of her connections with the nobility, if not actually the Court.

After squaring the Law, she sought fresh pastures more convenient to continue her profession, free from the City's archaic regulations. She was directed to examine the Paris Gardens Manor House, then untenanted, ruinous and deserted.

The contemporary description is very quaint:

> '. . . *at length shee is informed of a place fit for her purpose beyng wonderous commodiously planted for all accomodations: it was oute of the citee onlye divided by a delicate river. There was many hand-some buildings and many hearty neighbours . . . shee made for that coast, where shee founde abundance of naturall and artificiall entrenchements . . . it itselfe a little citee. Here shee enquires what strong hold or citadell or Mansion house so fortified and envyroned with all maner of*

> *fortifications that ere any foe could approache it hee must march more than a musket shotte on a narrow banke . . . between two dangerous ditches, then enters a port . . . a drawbridge and sundry pallysadoes . . .* '

(The more prosaic later Conveyance of 1660 confirms that it was a 'Mansion House within a mote . . . ' with ' . . . a Gate House, four pastures ditched about . . . '.) A contemporary map shows such a layout and its situation within the area of Paris Gardens, with pleasant walks, trees, shrubberies, and hedges, with a fine view across the river, and guarded by a series of ditches with small bridges over them, the ditches being filled from the river through a sluice gate while the tide ebbed and flowed. Another map shows the little boats moored in the ditches, all round the property like a moat. A quaint contemporary sketch shows the front door being guarded by an Elizabethan pikeman with a musket and steel helmet, with ladies disporting themselves in the garden.

Of course the local Law had to be squared, and Shakerley Marmion in his play *Hollands Leaguer*, some part of the action of which takes place outside the very brothel, dwells on this point. Of particular interest is the entrance of the Constable, come to claim his regular 'douceur':

BAWD:	Who was't?
First Whore:	The Constable.
BAWD:	. . . a pox on him . . . What would he have?
Second Whore:	You know his business.
BAWD:	Pox on the Marshall and his Constable, there cannot be a mystery in this trade but they must peep into it. Merciless varlets that know how many fall by our occupation and yet would have *their* venery for nothing . . .
Constable:	Hast Thou e'er a morsel that is not tainted nor flyblown?
BAWD:	Ay! but I have one I dare commend you for wind and limb.
Constable:	Come! let me have her then.
BAWD:	Please you, walk in, Sir.

Madam Holland took great precautions to ensure selectivity. Her patrons were amongst the highest in the land, including King James I and his favourite George Villiers, Duke of Buckingham, who used to disport themselves at Hollands Leaguer.[2] These precautions led to many playful allusions, such as in the Roxburghe Ballad entitled the *Joviall Broome Man* which also indicates that the charges as well as the ladies were too overwhelming:

> '. . . *At Hollands Leaguer there I fought*
> *but there the service proved too hot.*
> *Then from the Leaguer returned I*
> *naked hungry cold and dry* . . . '

The House must have been very luxuriously fitted out and decorated, for it was still known, fifty years later, as 'the Nobs' Island' amongst the vulgar inhabitants of Southwark. Not only was it expensive but she and her girls were expert in squeezing out the last penny from the clients, although the reports show that the clients got very good value before they left, exhausted in strength and pocket, since the food was excellent and so were the entertainments and amenities. She herself, although a small woman, was reputed still to be a beauty, of strong and imperious character and of extreme efficiency in the running of her House.

Certainly her normal precautions against unwelcome entry were very stringent. Would-be patrons had first to square the 'Cerberus', then the Drawbridge Gate man, after which they could cross the bridge and enter the premises. She greeted each in person, to ascertain their special wishes, but also to size them up as to wealth and spending capacity. She stood no nonsense. She would not allow anyone to shout or ill-treat her girls, nor any rumbustious or unruly activity, on pain of immediate ejectment. Nobody, of whatever social status, was ever admitted again if they had been guilty of any misbehaviour.

Likewise those who had no money were denied admission. Her motto was 'cash with order'; there was no credit, no matter how illustrious the client. In this way, although she offended some, she ensured that only the really rich and exclusive customers were admitted. It also enabled her to fill

[2] Edward Walford. *London, Old and New*. London 1877.

the several chests in her basement with more and more gold.

She had started up with four hand-picked professional whores, each gifted in her own way and much in demand amongst the cognoscenti. As the business expanded she embellished the premises even more luxuriously as well as by the acquisition of more girls. She recruited extra staff, and also a full-time doctor especially to look after the health of the girls, thus assuring the exigent clients that all the goods were fresh and clean. Her kitchen enjoyed a high esteem for the excellence and abundance of the food and drink. Her 'apple Squires' or wine waiters knew their jobs to perfection.

Nevertheless there must have been a canker in this rose garden. The strictness with which she controlled her girls led to very frequent turnover, for the casualty rate was high when perfection was demanded, with consequent dissatisfaction by those rejected or worn-out.

While her brothel certainly benefited by the proximity of the three theatres, The Globe, The Hope and The Swan – the latter was just across the alley and was said '. . . to shake handes with Hollands Leaguer . . . ' – the last two were not places of the highest class: in 1603 The Swan was so far reduced as to run a season for a foreign acrobat under a licence given by James I.

This may have caused the decline of the House and eventually debased its character. Apart from the drinking and carousing and gambling and dancing, the noise and the screaming, as well as occasional indulgence by noble clients in the pastime of 'whore-bashing', the exploits of her girls and the generally riotous behaviour began to attract notice in quarters hitherto acquiescent. These goings-ons aroused the ire of the pamphleteer Daniel Lupton, who about 1630 wrote a broadsheet entitled *London and the Countrey Carbonadoed* with a special paragraph, No.17 entitled 'Paris Gardens' in which he says:

> '. . . *this may better be tearmed a foule Denne than a Faire Garden . . . heeratte foule beasts come to itt and as badde or worse keepe it; they are fitter for a Wildernesse than a Cittee: idle base persons . . . the Swaggering Roarer, the Cunning Cheater, the Rotton*

Bawd, the Swearing Drunkard and the Bloudy Butcher have their Rendezvous here . . . '

While King James was alive she was quite safe. But Charles I's first Parliament instructed the Lord Chief Justice to put down prostitution and bawdy houses – although strangely enough the areas mentioned do not include the Bankside nor Paris Gardens – and this must have had some effect because it encouraged informers and blackmailers, and undoubtedly made the exactions of the local Constables and Bailiffs more onerous. She had other ill-wishers too, quite apart from any jealousy from the competitive brothel barons; the Lord Mayor and Sheriffs were on brothelry's tail and had only been frustrated by her noble and royal protectors. Her luck was running out and eventually some particularly outrageous piece of noise and licentiousness gave the local authorities the opportunity to intervene.

Some time in December 1631 ' . . . a Corporall . . . and a Stoute Bande of Halberdiers and Bil-men . . . ' were sent to arrest her and her girls. Now Dame Britannica Hollandia displayed her martial and courageous spirit, which had been the secret of her success for upwards of thirty years as Whore and Bawd. She showed herself to be a general and strategist of a high order.

She greeted the Law with defiance. She not only denied them entry but by enticing them on to the drawbridge, which was then suddenly dropped downwards (as specially devised) she plunged the unhappy and doubtless unwilling soldiers into the dirty stinking and muddy moat, in which they floundered about, while the girls shouted abuse and scorn at them and pelted them with various missiles including chamberpots complete with contents, to the encouragement and plaudits of the Southwark mob. Although the soldiers reformed several times, all their efforts were in vain and they were several times repulsed. Disheartened and discouraged at being shamed by a pack of whores they retired.

The Law could not allow itself to be flouted in such an outrageous and ignominious manner. A more impressive commando under the leadership of a Provost was despatched, and met the same degree of resistance and non-success. This beleaguering of Mrs Holland's fortress gave her house immortality as 'Holland's Leaguer' by which name it appeared in later conveyances.

The eventual triumph of the Forces of Righteousness must be assumed because in March 1632 an appeal was made to the Privy Council:

> *'Petitioners Hunt and Rogers of late bought the lease of a house . . . wherein Mrs Holland dwelt, who was reputed to keep a house of obscenity . . . albeit (she) went thence six weeks past . . . the said house and twenty others neere . . . shall be pulled down on Tuesday next, for the prevention of whiche yr. petitioners (ask) for a Watch that day in regard to the many thousands of scrolls and papers cast abroad in the City for aggregating the prentices to demolish the said houses . . . ask therefore for the Southwark Trayned Band all that day . . . to suppress such riot and commotion . . . '*[3]

This referred to the coming Shrove Tuesday when the apprentices had threatened to pull down all the twenty-odd brothels. The new landlords were anxious that their properties should not be destroyed.

In March 1617 the Apprentices attacked and wrecked the Playhouse in Drury Lane; and even in 1642 the anonymous *Satyre against Separatists* fulminates against ' . . . th' Prentices . . . for they who if upon Shrove Tuesday or May Day Beat an old Bawd or fight poore Whores . . . think themselves greater than (Jesus) . . . '.

So Felix Hunt and his friends had strong reasons to be afraid. However on this occasion they appear to have got the desired protection and no more is heard of Dame Holland or her girls; but Hollands Leaguer passes into history.[4] It changed owners in 1665 under that name, and when next heard of, the site is a tenterground being used by Widow Blunden. The site is still shown in Rocques map of 1746 in what was then

[3] Cal. State Papers (Dom). 1631-33. p. 221.

[4] The full history of Hollands Leaguer may be read in the author's book *Queen of the Bawds*. Neville Spearman. 1973.

called Holland Leger, and today is called Hopton Street. The Leaguer was still remembered in 1880 when Walford was writing his 'History of Southwark'. An old inhabitant described it to him as an oblong square surrounded by the tide which ebbed and flowed from the sluice-gate about 20 ft. from Cat's Dock Ferry, next to the famous Falcon Tavern frequented by Shakespeare and his boon companions. Old Walford sadly observed that there were still some houses of prostitution there!

Chapter Seventeen

Kings and Commonwealth

The advent of James I the Scotsman, made no sensible difference to the everyday lives of the ordinary people. When he came to the throne in 1603 it was a period of comparative peace and when the religious differences were for a time quiescent: and it is to his credit that he maintained internal peace (except for the troubles in Ireland which we have as a legacy still today) during most of his reign and gave the English people a much-needed breather.

As a Stuart he had the family proclivities for all forms of enjoyment, including gambling and wenching. As a Scotsman (in those days indeed a foreigner) he had to make a few adjustments. In poor Scotland he had been accustomed to little luxury and less servility from his nobles. Controlling a newer, larger and much richer and better organized kingdom was very, very different and he reacted by demanding personal attendance and personal service from the British Lords.

His Court has been described by G. Davies[1] as '... extravagant and disorderly, frivolous and indecorous, with hard drinking common and immorality winked at ...'. His personal habits and the physical state of the court left much to be desired. One incensed English Court Lady complained that she always came back from Court, lousy. James has been charged with homosexuality, in particular with his favourite George Villiers, Duke of Buckingham, but his heterosexual proclivities were also proclaimed in such famous whorehouses as Hollands Leaguer, where he was apparently a frequent visitor. The slander may have arisen from his friendly habit of embracing his favourites in public.

[1] Godfrey Davies. *The Early Stuarts*. Oxford, Clarendon Press. 2nd ed., 1959.

His heavy drinking conditioned much of his behaviour during his reign, apart from his gambling and his 'invention' of modern horse-racing; he was to be seen at the Bankside theatres and the bear-gardens, with George Villiers who was an incompetent administrator but an excellent boon companion. The general morals of the Court and of the wealthier citizens of London City are summed up by Heywood, in *Gynaikeion* written early in James I's reign:

'... *for concubines we need not travel as far as the Turk's Seraglio ... and toe find suche as we call Sweet Hearts, Friends or Good-wenches should we but search ... (any) citizen's garden houses ... (and) ... find plenty sufficient ...*'

On a different level James created some consternation amongst the aristocracy by the sale of peerages for about £10,000 a time, and the creation of knights by wholesale, thus swelling his treasury but debasing the quality of the British nobility to a degree not known since Edward II had demanded that every Citizen of London with an income of more than £40 a year must become a knight.

Under the king's 'enlightened' rule, the growth of whorehouses and whoring was phenomenal, and the case books of the Middlesex Sessions bulge with charges. Some are amusing or instructive enough to mention here. For example in 1608 Emma Robinson '... for thatte she is a notorious Common Queane and sittith vp at the doare till xj or xij a clok in the nyghte to entertaine lewd persons that resort vntoe her ...' and Barbara Jackson was '... whippt at the caretes tayle ...'.

On Shrove Tuesday 1612 there was a riot at the house of the Flemish whore-mistress, Mrs. John Leake in Shoreditch. Many apprentices were arrested and so was Mrs. Leake, and the case went on for months.

Ellen Allen was fined for that she was a bad woman 'and inticed a Dutchman to lewdness and while he was kissing her, her made (maid) stole his dagger ...'. Elizabeth Basse 'keepeth a notorious bawdy house whereby murther was lyke to have ben committed ...'.

In 1613 there are a very large number of cases indeed,

spread all over London and Middlesex, which demonstrate the tremendous increase in prostitution in the Northern and North Western area just outside the City walls, but also as far as Enfield and Barnet and many places in between. It seems to have been a veritable contagion. Even on the 'Saboth daye' people were 'using sinfull lust carnallie . . . '. One Robert Holland of St. Brides parish and a Master Cutler no less, 'had the use of Isabella Sowth's bodie on the Sabbath day . . . '. William Roger and his wife of Holborn were common barrecteurs and disturbers of the peace and kept a common bawdy house . . . his wife was carted in a ' . . . blew mantle lyke a Bawd and set openly in the stocks there to remain in prison until surety founde for her good behaviour . . . '. Thos. Marcroft and his wife 'bring half a dozen whores to bed in their house in Cow Cross at once . . . '. Alban Cooke of Hoxton was indicted for buggery ' . . . with a man under 20 years of age . . . ' while Richard Walker of Castle Baynard ' . . . was taken late in the nyghte abusynge himselfe in an alehowse . . . '.

There were cases of men keeping bawdy houses at which also illegal abortions were done on the whores. There were innumerable cases of soliciting and pimping, until even the tolerant James, in his 20th year, was compelled to issue an ordinance dated 4 December, 1622 . . . *Touching on Disorderly Houses in Saffron Hille . . . :*

> ' . . . *of longe tyme hath bene and is still much pestered with divers immodest lascivious and shamless weomen generally reputed for notorious common whores, Whoe are entertained into divers howses for base and filthy lucre sake akreweing to the private benefett of the Landlords and Tannants of suche houses . . . such women whoe doe usually sitt at the doores . . . doe allure and shamefully call in . . . such as passe bye to the great corruption . . .* '

and there is a special clause 'for the prevention of Connivance . . . ' to try and stop any further covering up by the Beadles and Headboroughs. It made no more difference to the situation than all the ordinances and threats of the previous five hundred years.

Despite frequent mass raids the situation grew even worse,

Cock's Lane.

so that James I was compelled again in the next year to issue another Ordinance (on 13 January, 1624) on the same lines, and the extent of the evil is spelled out in the names of the places raided: Cowcross, Cock's Lane, Smithfield, St. John Street Clerkenwell, Norton Folgate (just outside Bishopsgate), Shoreditch, Wapping, Whitechapel, Petticoat Lane, Charterhouse, Bloomsbury and Ratcliffe. Again the King spells out that henceforth nobody who had been committed 'of Bawdrys and Whordome' shall be released on bail, unless two sureties are found, 'one a subsidie man', and both sureties must be substantial citizens because hitherto many accused had skipped bail, and the sureties had vanished.

It is to be remarked that in neither Ordinance is there a mention of the Bankside stews nor Old Paris Garden: nor is there extant any comparable one for those areas, which may infer that the London citizens preferred now to do their lechery without crossing the water.

King Charles I, a religious man of high moral character, came to the throne in 1625. His reign was to prove a constant struggle with his Parliament and people and eventually the country was plunged into civil war, terminating in his own execution.

To King Charles' credit must be placed the directive of 9 July, 1625 in his 1st Parliament set out in the Journals of the House of Commons for that date:

> 'Mr. Jordan moveth: *"That divers places, viz., Clerckenwell, Pickehatche (in Finsbury) Turnmill Street, Golden Lane, Duke Humphreye's at Black-fryars are places of open bawdry."*
> Resolved: *"To acquaint the Lord Chief Justice with this complaint and to desire him to take some present Order for Reformation of it."* '

Once again, neither Bankside stews nor Old Paris Gardens are mentioned, although whoredom was still very active there. As far as the Bankside stews are concerned, there is the anomaly that Henry VIII's ordinances had been re-confirmed *in toto* by Elizabeth although, as we have seen, the brothels still went on without let and hardly any hindrance; and even now, in Charles I's reign nothing is said about them, while we know they were still flourishing mightily. Nevertheless the Lord Chief's activities did cause some harassment to the stews, as the Middlesex Court registers still attest.

Then in 1630 Charles I, describing his Parliament '. . . as a lot of cats that ever grow cursed with age . . .', dispensed with it for eleven years. These were bad years for the English people, as evidenced by the complaint of the King's own Sheriff of Dorset in July 1635 regarding the relentless collection of the hated Ship Money:

> *'. . . money was paid . . . like drops of blood . . . some sell their only cow which should feed their children. Some come on to the Parish . . .'*

and all this was in a period when there was no war.

When the King reluctantly was compelled to convene the second session of the Long Parliament in 1641 there appeared one Oliver Cromwell, then just over 42 years old, who was to make his mark immediately. In that year Parliament enacted that prostitution was no longer to be considered a crime but only a public nuisance, to be considered as gross indecency if committed in public, and by enforcing Common Law, Parliament abolished a host of mediaeval tortures and punishments and paved the way for fairer treatment of political and other enemies when brought to trial. Nonetheless Parliament also re-enacted the ordinance of 1625, although bull-baiting and bear-baiting were still to flourish almost until the end of the century.

The changing shape of the populations in London and Southwark manifested itself in the commotions of 1642. In August the plebs of London had ousted the Royalists from control. In Southwark the commons were wholeheartedly for Parliament. The relaxed ecclesiastical influence permitted a number of sects to spring up, including the Brownists, who met frequently and clandestinely in the small houses on the Bankside. The great issues of 1642 caused town and country to rush to arms, with the essential difference that it was a war of ideas and each side's supporters were under no compulsion except their own opinions. The bitterness of the division was expressed by Sir John Oglander:

> *'. . . thou would'st think it strange if I should tell thee that there was a time in England when brothers killed brothers, cousins cousins, friends their friends . . . when thou wentest to bed at night thou knewest not whether thou shouldest be murdred before day . . . '*

The embryo socialist policies of reform put forward by Levellers and Diggers fell on fertile ground, especially in the new non-conformist areas in London and Southwark, in the horrible conditions existing among the working people and the poor. Certainly the inhabitants of the brothels were affected, for Cromwell's revolution was both social and economic and at last offered some hope. The yeomen and townsfolk almost everywhere were for Parliament. There had been nothing like it since the days of John Ball and Wat Tyler and Jack-amend-all.

When the Civil War broke out therefore, both London and Southwark supplied thousands of men for the New Model Army, and after the battle of Edgehill when Prince Rupert's Cavaliers overwhelmed the raw Parliamentary levies at Brentford, just outside London, the London and Southwark Train-bands came streaming out all through the night, so that when, next morning the Royalist Commander beheld the grim hosts of Londoners blocking his path, he turned and withdrew to Oxford, never again to approach London.

Another blow against the Southwark Bankside was struck when in 1647 the victorious Parliament sold the stews, still then described as '. . . churche lands . . .' for more than £4,000 including 'all that tenement . . . (known as) . . . the Falcon Inn'. By this time too the surrounding lands and properties were being developed for commerce and industry and several of the ancient whorehouses on Bankside were being turned into warehouses.

In any case the Commonwealth was 'agin sin': Parliament quickly proscribed whoredom and brothels. The Puritan view of these and theatres is nicely summed up by that dour character William Prynne:

> *'. . . it hath evermore been the notorious badge of prostituted strumpets and the lewdest Harlots to ramble abroad to plays and to Playhouses whither . . . only*

branded Whores and infamous adulteresses did usually resort . . . '[2]

It is to be noted that there was no sympathy or understanding of the conditions of the whores nor any attempt to alleviate them by new social devices. Likewise no stricture on the men who frequented and thus maintained the institutions. Steadily going ahead, Cromwell's Parliament closed all theatres and gambling houses, and had actors whipped at the cart tails. There were heavy fines for swearing too. In April 1644 Parliament ordered that all Maypoles should be cut down because they were ' . . . a heathenish vanity . . . '. The Puritan Shrubbe – that hard honest man who had allowed his hand to be cut off rather than retract his stern warning to the old Queen Elizabeth against her marriage – described the 'Maie poole' as a ' . . . stynkynge idoll . . . '. Nude statues had their genitals covered decorously and anything that might profane the Sabbath Day was banned. In 1650 Parliament had even enacted the death penalty for a second offence in adultery, and this savage sentence was actually carried out in three instances, after which even Puritan juries refused to convict and the Act ceased to be invoked.[3] What makes this ordinance the more sickening is that at that time Cromwell himself had a mistress, Bess Dysart.

On the day in 1649 when Charles I was executed, London was free of any disturbance; the shops were all open as usual. In Southwark, the King had few mourners. In April 1651 Cromwell's patience with the treacherous Royalists and their Parliamentary supporters was exhausted. He came to the House, put on his hat, left his seat and walked up and down pointing his finger and blaming individual members for their part in fomenting anarchy. Some he called drunkards, some whoremasters; even his close friend and comrade-in-arms Sir Henry Vane, he dubbed a Juggler (a sinister term of abuse then). This was the occasion for his never-to-be-forgotten remark 'Take away these baubles . . . ', with which words the Long Parliament came to an end and the Commonwealth

[2] *Histrio-Matrix* or *The Players' Scourge*. 1633.
[3] G.M. Trevelyan. *English Social History*, p. 231.

began.[4] Another, and quite different type of Welsh gentleman began to rule the land.

So great was the revulsion against bagnios and stews that when, in the first year of the Commonwealth, the well-known abortionist Dr. Chamberlen petitioned for the opening of bagnios all over the country because they were urgently needed for bathing, washing and sanitary use, he was refused only because of the infamous connotation of the words.[5]

In 1655 it was reported that '. . . seven beares had been shot to death by souldiers next the Hope Theatre . . . ' and in the following year the theatre was pulled down. Nonetheless it seems that Cromwell personally was no killjoy, and he had successfully resisted the ultra-puritan demands from his radical fringe; '. . . the asperities of puritanism tended to disappear at Cromwell's Court . . . at the marriage of his daughter in November 1657 there was musick and frivolity and mixed dancing . . . '[6]

Taverns were flourishing during the Commonwealth period also, rather less flamboyantly than before. In fact they had to meet a dreadful challenge in 1652 when the first Coffee House was opened for '. . . the refreshment, and the purveying of newes . . . '. The establishments spread like wildfire, and before long became places of assignment, although at first it was thought that coffee was a sexual destimulant. Indeed in 1674 there was a Women's Petition to Parliament against Coffee Houses because '. . . they make our men as unfruitful as the desert whence the unhapy berry be brought . . . '. Little did these ladies know the debauchery awaiting coffee-drinkers, when Coffee Houses became the scene of the nasty sport of 'whore-bashing'. All in all, however, Bawds and Bawdy houses are not so much in evidence in Commonwealth days, although there are many Court records of clandestine (and not so clandestine) prostitution and brothels.

The historian Hall, writing in 1656, attests to this in his couplet:

[4] M. Ashley. *Greatness of Oliver Cromwell*. 1957.

[5] L. Wright. *Clean and Decent*.

[6] Godfrey Davies. *The Early Stuarts*, p. 265. Oxford, Clarendon Press. 2nd ed., 1959.

> '. . . *lousy cowls come smoking from the stewes*
> *to raise the lewd rent to their Lord accrues . . .*'

although it may be read just as accurately in two ways; i.e. that priests were furtively visiting the whores' attics so helping them to pay the rents to the Lord of the Manor, or it may refer to the smoking chimney cowls from these dirty attics rack-rented out to poor whores by rapacious speculative landlords like Langley, Henslowe, and Alleyn in the past.

Chapter Eighteen

Leisure for Lords, Hell for Harlots

The Restoration in 1660 was the resultant violent reaction against the excessive Puritanism of the Republic and the anti-clericalism which prevailed, which was so great that it was said that had Cain been alive and come to London, he would have been fêted. It took some exaggerated manifestations, such as the erection of a giant Maypole in London City whose phallic implications were obvious. The harsh laws against fornication, prostitution and brothels were repealed almost immediately.

To understand how the Court of Charles II became in effect one large brothel, it is essential to remember that the King and most of his *entourage* had been brought up in France and had known and participated in French education and frivolous entertainments, as well as debauchery of a high order, as the prerogatives of high birth. The gulf between the French royalty and their commons was unbridgeable. Thus on his return, Charles II encountered that period in English history when it was said, '. . . The Puritans had made men eat religion with their bread until the taste of it had sickened them! . . .'.

The populace had forgotten the benefits which Cromwell's rule had brought to the mass of ordinary people. Only the promise of relief from oppressive dogma was uppermost in the minds of the merchants, the nascent middle classes and the upper classes. The commons had little say in the matter and were still in the main anti-royalist. Still, they were not consulted anyway.

Consequently, all stops were pulled out and there was not any form of sexual lubricity which was not encouraged by a profligate king and a debauched Court. The men who thronged King Charles' Court laughed at virtue as hypocrisy and as they themselves were for sale, believed that every man and woman had their price. Not surprisingly this laxity spread by example to all walks of life. Extreme tolerance begat licence.

But the times also had changed. The English people of Charles' time were not by any means the same as at the beginning of Elizabeth's reign. The rising gentry had made money in her time and the London merchants had turned into immensely rich magnates to whom every government had been forced to turn for money in every crisis.

The re-opened theatres were lavishly decorated and lovely women and nubile girls took the place of boy actors. The emergence of actresses meant that the theatres became akin to brothels; every actress no doubt dreamed then – as now – of securing a rich, young, handsome lover or husband to raise her to affluence, if not to the nobility.

The orange sellers, comely wenches of all sorts, were available as whores also. In the seating the audience were divided by classes and so were the strumpets. The 'pit' was patronized by the fashionable and the aristocrats, who likewise shared the best harlots. The middle gallery was patronized by the merchants and middle class professionals, with suitable grades of strumpets. The upper gallery held *hoi polloi* and, of course, the common whores who were also known as 'punks' and 'trugs' or 'tweaks' and a variety of uncomplimentary and mostly obscene epithets.

Disturbances, fighting, barracking and brawling frequently held up the performances, and the criticism was noisy and uninhibited; this added to the spice of the entertainment and a good time was had by all.

Pepys himself was a modest lecher, contenting himself with maids when the mistresses were not available to him. He was kept abreast about theatrical gossip and scandal by 'Orange Moll', the very efficient organizer of the Orange Girls in Drury Lane Theatre, and an equally efficient Bawd. One of Pepys' mistresses was Knipp, herself a popular whore, and an actress, who on 23 January, 1666, introduced him to 'Nelly, a most pretty Woman . . . '. Pretty and sweet she may have been, but she had been trained as a whore ' . . . in Madam

Ross' brothel . . .' She was to become the archetype of the whore with the heart of gold, but her main allure was that she could entertain the King with a complete disregard to convention, and he could treat her as a strumpet and a pal. Not that Nelly was a favourite at Court, witness the scurrilous and lewd *Panegyrick vpon Nelly* by the egregious Earl of Rochester.

He called her 'Cinder Nell' to equate her with a Cinderella dragged up from beggary:

'. . . *E'en in her native Dirt, her soul was high*
E'en while she cinders rakes
her swelling Breast
with thoughts of Glorious Whoredom
was possessed . . . '

ending the stanza with the lewd *double-entendre:*

'. . . *still did she Dream, nor did her birth withstand*
of dangling Sceptres in her Dirty hand . . . '

Rochester's *Satire Vppon the King* earned him yet another banishment from the Court for it included the lines:

'. . . *witness the Royal Heire sprange from the Belly*
of Thy anoynted Princess, Madam Nelly . . . '
. . . *by Madam Ross exposed to the Town,*
I mean, to those who would give Half-a-Crowne . . . '

with perhaps the most devastating line as payoff:

'. . . *however weak and slender be the String,*
bait it with Cunt and it will hold a King . . . '

He was in fact banished from the Court no less than five times, but the tolerant and debauched King much liked him and his biting wit even though it was so often directed against him.

Nelly of course was popular with the populace from her witticism that she was the 'Protestant whore', and Pepys recounts her altercation with Mrs Becky Marshall, Lord Buckhurst's mistress when she riposted:

'. . . *I was but one man's mistress, though I was brought*

up in a Brothel to fill strong waters to the gentlemen, and you are a mistress to three or four altho' a Presbyterian's praying Daughter!'

Even the name 'Sweet Nell of Old Drury' has a sexual connotation not generally known. Drury may have been the name of the founder of the theatre, but in fact anciently 'druerie' or 'drowerie' meant sexual love, particularly carnal or illicit love. As early as 1225 the 'Ancren Riwle' disparages the carnality of married love in the phrase ' . . . uor (for) the deorie driwerie (dear carnality) he haueth for his deore spuse . . . ', and another religious tract of 1275 castigates ' . . . theos prude leuedies (proud lewdnesses) that drywories & brekyth spusynge (that instil carnal love and wreck marriages) . . . '. Nelly was only carrying on a tradition expressed in 1300 ' . . . a litel lust, a drowri thatte ys bot a duste . . . '.[1]

Significantly, it was the outspoken Earl of Rochester who revived that very old word 'cunt' after some 250 or so years of suppression. It is clear from its context and frequent repetition that the word then became quite common at Court. Its provenance is very ancient, since it was in use in Roman times originally when describing syphilis as '*Morbus indecens aie cunnientis*', derived from '*cunnus*' the genital slit or *vulva*.

In *Satire II* Horace remarks:

'*nolim lauderier, inquit sic me, mirator Cunni Cupiennius albi* . . . ' (I should not wish to be praised for looking at a cunt under a white robe) which is in accord with the line 70 in the same satire:

'*magno prognatum deposco consule Cunnum velatunque stola* . . . '

(a cunt clad in a stola for the great Consul).

The meaning of these two lines is that fornication was being offered by a Matron dressed in a stola; while a Meretrix (whore) was only allowed to dress in a toga at that time.

In his *Satire I* Horace makes a very outspoken remark about Helen of Troy ' . . . ante Helenum cunnus teatorerrima

[1] O.E.D. *Cursor* MS.23786. Edinburgh.

belli causa . . . ' which may be translated either as ' . . . before Helen's cunt caused the war . . . ' or 'before Helen's time, cunt was the vilest cause of war . . . '.

Its use in English has likewise been consistent, and was freely used in mediaeval times. The word stems from 'cunnus' through Old Icelandic 'kunta', later Middle Low German 'kunte' thence into Old English as cunt or cunte, cownte and queynte (where the qu has a 'k' sound). It is obvious that word was in common use long before it was documented in writing as all records prior to 1000 A.D. are rare. The first written record is dated 1325 and is the proverb ' . . . geve thi cunt to cunning and crave affetir wedding' in the sense that if you use your cunt artfully it will lead to a wedding.

In the medical sense the word makes its appearance in Lanfranc's treatise ca. 1400: ' . . . in wymmen the necke of the bladdre is schorte & is maad fast to the cunt . . . ' and in a Glossary dated 1425 'Vulua (*vulva*) – a counte or wombe'.

Chaucer uses it quite colloquially twice in the *Wife of Bath's Tale* when describing her marital adventures:

' . . . what eyleth yow to grucche thus and grone?
Is it for ye wolde haue my queynte allone?' (line 444)

and earlier when she has derided her old previous husband:

' . . . for certayne, old Dotard, by yowr leve
ye shul haue queynt right y-nough at eve . . . ' (line 331)

One very pertinent reference from Chaucer's *Miller's Tale* line 3276:

' . . . and pryvely he caughte hire by the queynte . . .'

which would accurately describe the activities in any Gropecuntelane.

In a religious context at the same time are two epigrams from Layard:

' . . . frerie hase . . . sworne ilkane to others sal never no counte betyne mans bycomen ther brother . . . '

which is to say that the Friars or brethren have sworn to each other that they will never allow a cunt (a woman) to come between them. The second example seems to come from a weary old Don Juan 'bete the cownte with your neffes (fists) when y may doe no more . . . '.

About the same time in the religious poem *Castell of Perseverance* occurs the couplet (page 38, line 1190):

> ' . . . *therefore Mankynd, my leue lemman i' my cunte thou schalt crepe* . . . '

'Mankind, my dear love, into my cunt shalt thou creep,' in the sense that mankind is God's beloved and can seek shelter again as in the womb.

The word 'cunt' is seldom met in written English after about 1400, although the French and Italian words remain commonly current for centuries after that, in their countries.

Thus for centuries it was used in the straightforward objective sense, and only in about 1500 do we find a reference to 'a sluice-cunt' meaning a very large one, with a vulgar or lewd inference. Thereafter it tends to be used in such wise, although at the same time in Wright's *Anglo-Saxon Glossary* appears under *Nominales: 'Hec vulva* – a cunt: *Hic Cunnus, idem est.'*[2]

Writers and playwrights frequently made use of similar sounding words in the 16th century and even Shakespeare was not averse to such salacious punning, as in the following famous scene:

Hamlet: Lady, shall I lie upon thy lap?
Ophelia: No! my lord.
Hamlet: I mean, my head upon your lap.
Ophelia: Ay! my lord.
Hamlet: Do you think I mean country matters?
Ophelia: I think nothing, my lord.
Hamlet: That's a fair thought to lay between a maid's legs! . . . '

thus making sure that nobody would miss the allusion. Shakespeare is one of the sexiest dramatists in the English language and in his plays there is a continuous stream of *double-entendres*, lewd puns and open allusions to sex.

[2] The early examples are from *Middle English Dictionary*. Kurath and Kuhn. University of Michigan, 1961.

Only when John Wilkes M.P. appeared on the scene somewhat later was a courageous attempt made to strip the veil of hypocrisy away and expose all the mouthing about lechery as a sin by pointing out in the very plainest of plain English:

> *'Fucking's the end and cause of human state, and Man must fuck or God will not create . . .* '[3]

For himself, Wilkes said he was content to ' . . . hope humbly then, clean girls: nor vainly soar, but fuck the cunt at hand – and God adore!'. It was not his use of these common words which aroused the ire of the Establishment but his temerity in equating man's sexual performance with that of the jackass or the stallion when in rut. He was imprisoned not for obscenity but for Blasphemy! None of his contemporaries could cavil at his language for they used the same words and phrases habitually in Court, in Parliament and in the Church. In fact his whilom friend, Bishop William Warburton, was his translator from the Latin in even coarser terms. It is thus curious that shortly afterwards such words became taboo for middle-class usage only, while leaving them to the nobility and the proletarians in the intervening years!

It is extremely interesting to note that a lecher and profligate of the first rank, like Rochester, and a poet of no mean order to boot, while praising whores for their usefulness, always describes them as dirt, and blames them for almost every ill in society. This ambivalence is clearly exposed in his poem entitled *The Debauchée*, a vignette of the life of a Courtier at Charles' Court:

> *'I rise at eleven, I dine at two*
> *I get drunk before seven, and the next thing I do*
> *I send for my Whore, when, for Fear of the Clap*
> *I come in her Hand and I spew in her Lap.*
> *Then we Quarrel and scold till I fall fast asleep;*
> *when the Bitch growing bold, to my Pocket doth creep;*
> *she slyly then leaves me – and to Revenge my Affront*
> *at once she bereaves me of money and cunt . . .*

[3] *Essay on Women.* John Wilkes. M.P. 1750 (Privately Printed) Guildhall.

I storm and I roar and I fall in a Rage
and, missing my Whore, I bugger my Page . . . '

The general looseness of morals attributed to English women at that time is described in another *Roxburghe Ballad* entitled *Cuckold's Haven.*

Other examples of the general coarseness of life and speech are supplied by Pepys' Diary. On 19 October, 1666, he refers to a young Commander of his acquaintance who ' . . . do presently sware that a citizen's Wife that would not take half-a-piece (half a sovereign) before, would now be content with half-a-crown . . . '.

On 10 June, 1666, he describes himself, not too facetiously, and his chief, Lord Brounker, as ' . . . pimping for a new Mistress for the King . . . '.

But perhaps the most revealing entry is that of 8 December, 1666:

'Great Proviso passed the House of Parliament, which makes the king and the court mad, the king having given orders to my Lord Chamberlain to send the playhouses and the brothels to bid all the Parliament men there to go to the Parliament presently . . . '[4]

On 23 June, 1667:

' . . . *The Duke of York hath not got Mrs. Middleton but now says he want her not, for he hath others and hath always had . . . hath known them brought . . . into his closet . . . Nay, had come out of his wife's bed and gone to another laid in bed for him, that Mr. Brounker (later Lord Brounker) is not the only pimp . . .* '

On 24th March, 1668, *à propos* the Shrove Tuesday tradition:

' . . . *Tumult near Moorfields, the 'prentices pulling down the brothels . . . which is one of the great grievances of the nation . . . It was only for pulling down the brothels, none of the bystanders finding fault, but rather the soldiers for hinderling them. To the*

[4] Henry II was cleverer; his ordinance kept the stews closed while the Court was in session, thus helping to curb absenteeism.

> *which the King made a very poor cold insipid answer "Why? Why do they go to them then?"'*

The soldiers were there, of course, to prevent damage to property which belonged to influential citizens, for the very next day Pepys notes:

> '*. . . the 'prentices not yet put down . . . some blood hath been spilt (by the militia) and among others the Duke of York was mighty merry at that of Daman Pages (Mrs. Page) the great Bawd of the seamen, and complained merrily that he hath lost two tenants by their houses being pulled down, who paid 15/- a year for their wine-licences . . .*'

The Duke of York was of course, the King's brother, and the properties being protected rather unsuccessfully by thc militia were those in which he and his friends had a financial interest. Nobody was concerned with the fate or wellbeing of the women thus threatened or attacked. The King's plaintive remark was only directed against the fact that they chose whorehouses to despoil, and not because he thought that apprentices frequented such places.

But Pepys, whose latent respect for Oliver Cromwell grew steadily as he grew older, because of the shameless debauchery and reckless waste of money, as well as inefficiency and corruption in every sphere, was constrained to note in his diary:

> '*. . . that some . . . had the confidence to say that the (the apprentices) did ill to content themselves in pulling down the little brothels and did not go and pull down the great one at White Hall . . .*'

Pepys' mention of Damrose Page is very interesting, for that lady, and another, named Priss Fotheringham, were the two most famous Bawds of the time, matched only by the other supplier of nubile whores to the Court, the infamous Mrs. Creswell. A series of broadsheets published in 1660 under the title of *The Wandering Whore*, while ostensibly fulminating against prostitution, gives with each issue an expanding list of 'Crafty Bawds and Maidenhead-fellers': (in which the first two women occupy places one and two) 'Common Whores, Nightwalkers, Pickpockets, Wanderers and Whipers', and lastly 'Foylers, Kidnappers, Decoyes, Hectors, Pimps and Trappaners'.

From this it is clear that a very large number of these establishments must have been operating in Commonwealth times, since in 1660 they are already all well established. Both Damarose (or Damrose or Daman) and Priss had already spent some time in Newgate before the Restoration. The publication above mentioned was a nexus between a loose – in both senses of the word – organization called 'The Half-Crown Chuck Office' so-called because the whores (reputed mostly to be Dutch) were skilled in that exercise which consisted of standing on the head with the *vulva* gaping wide, and allowing the assembled gentlemen to chuck in half-crowns until the orifice, and indeed the whole vaginal canal, was filled with coins. Later the words 'chuck' and 'cunt' became synonymous. The complementary establishment was the 'Prick Office', and the little journal performed the useful function, of marrying them up. Mrs. Creswell's fame also is based on the fact that she kept a 'stable' of young fresh girls always available, who could be despatched anywhere on request. She operated at one time in Lewknor Lane in Lincolns Inn, and later in various places nearer the Court, whose demand for her goods appears to have been insatiable. From 1655 onwards she had been operating in St. Bartholomew's area, then in Shoreditch, ' . . . for which she paid a £100 for a fine and a rent of £40 per annum . . . ' according to the Charge Sheet of the Middlesex Sessions held at Westminster in October of 1658. She was remanded in the Gatehouse prison until the next Quarter Sessions.

Other lesser-known *Lenas* were Betty Farmer, 'Thomas Beard's wife and savages Mobb'; Mrs. Easton, 'a Maidenhead feller on the Ditch-side'; Jone Harman 'a running bawd'; Mother Cunny; Baud Paskin at the Armitage and Bess Mundel, who 'keeps three bawdy houses in Dog & Bitch Yard'. A couple of Bawds-cum-midwives are listed, and only three men *Lenos*.

Amongst the Common Whores were Johanna Witte, 'a buttock-whore'; Mrs. Debenham and Mrs. Clarke, 'two crack-brain'd whores; Mrs. Westover, 'Bandstring seller to the offices in Chauncery Lane'; the 'Queen of Morocco': 'Butter & Eggs': Mrs. Flower, 'Pocky'; Mrs. Bourne, 'a scribes wife'; Thomas Langley's Mobb; Frank Riggs, 'a theeving whore'; and the *pièce de résistance* Fair Rosamund Sugar-cunt.

There is also a long list of Pimps, the descriptions of one or two being amusing. Pimp Singleton, 'the extempory poet'; Wil Pease, 'an extorting pimp, who is burnt in the hand'; Roger Kissner, 'with a Wen on his eye'; Jack Miller and Tim Thornber, 'Newgate Birds'; Sam Pink, 'a slovenly pimp'; Winch, 'the nailer; Ralph Ashington, '*alias* Shitten-arse; and of course, Fair Rosamund's pimp.

As a matter of interest no less than 100 whorehouses appear on the list, under the Madam's name: about ten have tavern names; and there are about 200 whores listed as independents, with some 50 pimps. This gives just an inkling of what was going on. Of great interest is the reference to several 'Mobbs' which indicates that brothel-keeping was just as well organized with a 'ring' of whoremasters, as today. One important name is missing however that of Madam Ross, who trained Nell Gwynne.

One curious Restoration entertainment was the *Showboat*, originally called *The Royal Diversion* and for some time actually anchored off the Bankside. It soon became known as *The Folly*, a pleasure boat wherein the currently fashionable Italian Musicke could be enjoyed, but very soon it became a resort of whores and as such is mentioned by Pepys, who visited it in 1668. Eventually it fell out of favour, lay derelict for some years, and ended its days as a meeting place for respectable citizens in Queen Anne's time. Indeed towards the end of its life it was visited by Queen Mary II.[5]

One truly noble deed will always resound to Charles' credit: the ending of the atrocious persecution and punishment of witches. Even in 1645-47 no less than two hundred of these unlucky creatures had been horribly executed, many of them being nothing worse than aged common prostitutes who had earned the enmity of their 'virtuous' sisters; some

[5] H.B. Wheatley. *London Past and Present*. Vol.I. John Murray, London 1891.

BILLIARDS
I T E
16 90
Old Doorway & sign at the "Half Moon" Boro. [E. Morant Cox.]

Soliciting outside the Half Moon.

may have been failed midwives; most were half-senile old women and nothing more. The King's marked tolerance was never more rightly directed than in this measure.

At this time a new type of citizen was emerging in Southwark, who, dominated by working-class noncomformist religious influences, was not disposed to accept brothels and prostitution as neighbours. The continuing civil and economic disabilities drove thousands of citizens to emigrate to the new American colonies where they would be free to practise their religion and have a chance to improve their economic freedom and reach prosperity. Hundreds of whores were also shipped out to America to provide the settlers with women; and although this was supposed to be a punishment undoubtedly it gave a new and better life to hundreds of them.

Moreover the measures taken by Charles I and the Commonwealth had taken toll of many of Southwark's stews. They were never to recover fully, although numerous charges of keeping Disorderly Houses appear in the Court Books until about 1670. The orrible synne was moving westward to Covent Garden and its purlieus. Some brothels obstinately remained, such as the 'Half Moon' first shown in the 1542 map, which was rebuilt in 1690 and was still going strong in 1750.

Chapter Nineteen

'Cunno Opt. Min.'

The death of Charles II in 1685 may be said to be the watershed dividing this history of English bawdry from the next bout under the Hanoverians. By this time the glory of the Bankside and Paris Gardens whorehouses had waned. The Surrey and Middlesex Court records are still full of reports as to the sinful misdeeds of the citizenry, but it is clear that the focal point for the orrible synne had now shifted irrevocably westward, although until the end of the century the area outside the city walls in a great arc from Holborn, Cripplegate and Smithfield via Finsbury and Shoreditch, Petticoat Lane and Whitechapel, and further east along the riverside to Wapping and Ratcliffe, are frequently mentioned. None of the cases are worth repeating since they reflect the same situations as before. A few years later the centre was to shift to the Pleasure Gardens at Vauxhall and Ranelagh, thence over the new Westminster Bridge to the West End where it remains to this day. The whores on the City perimeter moved out in the direction of Kings Cross and Holborn, where Whetstone Park and Lewknor Lane became synonymous with whoredom much as the erstwhile Bankside stews had been for the previous five hundred years. The same collusion between whoremasters and police chiefs is frequently aired in the Courts. One particularly juicy incident was in 1671 when the Constable and Headborough were charged with not only failing to search and apprehend the Brothel keepers, but receiving money from them and '. . . later had dinner with them at the Bear Tavern where many unseemly and unhandsome doings and actions and passages passed between them and the said lewd people

Bankside in 1710 showing the Cardinal's Cap.

. . . '.[1] Officialdom also showed its exasperation with some of the recalcitrant women in October 1683 when:

' . . . many assaults and batteries . . . arise from scolding and backbiting and reproaching . . . (the Jury) are of the opinion that the olde legall wayes of a duckinge stoole might prevent these quarrellings: shame may doe that which . . . other punishments will not . . . '

Public whipping through the streets was still carried out right up to the middle of the next century, even though harlotry was no longer a felony. But the City and Southwark were at last cleansed of the stynkynge orrible synne, not indeed by the six hundred years of proscription, harassment and punishment but by the more powerful influences of Banking, Insurance and International Business and the consequent property developments and intensive industrial developments, especially in Southwark, in which the Bankside warehouses finally ousted the last (but one) of the ancient stews. The Cardinal's Cap remained, although it too became a warehouse with its own wharf, and still stands there to this day. Not only was there no room for whorehouses, there was no time to enjoy the whores locally.

Only the shades of the old Bishops of Winchester and of St. Thomas à Becket now hovered over their handiwork, accompanied by the shades of such as clarice la Clatterballock, Ionette of the stews, Longa Margarita and the Queen of them all, Dona Britannica Holland. King Henry II who legalized the sin, Kings Henry VII and VIII who stopped it temporarily, can likewise rest in peace. They had wasted their time and efforts, for they forgot to heed the motto over the frieze of the ancient Temple of Priapus at Lampsacus 'CUNNO OPT.MIN'.

[1] Both instances are from the Middlesex Sessions Records of those dates.

Iconography

Ad Sorores IIII (At the Four Sisters). Architrave over the entrance of a Roman brothel, showing three working whores and the Lena. Centuries later, the London brothels were obliged to have their signs painted on their walls 'so that they be known for what they are' according to Royal Ordinance. Courtesy of Staatsbibliothek Bildarchiv, Berlin. Page 16.

Street corner statue of the god *Hermes*, popularly known as 'Herms', reputed to bring good luck and fertility. Courtesy of Antikensammlung der Städt Museum, München. Page 21.

London about the year 200 A.D. Painting by A. Forestier. Courtesy of the London Museum, Kensington. Page 25.

Soliciting outside a Roman Lupanar. Engraving by Cabasson, Paris. Page 26.

A reconstruction of the 'red Light' district around Cripplegate and Aldersgate, and its relation to the ancient Roman fort and the City Wall. Based on data in contemporary documents, and specially drawn for this book, by the author and C. Davidson. Copyright: Calder and Boyars. Page 27.

The preamble to the Ordinance of King Henry II dated 1161 A.D. officially regulating the running and conduct of the brothels on Bankside, in Southwark. Bodleian MS.e MUS.229. Courtesy of the Bodleian Library, Oxford. Page 51.

King Richard I, Lionheart, arrested in a Parisian Brothel. Print by J. Veyassant. Paris. Courtesy of the Wellcome Institute, London. Page 59.

The Lock Hospital in Southwark founded in 1321 A.D. by a Patent of King Edward II as a 'Lazar House' on the site of a leprosarium established long before. Later, all hospitals for the treatment for venereal diseases were known as 'Lock Hospitals'. Courtesy of the Guildhall Library. Page 73.

A Mediaeval Brothel. Attributed to the Westphalian Master of 1464. A young nobleman, accompanied by his Jester, who pretends to be shocked but still peeps through his fingers. Engraving in the Bibliothek Albertina, Vienna. Page 83.

Preparation for drowning a harlot in a cage, carried out in French cities in the 15th century. Print by A. Cabasson, Paris. Courtesy of the Wellcome Institute, London. Page 100.

Ordinance Pour Remouver les Estues from the City of London to the 'assigned places' on the Bankside in Southwark and Cokkeslane in Finsbury, in 1417 A.D. (Letter Book I, folio cxciii.5. Henry V.) Courtesy of the City of London Records Office. Page 103.

For to Eschewe the Stynkynge and Orrible Synne of Lechery. The *Proclamation contra Meretrices vagant' circa Civitatem* – 'Against Whores Soliciting in the City', issued in the name of King Edward V in 1483. (Letter Book L, folio 189 b. I.Edward V.) Courtesy of the City of London Records Office. Page 120.

An honest Stew. A mediaeval Bath House for Women. A painting in the Muzeum Slaskie, Muzeum Narodowe we Wroclawiu. Courtesy of the Wellcome Institute, London. Page 124.

A Woman encaged on Old London Bridge in the time of Queen Mary I. From Foxe's 'Book of Martyrs'. Courtesy of the Guildhall Library. Page 131.

The Clink Prison ca.1550. Page 134.

Henry VIII's Ordinance *Ordering the Brothels to be Closed* 13th April 1546. Steele MS.288. Courtesy of the Society of Antiquaries, London. Page 141.

The Stews as an Amorous Rendezvous, in the Middle Ages, attributed to the Master of the Mediaeval House Book, ca 1450. Courtesy of the Wellcome Institute, London. Page 154.

The Bankside Stews in Tudor times, during an Ice Fair. Courtesy of the London Museum, Kensington. Page 184.

Reconstruction of the locations of the brothels on Bankside, just prior to Henry VIII's closure, based on contemporary documents. The locations of the Antelope, the Boar's Heade and the Flower de Luce are uncertain. The Horseshoe was an inn. Specially drawn for this book by the author and C. Davidson. Copyright Calder and Boyars. Page 187.

Cock's Lane about 1710. As Cokkeslane it is mentioned as early as 1241 A.D. in Ancient Deeds No.A.1661, and as an 'assigned place' ca. 1286. Courtesy of the Wellcome Institute, London. Page 219.

The famous 'Half Moon' brothel in Southwark, first mentioned in an old map of 1542, as reconstructed in 1690. It shows one of the whores soliciting as late as 1800. An old drawing by E.M. Cox. Courtesy of Guildhall Library, London. Page 237.

The Bankside in 1827, showing the Cardinal's Cap with its 1710 facade, and a surviving Elizabethan building adjacent. Under the name of 'The Cardinallshat' it existed as a brothel from time immemorial until it became a tavern about 1627. The building still exists on Bankside. It bears a plaque with an indecypherable coat-of-arms, which however includes three 'bekets' or choughs. From Thomas Pennant's Collection of Prints in Guildhall Library. Courtesy the Guildhall Library, London. Page 240.

Index

INDEX